The Secular
Northwest

The Secular Northwest

Religion and Irreligion in Everyday Postwar Life

Tina Block

UBCPress · Vancouver · Toronto

25 24 23 22 21 20 19 18 17 16   5 4 3 2 1

Printed in Canada on FSC-certified ancient-forest-free paper (100% post-consumer recycled) that is processed chlorine- and acid-free.

Library and Archives Canada Cataloguing in Publication

Block, Tina Marie, author
  The secular Northwest : religion and irreligion in everyday postwar life / Tina Block.

Includes bibliographical references and index.
Issued in print and electronic formats.
ISBN 978-0-7748-3128-4 (hardback). – ISBN 978-0-7748-3129-1 (pbk.) –
ISBN 978-0-7748-3130-7 (pdf). – ISBN 978-0-7748-3131-4 (epub)

  1. Secularism – British Columbia – History – 20th century. 2. Irreligion – British Columbia – History – 20th century. 3. British Columbia – Religion – 20th century. 4. Secularism – Washington (State) – History – 20th century. 5. Irreligion – Washington (State) – History – 20th century. 6. Washington (State) – Religion – 20th century. I. Title.

BL2530.C3B56 2016   200.9711   C2015-908706-6
                                                     C2015-908707-4

Canadä

UBC Press gratefully acknowledges the financial support for our publishing program of the Government of Canada (through the Canada Book Fund), the Canada Council for the Arts, and the British Columbia Arts Council.

This book has been published with the help of a grant from the Canadian Federation for the Humanities and Social Sciences, through the Awards to Scholarly Publications Program, using funds provided by the Social Sciences and Humanities Research Council of Canada.

Printed and bound in Canada by Friesens
Set in Galliard and New Baskerville by Apex CoVantage, LLC
Copy editor: Jillian Shoichet
Indexer: Timothy Pearson
Cover Designer: George Kirkpatrick

UBC Press
The University of British Columbia
2029 West Mall
Vancouver, BC V6T 1Z2

www.ubcpress.ca

Dedicated in loving memory to Nels Block (1926–2010) and Kyle Block (1987–2013).

Contents

Tables

Acknowledgments

It is a great pleasure to thank the many people who have guided and supported me in the completion of this book. I owe a deep debt of gratitude to Lynne Marks for her patient, skilful guidance of my work and for her constant support during my transition to life as a history professor. She was and remains a cherished mentor and friend. Many other scholars at the University of Victoria offered important encouragement and feedback, including Peter Baskerville, Eric Sager, Elizabeth Vibert, Rennie Warburton, and Wendy Wickwire. I am also grateful to Robert Orsi for his thoughtful comments on this project in its earlier form. I would like to acknowledge David Marshall, whose undergraduate course on the history of religion in Canada ignited my interest in this area. In the process of completing this book, I was very fortunate to join the warm, collegial environment of Thompson Rivers University. A special thanks to my colleagues in the Faculty of Arts and, most particularly, the Department of Philosophy, History, and Politics, for their ongoing support, advice, and friendship.

This project would not have been possible without those women and men who so kindly agreed to be interviewed about their "secular journeys." I am overwhelmed by the generosity of those individuals who so willingly shared their time and memories with me, and remain forever in their debt. During the course of my research I received invaluable assistance from the staff at several archives and libraries. I would like to thank the patient and knowledgeable archivists and librarians at the United Church of Canada and Anglican Archives at the Vancouver School of Theology, Library and Archives Canada in Ottawa, the University of Washington Manuscripts and Special Collections Division in Seattle, and the British Columbia Archives in Victoria. This book was made possible, in part, by generous financial support from various sources, including the Social Sciences and Humanities Research Council of Canada, the Imperial Order of the Daughters of the Empire, the BC Heritage Trust, the University of Victoria, and Thompson Rivers University.

It has been an immense pleasure to work with UBC Press in the preparation of this book. A special thanks to Darcy Cullen, Ann Macklem, and Nadine Pedersen for their kind assistance and encouragement during this process. I am very grateful to the anonymous reviewers for providing such constructive, thorough feedback on the original manuscript. Their suggestions helped me to think in new ways about aspects of this project, and made for a much improved final product. Of course, any errors that remain are entirely my own. Over the years, I have presented parts of this research at various conferences, and am grateful for the feedback that I received from commentators, especially John Belshaw. Portions of this book, reproduced here with permission, were originally published in "Religion, Irreligion, and the Difference Place Makes: The Case of the Pacific Northwest, 1950–1970," *Histoire sociale/Social History* 43: 85 (2010): 1–30; "'Toilet-seat prayers' and Impious Fathers: Interrogating Religion and the Family in Oral Histories of the Postwar Pacific Northwest," *Oral History Forum d'histoire orale* 29 (2009): 1–27; and "'Going to church just never even occurred to me': Women and Secularism in the Postwar Pacific Northwest," *Pacific Northwest Quarterly* 96 (2005): 61–68. I am grateful to these journals for their consideration.

This book has been many years in the making, and along the way I have been sustained by friends and family. A special thanks to my friends in Kamloops, Victoria, Ottawa, and beyond for their encouragement, companionship, and perhaps most importantly, for reminding me of life beyond work. I am so grateful to my family for their loving support over the years. Barbara White provided me with the comfort of family and a home away from home in Victoria. I would like to thank Murray and Diana Lowick for their love and generosity, and the Ruhe/Hovdebo clan for their support over the years. I feel lucky to have joined the Fuller and Ohlhausen crew, and am grateful to them for their love, acceptance, and warm family gatherings. My wonderful brothers, sisters-in-law, nieces, and nephews keep me grounded, and have all supported me in various ways. My mother, Dorothy Block, has provided me with steadfast love and encouragement throughout my academic career. I cannot thank her enough. During the completion of this book I was deeply saddened to lose my much-loved father and nephew, two men who, despite their difference in age, shared a similar love of knowledge. This book is dedicated to them.

Lastly, I would like extend my deepest thanks to Troy Fuller – this book would most certainly not have become a reality without his constant support and encouragement. I thank him for his love, humour, generosity, and friendship, and for sharing this and every journey with me.

Introduction

In 2003, I met with Joe, who has long considered himself both non-religious and anti-church. In our conversation, he recalled his move to British Columbia during the 1960s. Born in 1932 in northeastern New Brunswick, Joe was raised Roman Catholic and regularly attended Sunday school as a child. At the age of twenty he married, and took a job as a technician with the army, an occupation that involved frequent relocations across Canada. During the 1960s, Joe's work took him to the "hub" of Vancouver Island, Nanaimo, where he settled with his growing family. He and his wife had the first few of their eight children baptized and, in the early years of their marriage, attended church sporadically. Joe recalled that their involvement in the church petered out, in part, because of Joe's growing disenchantment with church hypocrisy. When I asked Joe if his wife shared his views on religion and the church, he replied: "Oh I don't think ... she probably never had any, and neither did I. At first you have that old died-in-the-brain deal, oh I must conform, until you realize that no, you don't have to conform."[1]

Neither Joe nor his wife considered themselves Christian, although they were also not atheists. By contrast, another of my interviewees, Frank, began identifying as an atheist as a young child. Born in 1926, Frank grew up in Shelton, Washington, and settled during the 1950s in Seattle, where he worked as a longshoreman. He remained single throughout his life. While his parents were believers, they were not churchgoers; as a youngster Frank was sometimes "corralled" by his neighbours to attend worship at a nearby Baptist church. "My mother never had any objection to that," Frank recalled. "She probably thought it would help me be a good person." As an adult, Frank occasionally associated with Buddhist and Unitarian groups, though he did so for social rather than spiritual reasons. Frank never wavered in his atheism, but sometimes he was less open about it, due to the persistent stigma attached to non-belief. "I didn't stick out my neck, you know," he admitted.[2] Although

1

their experiences differed, Frank and Joe, along with the forty-two other individuals I interviewed for this study, were part of the religiously uninvolved majority in the postwar Pacific Northwest. *The Secular Northwest* is about this majority.

In the postwar period, the Pacific Northwest was not populated exclusively by atheists, agnostics, freethinkers, and active secularists. This was not a universally secular region, but residents of British Columbia and Washington State were far more likely than other Canadians and Americans to reject, dismiss, and ignore religion, particularly in its organized forms. The unique secularity of the Northwest has drawn frequent comment in the wider media. In 2003, the Victoria *Times Colonist* reported that having "no religion is still the No. 1 religion in BC." One year later, a Seattle journalist remarked: "In the Pacific Northwest, we're the most irreligious folks in America." Prominent pollster George Gallup has suggested that the unchurched character of Washington may, in fact, "be the ethos of the state."[3] The Northwest's distinct secularity has a long history. According to the Canadian historian Lynne Marks, "in many ways BC was 'born secular.'"[4] While scholars have traced the Northwest's secular culture back to the nineteenth century, and linked it in part to the region's transient and masculine population, there is no general consensus regarding the roots of this culture. While we still have much to learn about the historical development of Northwest secularity, we do know that people have puzzled about this secularity since the early days of European settlement. Such puzzling intensified in the decades following the Second World War, as secularizing currents deepened and organized religion came under increasing critical scrutiny. Through the 1950s and 1960s, religious leaders bemoaned the "cold religious climate" of the Northwest, and categorized the region as a critical mission area.[5] Over the years, the secular character of the Pacific Northwest has been the subject of much comment, but little critical investigation.[6] *The Secular Northwest* is the result of my exploration of this regional phenomenon in the postwar era.

Most Northwesterners did not join, attend, or otherwise actively participate in organized religion in the postwar years. They generally accepted religious non-involvement as normal, and at times even celebrated it as intrinsic to the "hardy" Northwest lifestyle, with its emphasis on self-reliance. Of course, religion is not something that happens only in connection with institutions. Rich and varied spiritual practices took shape outside of, and often quite separate from, religious institutions in the region. This book focuses on the religiously uninvolved majority, which included non-believers like Frank, but also people like Margaret, who drifted from the church in the postwar years though she remained Christian, and Susan, who disdained organized religion but considered herself deeply spiritual. In the following pages, we will encounter people who rejected or ignored organized religion yet embraced the sacred, as well as people who denied the spiritual altogether. This book, then, introduces us to people with quite disparate histories and experiences. Regardless of their varied social locations and spiritual outlooks, Northwesterners were part of a regional culture that placed relatively little importance on formal religious connections. This was a culture produced and sustained largely by ordinary people in the spaces of everyday life. Although their perspectives on religious institutions ranged from indifference to hostility, my interviewees shared in making noninvolvement in such institutions a normal and accepted part of life in the region.

In this book, I investigate the shape, meaning, and significance of the Northwest's secular culture, focusing specifically on British Columbia and Washington State between the 1950s and the 1970s. When I embarked on this project, I did not begin with the question, why was this place distinctly non-religious? Such a question presupposes the existence of a uniform, shared definition of religion. Since no such definition exists, I began, instead, with other questions: Was this region less religious than other places? Or was it just religious differently from other places? In what ways was the region secular, or differently religious, and according to whose definition? From the perspective of Christian leaders, the Pacific Northwest was a distinctly secular place because such a large proportion of its residents stayed away from the churches. Church officials in the Northwest and beyond bemoaned the tendency of people to disassociate church involvement from religiosity. In 1958, an Anglican writer for the *Canadian Churchman* affirmed that those who saw churchgoing and religiosity as separable were, quite simply, "muddle-headed and incorrect." The writer offered what he considered to be the true definition of religion: "Religion consists of being trained by regularity at church and prayer and a definitely planned spiritual growth and development."[7] Church-centred definitions of religiosity fail to capture the diverse spiritual experiences that have flourished outside of the institutional realm. Residents of the Pacific Northwest were not always religious in expected ways, and non-institutional forms of spirituality were

prevalent in the region. Scholars have done much to challenge definitions of religion that rely exclusively on church involvement. Secularity,
however, continues to be equated with unbelief. Just as church participation is not the sole measure of religiosity, unbelief is not the sole measure of secularity. Few Northwesterners called themselves atheists, or
adhered to any formal doctrine of secularism. Many, however, were part
of a regional culture that placed little emphasis on organized religion,
and that accepted and allowed for multiple, intermittent, and informal
ways of engaging and rebuffing the sacred.

Born in 1943, Sandra eschewed organized religion, and described herself as both anti-church and spiritual. She spent most of her childhood
in Montana, but eventually settled in Seattle during the 1960s. In our
interview, she recalled being struck by the "incredible variety of thought"
in Seattle: "There's all kinds of different churches, there's all kinds of
different political groups, this is a very politically active part of the country. So, anytime someone presents some argument, somebody else says
well this is another take on it, and this is another take on it, and this is
another take on it. So, it's very easy to escape from." Sandra commented
on the unimportance of churchgoing to many in the region: "there's
such a large number of people to whom [churchgoing] makes no difference."[8] Like Sandra, many residents of British Columbia and Washington were content in their distance from religious institutions and
embraced, as part of the Northwest identity, the fluidity of sacred and
secular in the region. In this study, I conceptualize secularism in a way
that captures both this distance and this fluidity. According to sociologist
Barry Kosmin, the study of secularism is a new field that "lacks common
language or tools of analysis."[9] I use the term "secularism" flexibly, and
interchangeably with other terms such as "irreligion," "secularity," and
"non-religion," to refer to the many ways that people avoided, resisted,
or lived comfortably without religion, particularly in its organized forms.
Framed in this way, secularism includes, but does not equate to, unbelief.
The concept of religion itself bears no stable, universal meaning. In the
following pages, I focus on Christianity, as this was the dominant religious tradition in the region. I do not equate religion with Christianity,
however, nor do I take the term to mean any worldview, code of ethics, or
system of meaning. Rather, I use "religion" to refer to beliefs, structures,
and practices that people associated with the supernatural, the sacred, or
the otherworldly, or that, quite simply, they understood to be religious.
I have deliberately kept the boundaries of religion open in an effort to

foreground the experiences and understandings of ordinary Northwest-erners such as Sandra.

The postwar Pacific Northwest was characterized by a secular, or reli-giously uninvolved, culture, which embodied some common norms and parameters. Many Northwesterners shared in living without, and plac-ing relatively little significance on, formal or organized religious con-nections. Even those who led and joined churches knew that religious involvement did not confer social acceptance in the Northwest as it did elsewhere. However, Northwesterners well understood that public athe-ism crossed the boundary of social acceptance. Most residents of the region did not define themselves as atheists or unbelievers, and most at least sporadically participated in religious practice throughout their lives. The region was also home to a significant, and often overlooked, minority of individuals who were ambivalent about or disinterested in religious belief, and who considered themselves neither spiritual nor atheistic. Despite such diversity, most Northwesterners shared a sense that their region was, and should continue to be, a place where formal religious involvement mattered little. Although scholars have explored the ways in which distinct religious cultures, based on shared meanings and practices, have taken shape in various times and places, the secular culture of the Pacific Northwest has drawn scant attention.[10] "Religion matters," Callum Brown writes, "because it shapes people's lives." It fol-lows that denying, doubting, or drifting away from religion also matters. Brown urges historians to take these secular journeys seriously and to treat those who undertook them "not merely as lost flocks of the Chris-tian churches" but as people carving out new, often positive, and decid-edly non-religious ways of being in the world.[11] In foregrounding the Northwest's secular culture, this book offers insights not only into how people in the region viewed and approached religion, but also how they imagined their communities and went about their everyday lives. As we shall see, secularity shaped daily decisions about everything from leisure to parenting, and was entwined with regional ideals of tolerance and independence.

Northwest secularity was lived, created, and negotiated by all individu-als and groups in the region, but it was understood and experienced differently by people depending on their social location. As the anthro-pologist Claudio Lomnitz-Adler notes, regional cultures embody shared and divisive elements at once: "People understand that they share frames and idioms of interaction (a culture of social relations) and, at the same time, they know that these sets of practices have different implications for the different actors."[12] In this book I consider, in particular, the various gender, class, race, and family implications of the Northwest's secular culture. This culture took shape on two overlapping levels. First, secularity was reproduced in the myths, habits, stories, and symbols of the region. While always partial, contested, and contingent, regional discourses and imagery not only made organized religion an awkward fit in the Northwest but also marked out greater possibilities for secular practice. Second, secularity was made in the homes, neighbourhoods, and other everyday spaces of Northwest life. In daily actions and inactions, ordinary people helped to produce and circulate religious norms and expectations in the region. These two levels reinforced each other: everyday practices gave rise to shared cultural ideas and expectations, and such ideas and expectations framed, and occasionally delimited, individual practice. As scholars have shown in various contexts, the material and discursive realms were mutually constituted.[13] Northwest secularity was simultaneously made and contested on imaginative terrain and in everyday practices on the ground.

In exploring the secular experiences and identities of ordinary Northwesterners, I am inspired by the growing scholarship on popular religion and the social history of religion in North America and Britain.[14] This scholarship has turned the focus away from religious leaders and doctrines and towards the diverse, complex religious lives of ordinary people in everyday contexts. Recently, the concept of "popular religion" has come under criticism for implying a fixed, impermeable division between elite and working-class, clergy and lay religion. Historian Sarah Williams follows other scholars in pointing to the importance of "releasing the notion of popular religion from too close an association with ideas of class." Williams suggests that we conceptualize popular religion broadly as a cultural rather than exclusively class-based phenomenon.[15] She joins other scholars in challenging the idea, so prevalent in early studies, that religion was either irrelevant or oppressive to the working classes.[16] Current research on working-class religiosity offers an invaluable corrective to earlier studies, which overlooked religion, or depicted it as invariably antithetical to working-class interests. While many studies implicitly represent the working classes as secular by ignoring the place of religion in their lives, few examine working-class secularity as a subject in its own right.[17] At the same time, we know far more about the role of religion in the construction of middle-class identity than about the nature and meanings of middle-class secularity, particularly in the twentieth century. There was a significant working-class component to the Northwest's secular culture, but this culture was not produced and sustained by the working classes alone. Although constrained by wider class ideals, middle-class Northwesterners were very much a part of the region's secular culture. Regardless of social class, Northwest residents were not, as often depicted, unwitting secularists. They were creatively and often deliberately secular in ways that accommodated the some-times contradictory expectations of society, family, and self.

While some scholars use the term "popular religion," others have adopted the newer analytic concept of "lived religion," which is meant to capture the hybrid, shifting character of religion in all spaces of human experience.[18] Scholars of lived religion seek explicitly to avoid placing human behaviour into the discrete realms of sacred *or* secular, elite *or* popular, and other kinds of oppositional categories that have little reso-nance in the real world. According to Robert Orsi, the study of lived religion moves away from formal doctrines and denominations and "toward a study of how particular people, in particular places and times, live in, with, through, and against the religious idioms available to them in culture – *all* the idioms, including (often enough) those not explicitly their 'own.'"[19] *The Secular Northwest* contributes to this redirection, but departs from the usual path of inquiry by focusing mainly on how people lived "against" or without religion. Scholars of lived and popular religion have shed increasing light on the cultural meanings of religion, and on everyday spiritual practices, but we continue to know little about what it meant to ignore, disdain, or drift away from religion. Why did so many Northwesterners "live against" religion? How did secularity shape their everyday experience? Did it make a difference if one was a man or a woman, working or middle class, living alone or within a family? It is rare for a historian to ask these kinds of questions of secularity, a subject that is usually approached in relation to cultural institutions and elites rather than ordinary people. In the rich literature on secularization in North America and Europe, the ideas of religious and cultural leaders take cen-tre stage.[20] By contrast, scholars of lived and popular religion have shown that answers to the big questions in religious history are to be found not in the theological rafters, but in the practices of everyday life. In deci-sions about such things as what to do on Sundays, how to celebrate the holidays, and what to tell their children about religion, ordinary North-westerners produced and entrenched their region's secular culture.

My approach to this secular culture is informed, in part, by the influential work of British historians Callum Brown and Hugh McLeod. Such work breaks new ground in exploring the experience of ordinary people who left, or stayed away from, religion in Britain and beyond.[21] Brown and McLeod are also part of a growing contingent of scholars focused on that critical era of religious change, the postwar years. Canadian and American scholars have joined their British counterparts in identifying the 1960s as a decade of increasing secularization and declining Christian privilege – as a "hinge" era between the Christian-centric 1950s and the more overtly secular 1970s.[22] Scholars have been less attuned to how or whether these postwar changes played out in regional and everyday spaces.[23] National developments in religion did not pass over the Northwest, but they also did not determine the region's particular religious culture. Both region and nation experienced rising levels of institutional religious involvement in the 1950s, and decreasing levels in the 1960s; despite such developments, the relative secularity of the Northwest remained relatively constant. This does not mean, however, that there was nothing historically specific about the postwar era. For instance, cultural officials and ordinary people in the Northwest reflected upon, and helped to shape, the wider critique of the Christian churches that emerged in the 1960s. People in the Northwest and across both nations encountered new secular currents in the mid-1960s as *Time* magazine famously wondered about the death of God, and authors such as Pierre Berton railed about the self-satisfied, undemanding, "comfortable pews" of the Christian churches.[24] While events of religious significance occurred at points through the postwar decades, this era was itself distinct in the wider history of Northwest irreligion. A phenomenon with a deep past, Northwest secularity took on meanings specific to the postwar decades. It was, for example, less tied to labour radicalism and a demographic gender imbalance in the postwar decades than it had been in the nineteenth century. In gender, class, and a range of other ways, Northwest secularity was time- as well as place-specific.

Certain countercultural ideals of the 1960s, such as individualism and anti-authoritarianism, underscored and facilitated the secularizing currents of that decade. Introduced during the 1960s elsewhere, such ideals were longstanding elements of the Northwest's identity, and were central to its secular culture.[25] Many Northwesterners commented matter-of-factly on their region's indifference to, and disdain for, organized forms of religion. In our interview, Sylvia reflected on churchgoing in her hometown of Nanaimo: "I don't think anybody really cared. I think it got to the point where nobody really cared if you went to church. It didn't make any difference to the people you associated with, or to your work situation." Although she stopped attending church during the 1960s, Sylvia remained a believer. When I asked her to elaborate on her beliefs, she remarked: "I always felt there was something more."[26] Sylvia was among the growing number of people who, in the postwar era, "believed without belonging." In addition to the well-known work of sociologist Grace Davie on "belief without belonging," several scholars have examined the rise of religious "nones" and of the "spiritual but non-religious" in America, Canada, and Britain.[27] Such terms are fluid and imprecise, but together they point to the growing popularity of non-institutional forms of religion in the postwar world. Long the region with the lowest levels of religious belonging, the Pacific Northwest was at the forefront of this increasingly common way of engaging religion. The region was home to a wide range of informal beliefs and non-institutional spiritual practices, but also to a great deal of indifference to religion in all of its forms. According to Callum Brown, the new "no religionism" of the 1960s had more to do with growing disinterest in, and indecision about, religion than with atheism.[28] Imagined as an open, unconstrained, and anti-authoritarian place, the Northwest proved especially fertile ground for religious disinterest and indecision.

Mark Silk notes that scholars who explore the regional dimensions of religion are "in the business of opening conversations that have barely existed, rather than of having the last word."[29] *The Secular Northwest* joins these emergent conversations and suggests that place mattered to the religiously uninvolved culture shared by British Columbia and Washington State. Place is often treated as a container for wider processes rather than something that is itself in need of explaining.[30] While more attention has been given to the geographical dimensions of the sacred than the secular, scholars of religion often neglect the category of place. Samuel Hill hints at the reasons for this neglect: "It may be surprising to many that so apparently private, and perhaps culture-transcendent, an aspect of life is heavily influenced by where one lives, indeed the place to which one migrates."[31] As Hill implies, to suggest that where a person lives affects how, or indeed whether, they practice religion, is to acknowledge the extent to which human religious behaviour is shaped by everyday life. This contradicts the ingrained idea of religion as something "transcendent, not present in things," as something that is separate from, rather than made by and through, culture.[32] According to sociologist Rhys Williams, scholars of religion often ignore place because they focus on Christianity, "a self-proclaimed 'universalist' religion that aims to bring its truth to all peoples in all lands, regardless of geography."[33] Despite entrenched ideas about the universal, transcendent meanings of religion, decisions about the sacred were often grounded in place. Place shapes human behaviour, but it is not a meta-category. Place gives meaning to, but is itself differentiated by class, race, gender, and other social identities.[34] The class, race, and gender dimensions of place help to further illuminate regional religious behaviour. For instance, the Northwest's regional identity was premised partly on working-class values and expectations, including those around religion. In addition, the Northwest was gendered masculine, which not only helped to make religion an awkward fit in the region but also differentiated the secular experiences of men and women. The people who lived in the Northwest were not determined by the region's secular culture but, rather, helped to make it, and experienced it in class-, race-, and gender-specific ways. Nonetheless, even those who challenged this culture, such as church leaders, recognized its existence and shared an understanding of its habits, possibilities, and expectations: they shared, in effect, a sense of place.

To explore this uniquely secular place, I draw on three sets of primary sources: printed materials, quantitative data, and oral interviews. I delve into a wide range of archival and published printed sources for insights into the values and expectations associated with religion, secularity, and regional identity in the postwar world. I examine extensive local, regional, and national church records, including those of specific denominations such as the Anglican Synod of British Columbia, and those of ecumenical organizations such as the Washington and Northern Idaho Council of Churches. These sources, along with denominational newspapers, offer a lens to view how church leaders in British Columbia, Washington State, and beyond perceived and constructed religion and irreligion in the Pacific Northwest. For an alternative perspective, I turn to the records, correspondence, and newspapers of several Secular Humanist and Rationalist organizations within and outside of the region. Such materials help to further contextualize religion and secularity in the Pacific Northwest. I also move beyond explicitly religious and secularist writings to explore a range of travel literature, popular histories, and local newspapers published in the region during the postwar decades. This wider cultural media offers a useful lens on the dominant images, symbols, and myths associated with this cross-border region.

Qualitative sources such as popular literature and church records do not offer an unmediated window on the past. Such sources do, however, provide at least a partial view of culture, which, David Hall reminds us, "has multiple dimensions; it presents us with choice even as it also limits or restrains the possibilities for meaning."[35] In this study, I read the words of cultural commentators for what they might disclose about the "possibilities for meaning" in the postwar Northwest. Although they were directed at different audiences and guided by competing ideologies, church, secularist, and popular writings reproduced many common assumptions about the meanings of religion, irreligion, and the Pacific Northwest itself. The lived experience of Northwest secularity cannot be understood apart from how this secularity was imagined. The qualitative sources indicate that secularity was typically imagined as an element of the white, male wageworkers frontier. Cultural commentators shared in disseminating commonsense ideas about the innate piety of women, the natural irreverence of male miners and loggers, and the sacralizing effects of the family. Such ideas were often based more on unexamined essentialisms – on what was already "known" about the religious lives of women, workers, and families – than about what was actually happening on the ground. These ideas were not irrelevant in everyday life but, rather, formed part of the web of expectations that framed religious and non-religious behaviour in the Northwest.

I also consult a wide range of quantitative sources. The published Canadian census is among the most comprehensive of statistical sources on religion for this period. The census illuminates the demography of religion in Canada, and points very clearly to the uniquely non-religious character of British Columbia. In contrast, the United States census does not include questions on religion due to the requirements of church–state separation. To ascertain the religious demography of the United States, it was necessary to comb through several local, regional, and national surveys. For both countries, I consult extensive polls and studies conducted by independent, government, academic, and church organizations. These various statistical sources suggest that British Columbia and Washington State made up a distinctly secular place, especially with respect to religious affiliation and participation. Like other types of historical evidence, statistics must be approached not as disinterested facts but as selective constructions bound to the conditions of their making.

For instance, a typical census or survey question such as "What is your religion?" carries with it a host of normative assumptions, including those concerning the meanings of religion itself. This seemingly straightforward question evokes various social pressures depending on who is doing the asking and responding. Statistical evidence is contingent, shifting, and culturally situated. As sociologist Bruce Curtis reminds us, "censuses are made, not *taken*."[36]

Postwar churches regularly carried out and commissioned studies to measure various aspects of church participation such as membership and attendance. The impulse to quantify church involvement did not suddenly emerge after the Second World War. As historian David Marshall notes, in the latter half of the nineteenth century, Canadian churches undertook a "constant accounting which sought to measure the strength of the church."[37] The churches both shaped and reflected the growing emphasis on, and privileging of, statistical forms of knowledge associated with modernity.[38] In the postwar context, church leaders often turned to statistics to determine levels of religious practice, but their confidence in the numbers was belied by concerns that religiosity was unquantifiable. The clergy looked with distrust upon numerical increases in church involvement, and even in professed belief, because true piety – or that "great torture of soul," as one Christian writer described it – was thought to be beyond measure.[39] The statistics drew particular scrutiny during the 1950s, a decade of marked church growth. Commentators from within and outside the churches worried that the apparent revival of religion during the fifties was superficial and conformist. In 1956, a writer for the magazine *Christianity and Society* reflected on rising levels of religious belief: "Statistically, the increased figures are valid enough. But they raise a different question: do people believe more than before, or do they only believe they believe? Or believe they ought to believe?"[40] In that same year, a United Church clergyman from Toronto reported on "The Problem of Suburbia": "Everyone likes religion in the suburbs. Church going is almost rampant. Churches are filled twice on a Sunday morning. The admission of new members to church is only equalled by the spate of new church building." The report went on to ponder if such renewed interest in the churches was merely "a conventional suburban pattern with little or no spiritual meaning."[41] Similar concerns echoed through other churches. Despite their ongoing production of, and reliance upon, statistics, church officials worried that numbers revealed little about the depth of "spiritual meaning."

In 1959, a writer for an American Catholic weekly commented on the difficulties involved in measuring religion: "A religious boom is not like one in babies or in business. You can calculate the latter in terms of quantity. It is not always wise to do that with religion." The writer continued: "what percentage of these people really know what religion is all about? Does it mean for them living a good life, thinking good thoughts, 'feeling good' or secure, or a hundred other things?"[42] Many church officials shared this writer's suspicion that religion statistics, regardless of their purpose, were fundamentally flawed. For the clergy, the chief problem with religion statistics was that, regardless of what people did or said, few understood what "real" religion actually meant. Despite the normative assessments of church leaders, there is no fixed or universal definition of true religion against which individual levels of religiosity can be reliably measured. As well as causing anxiety among postwar clergymen, the flexible and indeterminate meanings of religion pose methodological challenges for the present-day researcher.[43] It is not possible to precisely calculate the religiosity of a particular person, or group, or place, but this does not mean that religion statistics should be abandoned. To categorically reject the quantification of religion is to risk reproducing the assumption that religion is somehow out there, separable from everyday life, forever beyond the reach of empirical study. Church leaders were disturbed by statistics on religion in part because they viewed numbers as too quotidian to adequately represent something that was meant to be transcendent and awe-inspiring. In this work, I resist the impulse to dismiss religion statistics on the basis that they reveal nothing about genuine religiousness. As scholars of lived and popular religion have demonstrated, the search for religious purity is futile: religion "takes life" within language, and at the level of everyday practice.[44] It is with this level that this study is concerned, and quantitative sources on religion offer one way of getting there.

While religion statistics should not be judged according to some nebulous ideal of authentic piety, they should also not be treated as frozen facts. Religious figures convey particular meanings that, in the North American context, have usually been determined by state, religious, or cultural authorities. Such authorities decide which aspects of religion are worth measuring, and reproduce in statistical form normative ideas about what it means to be religious. Thus, we are apt to encounter quantitative data on Christian but not occult practices, on prayer but not meditation, on participation in churches but not psychic fairs. Statistics on religion present not only a narrow but also a fixed picture of beliefs and behaviours that are shifting, fluid, and impermanent. As several scholars have demonstrated, conventional measures miss much of the texture and disorder of human experience in the religious realm. According to British historian Callum Brown, religion statistics are "discursively active" rather than hard facts that reveal the religious or secular essence of certain groups or places.[45] Like all historical sources, they offer an incomplete and selective view of the past. Approached in this way, and not as durable truths, religion statistics provide useful insights into regional and national patterns of religion.

When considered with critical caution, quantitative materials can suggest new lines of inquiry and add further texture to our understanding of the past. In this study, the statistical evidence challenges us to think in new ways about this regional phenomenon. While cultural and religious observers regularly attributed Northwest irreligion to working-class men, the statistics suggest a somewhat different story. The quantitative evidence points to a secularity that was broadly based, rather than isolated to a particular demographic group within the region. Class, gender, and other categories shaped and differentiated Northwest secularity, but they did not determine it. In the Pacific Northwest, working-class men were less religious than their counterparts in other regions, but so too were women and the middle classes. Statistical sources compelled me to broaden my view of Northwest secularity, and to bring new actors into the narrative.

The story of Northwest secularity is further complicated by the oral histories of the region's residents. This project partly derives from my interest in the secular journeys of ordinary people. It made sense, then, to talk to Pacific Northwesterners themselves. For this study, I conducted forty oral interviews with a total of forty-four people between June of 2003 and March of 2004. Pseudonyms are used throughout to protect the privacy of the interviewees. I carried out thirty-six interviews with individuals, three with married couples, and one with a mother and son. I spoke with people who were born in 1943 or earlier, and who had lived in British Columbia or Washington State for all or part of the period between 1950 and 1971. The majority of my interviews were conducted in five cities that approximately reflected the statistical average in terms of religious involvement in the region: Vancouver and Nanaimo in British Columbia, and Seattle, Olympia, and Port Angeles in Washington. In total, I interviewed twenty-two people who had lived in British Columbia during the postwar decades, and twenty-two who had lived in Washington State during that time. The vast majority of my interviewees were white and of European descent. I interviewed an equal number of women and men, and approximately the same proportion of working- and middle-class individuals. Most of my interviewees were exposed to Christian influences as children. Thirty-three had at least one nominally Christian parent, whereas eight described both of their parents as non-religious or atheistic. However, even those with non-religious parents celebrated religious holidays and rituals as children.

I endeavoured to interview people who, between 1950 and the early 1970s, fit one or all of the following criteria: 1) they considered themselves to be non-religious; 2) they did not attend or join a church or other religious institution; and 3) they left a church or other religious institution. While their religious identities varied, my interviewees shared a common sense of detachment from organized religion. I adopted what is often referred to as a "semi-structured" approach to interviewing.[46] Using a general interview guide, I asked my interviewees questions pertaining to a range of subjects, including the role, if any, of religion in their family lives, their reasons for turning or staying away from organized religion, and their thoughts on the place of religion in the postwar Pacific Northwest. Oral history is increasingly seen as a collaborative exercise involving the input of both interviewer and interviewee.[47] With this in mind, I used open-ended questions, and sought to allow my interviewees as much freedom as possible to take the interview in directions that were meaningful to them. I made every effort to provide them with detailed information about the interviewing process, and spoke candidly with them about the objectives of my larger project. Of course, as scholars who use oral history have long been aware, no amount of self-disclosure will erase all imbalances of power from the interview situation. The oral narratives in this study do not "speak for themselves," but rather are framed by my own interests and subjectivity: in the end, the power to interpret rests with the researcher.[48]

There is an extensive, interdisciplinary literature on the merits and limitations of oral history.[49] In oral history projects, questions invariably arise about whether or not the interviewees are representative. For this study, I located participants primarily through newspaper advertisements. Such an approach does not guarantee a random sample of the population since, as Valerie Yow notes, it "is the articulate who come forward to be participants."[50] Although the individuals in this study offer a range of class and gender perspectives, most of them encountered the world from positions within the racial and religious mainstream. Levels of involvement in all religions, not just Christianity, were comparatively low in the Northwest. However, non-Christians in the region who chose to disengage from religion likely met specific challenges, as they negotiated not only the dominant Christian society but also their own religious heritage. Although I do trace the racial and ethnic constructions of Northwest secularity, I do not pretend to capture the experiences of those outside of the white, Christian majority. Whiteness was central to understandings of regional and religious identity in British Columbia and Washington. Secularity was imaginatively construed as part of the quintessential Northwest identity – a regional identity premised, in part, on unquestioned assumptions of white dominance. Christian leaders and other cultural commentators likened the "godless" Northwest to foreign mission areas, and called upon racial tropes to situate and explain this regional secularity. For the most part, however, a reliance on Eurocentric frontier imagery meant that Northwest irreligion would largely be constructed as a problem particular to the white population.

For this project, I interviewed approximately fifteen individuals who identified as atheists, which is a greater proportion than in the Pacific Northwest as a whole. My atheist interviewees were, and are, more secular than most Northwesterners; their stories offer a rare lens on this small but significant group in the region. My interviews were not limited to active secularists or atheists. I also spoke with approximately sixteen individuals who identified as spiritual or religious, and thirteen who considered themselves neither spiritual nor non-believing.[51] I approach the oral narratives not as unmediated reconstructions of the past but as cultural constructions filtered through the present. Historian Sarah Williams suggests that in oral history analyses, "when the focus of the endeavour becomes the way in which memory is constructed and the manner of the telling is treated as equally important as that which is told, then the way is opened for the source to yield its unique value, which lies in the first instance in its expression of culture."[52] In this study, I look not only to what the people said but also to the "manner of the telling" for insights into Northwest culture. For instance, women and men spoke different languages of atheism, revealing the powerfully gendered character of Northwest secularity. Women talked more hesitantly and uncertainly about their unbelief, which, I argue, reflects the influence of persistent ideals of feminine piety. This gender discrepancy, along with many other subtleties of culture, would be missed if we looked only to statistical and published sources. Oral narratives reveal insights into the ingrained cultural symbolism of this region. My interviewees reproduced shared essentialisms of the Northwest, describing it as an especially rugged, tolerant, independent, and "unchurchy" place. Rather than debating the truth of such assertions, I interrogate them for what they reveal about the regional culture and imaginary. The Northwest's secular identity emerged, in part, through the stories that ordinary people have told and retold about the region.

In postwar writings, cultural and religious leaders regularly discussed the issue of Northwest secularity, but we rarely hear from the people themselves. Oral history offers a rare window on many otherwise hidden spiritual and secular impulses, thoughts, and practices. American and British scholars have been more apt than their Canadian counterparts to draw on oral narratives to enrich our understanding of popular religion and irreligion.[53] Oral history has the advantage of pointing the researcher in interpretive directions that may not otherwise have been considered. So as not to close down interpretive possibilities, and in an effort not to restrain "the messiness that leaks into everyday life," I structured my interview criteria very loosely.[54] My interviewees had all left or stayed away from religious institutions, but they ranged from the actively atheistic to the deeply spiritual. I interviewed people who described themselves as unbelievers, but who felt it was important to be married in a church; people who prayed regularly but who considered themselves anti-organized religion; people who went to church only to set an example for their children, and who left the church once their children were grown. The interviews reinforced my awareness that humans rarely fit comfortably into the neat categories that are set out for them. At the same time, the interviews also compelled me to take secularity seriously as an element of Northwest culture. Postwar observers often depicted Northwesterners as unwitting secularists – as a people inexorably drawn away from religion by external forces. The people themselves tell a different story, one in which they are agents, rather than passive observers, of secularism. In the view of many residents, the freedom to be religiously uninvolved was and is a positive and valued element of the Northwest lifestyle.

Northwesterners carved out religious and secular identities in relation to not only regional but also national norms. Most historians explore their subjects within the bounds of the nation-state; borders are regularly taken for granted, but their meaning and significance is rarely examined.[55] By adopting a comparative approach, this study brings the border into critical view, and offers new perspectives on the interplay between region, nation, and religion. The border mattered to religious meaning and experience. For instance, public atheism was more prevalent in British Columbia than in Washington due in part to the greater cultural constraints around unbelief south of the border. British Columbians have also been more likely than their Washington counterparts to reject organized religion. For various reasons, there have been wider secular possibilities north of the border. While not discounting national differences, I argue that British Columbia and Washington shared more in common, religiously, with each other than with their respective nations. In so doing, my work challenges the thesis of American exceptionalism. Proponents of American exceptionalism argue that there were (and are) fundamental religious differences between Canada and the United States.[56] In particular they contend that strict church–state separation has significantly distinguished the United States from its northern neighbour. I argue that region often superseded nation in the religious realm, even when it came to those things considered central to nationhood, such as relations of church and state.

Regions are now well understood to be shifting cultural constructions rather than concrete, stable entities.[57] There is no general, shared agreement in academic or popular discourse on what constitutes the "Pacific Northwest." While some use the term to refer to the states of Washington and Oregon alone, others include all or part of the states of Idaho, Montana, and Utah. Historian Richard Brown notes that it is something of a "geographical absurdity" to refer to British Columbia as the Northwest, since from a Canadian perspective this province is in the Southwest. Nevertheless, scholars regularly include all or part of British Columbia in their definitions of the Pacific Northwest.[58] British Columbia was also often included as part of the Pacific Northwest in the cultural media, tourist literature, and everyday discourse of the postwar era. While recognizing the contingent, contested, and indeed somewhat absurd character of all regional categories, I use the term Pacific Northwest to refer to the cross-border region of British Columbia and Washington State.[59] As several scholars have demonstrated, the border between British Columbia and Washington was highly permeable, and the two places in many ways constituted shared economic, cultural, and social terrain.[60] The years following the Second World War brought substantial economic growth to the region's service and manufacturing sectors, although resource extractive industries continued to predominate on both sides of the border. The population of the Pacific Northwest grew at a faster rate than that of both nations. Both British Columbia and Washington received a substantial influx of immigrants, and both became more ethnically and racially diverse. The Northwest shared in the baby boom, economic prosperity, and other national socio-economic trends of the era.[61] This study is not the first to point to the shared economic and social development of British Columbia and Washington, but the place of religion in this cross-border culture has largely evaded in-depth examination.[62] British Columbia and Washington shared much not only in the social and economic realms but also in the religious realm. Of course, both the province and the state embody internal divides, including those between country and city, the interior and lower mainland of BC, and eastern and western Washington. Despite such internal diversity, a distinct secularity permeated all areas, groups, and sub-regions of the Pacific Northwest.

My foray into Northwest secularity begins in Chapter 1 with an examination of how this secularity was approached in church discourse. Church commentators constructed Northwest secularity in ways that both reflected and entrenched wider class, gender, race, family, and regional assumptions. In Chapter 2, I situate the secular Northwest in comparative context, and explore the widespread critique of organized religion in the region. Fuelled by the global dechristianizing currents of the sixties, this critique took quick root in the Northwest, a region where formal religious connections seemed to matter little. In Chapter 3, I examine the ways in which class and gender shaped organized religious involvement in the Northwest. There was a significant working-class component to Northwest secularity, but secularism also slipped into more respectable, middle-class domains. Wider, middle-class ideals around churchgoing did not seem to hold the same power in the Northwest as in other regions.[63] Like class, gender mattered to the secular journeys of Northwesterners. My work brings a new regional perspective to the historiography of women and religion, and offers a rare look at women who challenged or ignored religion. Scholars have given little attention to the subject of women and secularism.[64] In an essay calling for more recognition of women's presence in American religious history, Ann Braude states: "In America, women go to church."[65] Braude correctly points out that women have generally outnumbered men in the churches, and that there is a need for greater attention to women's religious involvement.

At the same time, we know even less about those women who avoided, ignored, or rejected religion, in all of its forms. Although it was construed as a masculine problem, Northwest secularity was produced and sustained by both women and men. It was also nurtured by, and helped to shape, the masculine identity of the region itself.

Northwesterners were more apt than those in other regions to eschew formal religious connections, but few rejected religious belief entirely. Chapter 4 turns from a focus on organized religion to a closer analysis of belief and unbelief. The Northwest's secular culture was characterized by a disinterest in, and antipathy towards, organized religion, but perspectives on religious belief were more varied. Many Northwesterners saw institutions as irrelevant to religious understanding, and the region was at the forefront of the increasingly popular "spiritual but non-religious" category. Atheism was silenced and stigmatized in the Northwest as elsewhere, although this did start to change during the 1960s. Class and gender ideals compelled few to attend church in the postwar Northwest, but such ideals influenced approaches to religious belief. Regardless of class or gender, professed atheism remained rare in the region. However, religion in all of its forms mattered comparatively less in the Northwest, and the region embodied deep strands of religious disinterest, indecision, and ambivalence. Northwest secularity was tied, in part, to regional norms of family, the subject of Chapter 5. Secularity was partially created and disseminated within Northwest households, but the family was also the most common motivator of religious practice in the region. The ambiguities and tensions of this regional secularity were most apparent in the family realm, as Northwesterners struggled to reconcile their own secular impulses with the demands of parents, children, and extended family members.

Although class, gender, and family are important to understanding Northwest secularity, none of these categories alone explains this regional phenomenon. It is not possible to pin down a unitary cause of Northwest secularity, for this was a strand of regional culture that was created and sustained by multiple, overlapping factors. In Chapter 6, I suggest that Northwest secularity was in part a product of place. Religion is often conceptualized as universal, transcendent, and separable from ordinary, worldly things such as geography. However, place was and is central to how religion was understood and experienced.[66] People encounter religion from specific geographical as well as social locations. In suggesting that place shaped human experience, this study echoes, but does not replicate, the thesis of "western exceptionalism." Proponents of western exceptionalism have been criticized for arguing, without adequate comparative evidence, that the North American West attracted and produced an inherently more radical kind of people.[67] My study departs from this essentialist argument by situating the Northwest in comparative context and, following the work of cultural geographers, conceptualizing place as constructed, shifting, and contingent, rather than stable or natural.[68] Secularity was not somehow inherent to the land or people of the Pacific Northwest. However, intersecting demographic, historical, and cultural elements did help to make this a place of wide-spread disinterest in, and detachment from, organized religion.

In the postwar years, as in other eras, Northwesterners were some-times described as a people who had "left God on the other side of the mountains."[69] The Northwest was not a godless region, but there was something distinct about how religion was encountered and understood by those who lived there. In *The Secular Northwest,* I seek to unravel and explain this distinction and to provide new insights into Pacific North-west identity and culture in the postwar era. Northwest secularity was made in elite, official, and everyday spaces. In its making, this secularity reveals much, not only about Northwest identity and culture but also about the ongoing relations of gender, race, class, family, and place in the wider postwar world. In the following pages, we will learn about the secular journeys of ordinary Northwesterners like Joe and Frank, whom we met at the outset of this chapter. In the process, we will discover that being "on the other side of the mountains" did, indeed, matter to reli-gion and irreligion in the postwar Northwest.

1

Constructing the Secular Northwest
The View from the Churches

WHEN I ASKED JOANNE to describe what she and her family would do on a typical postwar Sunday, she replied: "Trying to think what we would do. I think Sunday was sort of the day that you caught up on everything, and sort of had a leisurely getting up, and then you probably would try to get the house somewhat clean, and get the shopping done, and ... and I think generally we would try to plan something social. But Sunday was not much different from any other day except that there was no school or work." Several interviewees echoed Joanne in describing Sunday as "not much different from any other day." Like Joanne, Linda associated Sunday with family and leisure but not with church: "I was frequently home alone on Sunday. And then he'd come home, and he'd have dinner, that's what we would do. And the kids would play with the other kids, all the kids – nobody was going to church, nobody was going to Sunday school. There was no pressure at all." Joanne and Linda were non-believers, but their Sundays were not unlike those of my Christian interviewees. For instance, Richard, who considered himself a Christian, recalled that on Sundays: "we'd sleep in as long as we could, and then figure out what to do for the rest of the day. Because Saturday and Sunday I didn't have to work, so we could go sight-seeing, we could go to museums, we could do things that we wouldn't do otherwise. Or we could leave them with a sitter, and just get out of Dodge." Margaret, also a Christian, reflected: "Well ... [pause] ... it was funny, about that time, two or three of our friends all started skipping church on Sunday. And, you know, we were getting on, and we figured well, we both worked all week, and we had this motor-home, we used to just go away every weekend. And being in Nanaimo, there were so many nice parks up there. So that was really how we got away from it."[1] These stories are not unique; despite a boom in church involvement immediately following the Second World War, by the 1960s more and more people were "skipping church on Sunday."

The growing tendency to see Sunday as "not much different from any other day" was a constant source of concern and frustration for postwar church leaders. These feelings were pronounced among church leaders in the Pacific Northwest, with the region's uniquely low levels of church membership and attendance. Church officials and commentators struggled to understand and explain the limited appeal of the churches in the Northwest. American church leaders regularly remarked upon the unusually "unchurched" character of the Pacific Northwest. In church papers, the American Northwest was often referred to as "missionary territory" and a place "where most of the people live without God."[2] Canada's westernmost province elicited similar comments in church circles north of the border. In 1966, a United Church minister observed: "This is the age of secularism and most people no longer feel any need of the church or obligation to it. This is more true of the province of British Columbia than of any other province of Canada, although this mood will increasingly sweep over the rest of Canada in the next few years."[3] Religious leaders in British Columbia and across Canada echoed this regional assessment. In Canadian church accounts, British Columbia was often likened to a foreign mission-field and described as a province where the "vast majority of the people are lost and unchurched."[4] Church discourse on the secular Northwest offers a revealing lens on the intersections of religion, irreligion, and region in the postwar world.

In this chapter, I draw on church records, reports, and periodicals at both the regional and national level. I consulted a range of sources, both Protestant and Catholic, for insight into how the churches approached and understood their work in the Northwest. Their accounts shed light on the realities of church work in the region, but they do not offer an unmediated picture of the Northwest's religious culture. In their efforts to explain the secularity of the Northwest, church writers and spokespersons drew on inherited and wider assumptions about who was typically irreligious and what it meant to be religious. Such assumptions were shaped and mediated by region, class, gender, and race. In the wider postwar world, the Northwest was constructed and imagined as a frontier.[5] Not surprisingly, it was to the familiar and enduring images associated with the frontier that church leaders most often turned when looking for answers to the Northwest's secular character. Irreligion was depicted as an unfortunate but inevitable result of the region's newness, isolation, ruggedness, mobility, and dependence on resources. Such depictions reflected not only common regional stereotypes but also ingrained race, class, and gender expectations. In church discussions, irreligion was typically described as a uniquely regional phenomenon and as something distinct from, although occasionally likened to, the difficulties associated with Christianizing "foreign" immigrant populations. Church leaders called often upon the Eurocentric category of the frontier to make sense of this "godless" region. Like other frontier characteristics such as individualism and mobility, secularism came to be seen as something made and perpetuated by whites in the region. Representations of Northwest irreligion hinged on unquestioned ideas not only about race but also about class and gender. Church commentators quite matter-of-factly referred to the working classes as anti-religious or, at best, indifferent to the churches. They also took for granted that men were less religious, and less inclined to become involved in churches, than were women. Church discourse on the secular Northwest drew on, and reproduced, normative assumptions about the inherent secularity of the working classes, men, and the frontier itself.

Secularism and the Idea of the Frontier

There has been a stimulating and ongoing debate in the Canadian and American historiography about the relevance of the concept of region to our understanding of the past. Although this debate is by no means settled, it is clear that the category of region was and is meaningful in North American society. As historian Gerald Friesen points out, "Canadians did not agree about the notion of region in the closing years of the twentieth century. And yet regional generalizations abounded in their daily conversation and in scholarly discussions."[6] Certainly, regional generalizations abounded in church discourse on religion and irreligion in the postwar Northwest. Of course, "the Northwest" to which I refer was internally divided by a significant political boundary. Nation mattered to religious identity, but when it came to discussions of Northwest secularity, church commentators on both sides of the border spoke rather similar languages and drew on shared cultural norms. As several scholars have argued, the idea of the frontier figured more centrally in the American than the Canadian social imaginary.[7] American church leaders were more apt than their Canadian counterparts to use frontier metaphors to explain the problems of church life in the whole of the Northwest, from its large urban centres to its smaller, more isolated communities. Canadian church commentators were somewhat more selective in their appropriation of frontier imagery, focusing their attention and their anxieties more on British Columbia's isolated resource areas than on its highly urbanized southwestern tip. In both countries, deeply held assumptions about the regional, class, gender, and race meanings of religion helped to determine where the churches would look for evidence of irreligion and, in many ways, what they would find.

According to American scholars Edward Ayers and Peter Onuf, regional identity is commonly understood as "at heart an inheritance from the past, a moral and intellectual 'heritage' that, if it is to endure, must be preserved from the ravages of modern life."[8] Despite the clear intrusion of "modern life," the Pacific Northwest of the 1950s, 1960s, and 1970s continued to be imagined as, at heart, a frontier. In 1956, a Presbyterian report affirmed that the American "Far West" was a region defined by its past: "History is still repeating itself in the west, or has never stopped writing the first chapters."[9] Although many areas of the Pacific Northwest hardly seemed new or rugged or isolated in the latter part of the twentieth century, the image of the region as quintessentially a frontier persisted. As the anthropologist Elizabeth Furniss argues, the frontier is not a particular place or a specific process but rather "an idea imposed on particular places and processes to provide a framework for understanding."[10] For church commentators, the frontier provided a malleable, ready-made explanation for the religious problems of the Pacific Northwest well into the twentieth century.

American church leaders identified the "still strong lingering spirit of the frontier" as a key determinant of irreligion in postwar Washington. In this period, the Washington and Northern Idaho Council of Churches (WNICC) reported that the "rugged, frontier individualism of early days persists in the Northwest and has affected, probably adversely, the strength of the Church."[11] American church commentators identified a "lingering" frontier spirit not only in the Northwest's remote resource areas, but also in its large urban centres, such as Seattle. The problems of church work in Seattle were regularly attributed to that city's apparent frontier characteristics – its newness, relative isolation, and distance from national centres. As one minister observed, "Seattle is the end of the frontier. Consequently, it has the highest number of alcoholics and suicides of any comparable city of its size in the country."[12] In American church circles, the frontier idea provided a convenient framework for understanding the problems of the Pacific Northwest, including those of metropolitan centres like Seattle. In their search for the source of British Columbia's secularity, Canadian church spokespersons generally turned to the province's remote resource communities, rather than to its cities. However, they joined their American counterparts in using the familiar, frontier idea to make sense of the distinct secularity of the region. According to one United Church minister, British Columbia's religious development was hampered by its position as "Canada's last frontier province."[13] In church discussions on both sides of the border, the Northwest was repeatedly defined as a frontier in the spiritual as well as the social, geographic, and economic sense.

Religious and cultural observers often attributed the Northwest's unusual secularity, at least in part, to the region's geographic isolation, scattered population, and rugged topography. In 1965, a writer for *Seattle Magazine* noted that the "Northwest's geographic isolation ... has much to do with the problems of its churches, because the centers of control and creativity in organized American Protestantism are all some distance away."[14] Church leaders often complained about the region's "remoteness from denominational centers" and its distance from the "mainstream of Protestant developments and fellowship."[15] In a 1960 work commissioned on the Oblate missionaries in BC, Kay Cronin noted: "Even after 100 years of civilisation there is still a vast area of British Columbia which comes under the heading of Frontier Missions as far as the Church is concerned – almost two-thirds of the province, in fact."[16] Protestant and Catholic spokespersons frequently attributed the problems of church work and the constant shortage of pastors in the Northwest to the region's isolation from church headquarters. According to a 1966 United Church report, the "geographical aspects of the Prince Rupert Presbytery cause unusual and difficult conditions for ministers and their wives and families principally because of the isolation."[17] Both secular and religious observers often remarked upon the perpetual lack of clergy in the region. Catholic leaders worried that "hungry souls must go without spiritual nourishment" due to the "undermanned" institutions of the Northwest; in 1951, the Archbishop of Vancouver commented on the great need for nuns to work in "the scattered parishes of this vast Province."[18] In 1960, an article in the *Fort Nelson News* titled "Wanted: Clergymen!" began: "'Where the hell can I find a Protestant minister?' Such was the enquiry we had the other day from a prospective groom. We advised him that they were pretty scarce in this land of opportunity."[19]

The problems of church life in the Pacific Northwest were attributed not only to the region's isolation from denominational centres but to its widely dispersed population. The WNICC noted that the churches faced unique difficulties in the Northwest because "the population is scattered. This fact tends to reinforce any isolationist, separatist tendencies of a highly individualistic population." The Council complained that outside "of city and metropolitan areas, the population tends to be thinly scattered. Such sparsely populated areas are difficult, if not impossible, to church adequately."[20] Similar concerns were expressed in church circles north of the border. At their annual convention in 1964, the Western Canada Lutheran Synod reported that in the British Columbia interior "there are many Lutherans and unchurched families widely removed by space from a congregation. Distance and sparse populations make a normal congregational life impossible."[21] The Northwest was regularly described as a "spiritual vacuum" and seen as existing on a religious as well as a geographic periphery.[22] In church accounts, the connection between geographic isolation and secularism appeared transparent and predictable. In emphasizing the vast and "empty" character of the Northwest, church leaders reproduced the racist assumptions underlying both frontier narratives and the project of colonization itself. While promotional literature often described the Northwest as an "empty wilderness" awaiting social and economic expansion, church leaders regularly depicted the province as a spiritual wasteland in need of Christian development. Both formulations ignored, and helped to legitimize the subjugation of, the rich cultural and spiritual life and history of the Northwest's Indigenous populations.[23]

The Northwest's rugged topography was often held accountable for the absence of a thriving church life in the region. In British Columbia, a Presbyterian official noted that "individual congregations ... are isolated by physical barriers," while an Anglican minister complained that the "lay-out" of the Cariboo region "is not favourable to the development of any but a scattered parochial life."[24] A 1959 Anglican report affirmed that "the Church's hold is always precarious" in northern British Columbia, "which despite modern communications and some development is still a very rough country entailing dangerous journeys along a treacherous coast and arduous trips into a forbidding interior."[25] In 1953, an American Lutheran journal printed an article titled "Geography, A Problem in the West," which described the difficulties of ministering "across the mountains and seas" on the west coast of North America.[26] New ministers in both British Columbia and Washington were warned of the "unbelievable" distances between parishes, and of the "rough" and "rugged" character of the landscape.[27]

Of course, the Northwest's "rough" and "forbidding" topography was more than just an imaginative construction. A rugged and complex terrain *did* confound easy movement through and around the region. Church work in the Northwest was affected in real ways by the region's isolated and scattered population and by its difficult terrain. The meanings attached to this terrain were, however, neither singular nor fixed. The American historian Thomas Tweed aptly observes that "mountains and rivers – components of the so-called natural landscape – are culturally constructed and socially contested spaces."[28] Church leaders did not invent the Northwest's natural landscape, but they did invest it with competing religious meanings. In 1955, the *Canadian Lutheran* offered the following description of northern British Columbia: "To one who sees not only with the natural eye, but with eyes enlightened by faith, the setting is most compelling. The great trees, the hills, and the mountains speak of the majesty and power of God. Yet there is no visible evidence that God is known and worshipped here."[29] An American Methodist leader observed that "we once called the Pacific Northwest country, 'God's great out-of-doors,' but now it's all too often a refuge or escape to all those who want to get away from hearing what the God of the 'great outdoors' has to say to man."[30] In Washington State, low levels of church involvement were often attributed to the prevalence of "nature worship" and to the fact that people were "so easily drawn toward the mountains, lakes, streams and sea-shore."[31] North of the border, Lord's Day Alliance (LDA) officials warned British Columbians: "the fact that you can find God in nature should not deceive you into thinking that you do not need the worship of the Church. Those who habitually excuse themselves from the church on the plea that 'the ... groves were God's first temples' are not the ones for whom nature has her true spiritual ministry."[32] The Northwest's natural landscape was assigned several religious meanings in church accounts. While its rugged and forbidding topography seemed to impede a normal church life, its size and beauty were presumed to embody an inherent spirituality. Church leaders construed the region's landscape as both beautiful and treacherous, as at once inspiring and confounding religious pursuits. This ambivalence was captured in a cartoon that appeared in the *Vancouver Sun* during the Archbishop of Canterbury's visit to British Columbia in 1966. The cartoon, set against a scenic background, shows a local pastor telling the Archbishop: "Our problem in British Columbia, your grace, is the widespread local belief that this IS Heaven."[33]

"A rougher, more itinerant kind of people":
Class, Mobility, and Irreligion

While the Northwest's very physical geography seemed to hamper the development of a regular church life, it was the region's economic base that proved most concerning to church officials. In 1955, the Roman Catholic Archbishop of Vancouver reported on the "marked lawlessness" and "desecration of the Sunday" that accompanied the "big material development in transportation, oil, gas, pulp, lumber, and construction" in British Columbia.[34] Concerns about the spiritual impact of the province's material growth are also evident in a 1967 *United Church Observer* article describing the work of Union College, the United Church theological college at the University of British Columbia. In this article, Rev. E.M. Nichols of Union College remarked on some of the difficulties of ministering effectively in British Columbia: "Other provinces are booming ... but on top of a fairly established rural life. In British Columbia the resource bases of the economy are lumbering and mining, not agriculture. This means a rougher, more itinerant kind of people." Nichols went on to observe that, due to these frontier, resource-based conditions, in "almost all of BC ... the queer ones are the ones who go to church."[35]

It is not surprising that Nichols attributed British Columbia's uniquely secular character in part to the relative absence of agriculture in that province. In postwar church writings, farm families were repeatedly and nostalgically referred to as "the backbone of Canada's religious life."[36] Observed Anglican Reverend Allan Read, the farmer "is unable to work without coming face to face with the deep mysteries of birth, life, growth, death and rebirth, the wonders of seasons, sunlight, rain and many other natural phenomena. These factors help to make the farmer responsive to religious teaching." Farming was imagined as an intrinsically spiritual occupation; church leaders presumed that agricultural and religious decline went hand in hand. Reverend Read affirmed: "Soil erosion means soul erosion."[37] In their efforts to make sense of British Columbia's secular culture, church leaders called upon inherited notions about the secularity of resource extraction and the religiosity of agriculture. They also overlooked the role of farming and rural life in British Columbia, and situated resource extraction at the centre of the province's identity, economy, and culture.

Although agriculture and rurality figured more prominently in the regional identity of Washington than in British Columbia, the state was also associated with resource extraction. According to historians Robert

Ficken and Charles LeWarne, cultural commentators have regularly portrayed Washington State "as a backward raw material colony, dependent upon manufacture and export of lumber, pulp, and paper."[38] Like their Canadian counterparts, American church officials often attributed the low levels of churchgoing in Washington to the state's reliance on resource extraction. In a lecture to a meeting of clergy in Spokane in 1975, Episcopalian minister Thomas Jessett traced Washington's unchurched character back to the nineteenth century:

> Washington ... was settled primarily by men who were mainly interested in exploiting its natural resources. Lumber, coal, fish and oysters were shipped to the profitable California market. Pope & Talbot, a California conern [sic], still owns large acreages in this state. It is no surprise, therefore, to learn that Washington had only 36 churches seating a mere 4,000 persons and valued at only $4,000.[39]

For Jessett, the relative lack of churches in Washington was unsurprising given the economic motivations of the men who settled in the state. That the connection between resource work and irreligion required no explanation illustrates the extent to which this connection was taken for granted. Religion, it was widely supposed, was far from the minds of those who were intent on exploiting the natural resources of the Pacific Northwest. This supposition emerged in the era of settlement, and continued to circulate in the region's postwar imaginary.

Like their counterparts north of the border, American church commentators reproduced normative assumptions not only about the secularizing effects of resource extraction but about the inherent spirituality of farming and country life. Described as the "seedbed of the Church," rural living was presumed to embody "special spiritual meaning" derived from "its nearness to nature, its slower pace, its opportunities for quiet reflection."[40] While church writings suggested that working the land made one more religious, this did not seem to apply to the seasonal agricultural workers of Washington State. Each year, thousands of migrants travelled from both within and outside of Washington to harvest the agricultural crops of the state. African Americans, Indigenous peoples, and Mexicans made up a large proportion of the state's migrant population. Marginalized by virtue of their race and class, these migrants were the subject of much discussion and concern in church circles. Despite their apparent "nearness to nature," Washington's agricultural migrants were referred to as "riff-raff" and seen as disinterested in, and occasionally hostile to, religion and the churches.[41] Unlike the independent farmer, who was believed to be ever conscious of the "gift of God in the earth beneath him," the seasonal agricultural labourer was understood to be spiritually impoverished and part of a "menacing rural proletariat."[42] As this example shows, assumptions about who is typically religious are not timeless truths, but rather contingent cultural constructions. Agricultural labour was considered naturally sacralizing, provided that those performing the labour were not transient, and that they met certain expectations of class, race, and respectability.

In discussing the problem of Northwest secularity, church officials drew on and helped to reproduce what was already known about religion's place in, or absence from, industrial, resource towns. An article in a 1965 edition of the *Western Regular Baptist* noted of the town of Kimberley: "The people have a typical mining community's outlook on life with little room for spiritual or eternal things."[43] As this comment suggests, spiritual indifference was perceived as a "typical" feature of mining communities. The Baptists were certainly not alone in pointing to the secularity of British Columbia's mining and logging towns. Reverend Redman, field secretary of the BC-Alberta branch of the LDA, often grumbled about the irreligious character of British Columbia's resource communities. Redman described Port Alberni as a town "that is not particularly favourable to the Church as a whole, and one in which Sunday is merely a recreation day." According to Redman, the "industrial nature" of the Kootenays meant that it was an area requiring "constant vigilance" on the part of the LDA. British Columbia's company towns, with their "pathetically small" church congregations, drew frequent and anxious comments from LDA workers.[44] American church leaders and spokespersons likewise described the secularity of resource-extractive communities and company towns as inevitable. The WNICC attributed the low levels of church involvement in Washington in part to the individualistic attitude of people living in "lumber towns, mining villages, reclamation projects, new construction centers, and military installations."[45] An American Lutheran journal similarly invoked frontier stereotypes to explain this regional secularity: "In the first place the spirit of the west has been one of material gain and conquest. Here are raw materials in abundance to be exploited – timber, mineral deposits, and fish in the ocean. The spirit of the gold rush days has not died."[46] In church circles, the resource frontier was depicted as embodying and inspiring material – rather than spiritual – endeavours.

On both sides of the border, church writings identified transiency as a key impediment to the development of a stable religious life in the Pacific Northwest. In 1971, the United Church reported that in the Cariboo region of British Columbia "the people are transient, moving from an expansion in mines, to expansion in pulp mills, to other expansions. New people are not yet established and committed to the churches."[47] In 1967, the *Canadian Register,* a Catholic periodical, reported that the "continuous change-over" of construction workers on the hydroelectric project at Mica Creek made it "difficult to expect the workmen to take responsibility for building a church"; to deal with the constant flux of workers, an interfaith chapel was established at the site.[48] Church leaders complained that the transiency of "instant" towns such as Kitimat made it "almost impossible to keep a church roll" and worried about the spiritual "apathy and indifference" of the mobile population of the Queen Charlotte Islands (now Haida Gwaii).[49] In 1966, the *Catholic Northwest Progress* reported that being a priest in one of British Columbia's instant towns meant administering "the sacraments in a kitchen where the paint is barely dry on the walls" and delivering "the new Mass blending with the sound of hammer and saw, pulp mill equipment and loggers' trucks."[50] In a discussion paper on the state of the church in the Northwest, the WNICC concluded that mobility "has negated the traditional avenues of 'belonging' which characterized the stable community of the past – a framework in which the church was central. Many people on the move don't readily seek community in the church."[51] Clergy in Washington noted matter-of-factly that "moving is hard on religion" and that "when people move, they are often lost to the Church."[52] Mobility was seen as the chief obstacle to the spiritual growth of the agricultural labourer. As one minister claimed, "mobility leaves migrants with emptiness of soul as well as emptiness of purse."[53] North of the border, the *Western Regular Baptist* described Prince Rupert as a place that was "dead spiritually" and where it was "respectable not to go to church." To the author, this irreligion was predictable in a town where a "transient population and a greedy materialism are handicaps that must be accepted."[54] Mobility was understood as an inherent feature of resource extractive communities, and as a fundamental barrier to church growth. It was also seen as intrinsic to life in the Pacific Northwest.

The transient nature of the Northwest's population made it difficult to keep a stable church roll, but it also signalled a more fundamental problem with the region's religious life. For church leaders, the problem was not simply *that* people moved but also *why* they moved. Drawing on regional frontier stereotypes, church officials assumed that people moved to and within the Pacific Northwest in part to escape social ties, including those associated with religion and the church. A United Church report on the Cariboo region of British Columbia observed that in that "pioneering country" people "are often slow to associate themselves with the Church or any organization that reminds them of the 'past social pressures' from which they are trying to escape."[55] Postwar observers described mobility as part of the quintessential Northwest lifestyle, a secularizing phenomenon with a deep past. One Episcopalian rector put it bluntly: "Grandpa was doing his own thing when he moved to Seattle, and part of that was not being a Methodist if he didn't want to be."[56]

In postwar cultural and religious media, the Pacific Northwest was imagined as a place of freedom and dynamism, a place without strict social conventions. Viewed as the last frontier, the Northwest was presumed to attract and produce a particular kind of people – "a rougher, more itinerant kind of people." In the Canadian context, like the "hardy fisherfolk" of the east coast so eloquently rendered by Ian McKay in *The Quest of the Folk,* the people of British Columbia's resource frontier were essentialized as a "special kind of Canadian." While McKay's "Maritimers" were set apart by their "natural simplicity, rootedness, and traditional ways," British Columbians were imagined as transient, rule-defying, and freedom-seeking.[57] Regional stereotypes were also widely circulated south of the border, where the restless and independent westerner was juxtaposed against the rooted, traditional easterner and the "backward-looking" southerner.[58] Church commentators often called upon these shared regional images in their selective assessments of Northwest secularity. They also constructed mobility as invariably secularizing, overlooking the fact that the process of moving – both within and between nations – could be a fundamentally sacralizing one. "Life without roots," remarked one United Church minister, "cannot breed and nurture religion. God's fruit cannot grow on shallow ground."[59] Postwar church leaders took for granted the link between mobility and secularity. For them, transiency went hand in hand with irreligion, and was central to understanding the secular character of the Pacific Northwest.

Constructions of the secular Northwest reflected and reproduced deeply held ideas, not only about the frontier lifestyle but about class, gender, race, and family. Certainly class was central to the understanding of who was typically religious and who was most likely to occupy the church pews on Sunday. Postwar church leaders agonized over the fact that their institutions seemed to hold little appeal beyond the middle classes. They widely assumed that the working classes were lost to the church and indifferent to religion. In Canada, the United Church worried that its congregations were becoming "clubby chubby collection[s] of respectable people," while the Presbyterians fretted that "the interests of the churches and of the labouring man seem ever more widely to diverge."[60] American church leaders shared similar concerns, pointing to the "painful fact that wherever industry spreads, the Church usually does not spread" and bemoaning that the "workers have been lost to organized Christianity."[61] In a 1962 report, United Church minister Robert Christie contemplated the impact of industrialization on Canada's religious life:

> As the occupational pursuits of the majority of Canadian workers begin to fall within the orbit of industry, so does the society which they collectively create. They and it become progressively materialistic, hedonistic and unashamedly pagan. History traces the progression of this coarsening effect in older, highly industrialized countries as surely as it reveals its scattered onset in this young and prosperous land. Always, it seems, this expansion of industry and the creation of a largely industrial society has been paralleled by a recession of the Christian church, institutionally and formally. Industrial workers "stay away in droves" from places of the public worship of God until their early fellowship with the church (if any) is forgotten and the lines of communication are broken down and obliterated.[62]

Christie, like many others in postwar church circles, perceived working-class alienation from the church as an unfortunate yet inevitable consequence of industrialization.

Concerns about working-class secularity were not unique to the west coast or to the postwar years. Such concerns did take on a sense of urgency in the Pacific Northwest, however – a region widely understood to be a workingman's resource frontier. The familiar boast "We left God on the other side of the mountains" was understood to reflect the sentiment of the region's miners and loggers, not of its middle classes.[63] The churches were presumed to have their greatest appeal among the "well-to-do middle classes," not among industrial workers and agricultural migrants.[64] Church reports of the 1950s, 60s, and 70s described the working classes of the Northwest as resistant to, or at best disinterested in, the churches and Christianity. In British Columbia, LDA officials complained that workers consistently chose work or leisure over worship on Sundays.[65] Alliance officials also suspected that British Columbia workers were guided by material rather than spiritual concerns, and were too easily drawn away from the churches by the prospect of higher Sunday wages.[66] Church members were urged to do what they could to appeal to the working classes. In 1951, an editorial in the *BC Catholic* congratulated "Catholic laity who are doing their apostolic work among and for the organized laborers," and remarked that the "importance of careers in the labor field cannot be overstressed, and above all, careers for Catholic young men, well versed in their Church's teachings, who alone carry the true torch of Christian guidance for the working man."[67] In an effort to reach the workings classes, churches on both sides of the border initiated industrial chaplaincy programs in the years following the Second World War, which involved clergy taking jobs in the mines, mills, and factories of the region. Michael Boulger, a United Church minister who worked at a Vancouver Island copper mine in 1966, reflected on his experience: "Outside our respectable, clean-shaven fellowship live a multitude of people who have not heard even the slightest echo of the precious gospel message. These miners are members of this crowd of spiritual outcasts."[68] Boulger, like other industrial chaplains, found that church was a hard sell among these "spiritual outcasts." Class expectations underlined the approach of the churches to the "problem" of Northwest secularity. Church leaders, convinced of the naturally secular character of the working classes, were preoccupied with the spiritual life of those who worked in the resource-extractive industries of the region.

"Why don't the men come?" Gender, Family, and Church Involvement

Class, race, gender, and family must be considered not only as demographic categories but also as part of the wider web of meanings through which ordinary people made sense of themselves and each other. Church officials and commentators drew on and helped to establish and entrench the normative class, race, gender, and family meanings of religion. In 1966, a British Columbia minister commented upon the class dimensions of church involvement:

> It is a well-known fact that most of our strong and active urban congregations are in middle class communities, or draw their strength from the middle class constituency. In urban industrial working class areas where the Protestant

churches are composed largely of working people, there are invariably far fewer and smaller congregations than in middle class communities of comparable size. In these congregations the male heads of families are often conspicuous by their absence.[69]

As this passage suggests, class was understood to be a significant determinant of religious behaviour; gender was also important. Church leaders in the postwar decades complained often about the absence of men from the churches. In 1955, the *Canadian Churchman* asked: "Why are there so many more women than men in church on Sunday? Why don't the men come?"[70] In 1951, the *BC Catholic* reported that the "record of all parish organizations shows that the women are better 'joiners' than their male counterparts."[71] In the American context, it was widely acknowledged that women were the "heart of the church" and that only an "unusual congregation" would have "as many men as women in attendance."[72] On both sides of the border, pastors ruefully referred to the evening service as "ladies' night," and readily admitted that women consistently outnumbered men in church organizations and in the Sunday morning pews.[73]

Church leaders were anxious about the spiritual lives of men generally, but they expressed special concern for single men without families. In the postwar era, as at other times, the traditional nuclear family was valorized as "the bulwark of the Christian faith."[74] The family setting was considered particularly essential for nurturing male piety, as men were considered far less religiously inclined than women. Ministers feared that to question a single man about his absence from church would be to summon the quizzical response: "Church? I'm single! Why should I go to church?"[75] The religious lives of married men generated somewhat less anxiety among church officials, who expected wives to use their "quiet but powerful influence" to bring their husbands to church.[76] A cartoon that appeared in the *Presbyterian Record* captured the common perception that married men went to church only when compelled to do so by their wives. The cartoon, which shows two men playing a game of golf, was underlined with the caption: "I almost went to church today, but my wife took sick."[77] Despite their hopes for married men, ministers acknowledged that the Christian church remained a women's domain. In both British Columbia and the American Northwest, church leaders regularly bemoaned men's "lack [of] serious interest in the life of the church" and observed, with chagrin, that many "a man has his religion, such as it is, in his wife's name."[78]

In the postwar decades, as in earlier times, men, the working classes, and unmarried people were understood to be intrinsically less pious than women, the middle classes, and those living in families. Given this class, gender, and family framework, it is not surprising that single working-class men bore much of the blame for Northwest irreligion. Working-class alienation from the church was a gendered issue, commonly defined and understood as a problem of the "working man." While the secularity of the working classes in the Northwest more generally caused concern, the spiritual lives (or lack thereof) of male workers generated particular anxiety. Reverend Wayne Mackenzie reflected on the difficulties he encountered in British Columbia's logging camps: "The single men in the camps won't come out to services ... We announced a round table discussion in one camp and the only people who showed up were the cook and his wife. We planned services in another, but only five women and one man came, so we had a discussion."[79] Mackenzie joined many of his contemporaries in acknowledging that the Christian churches remained the province of women in the Northwest's resource areas. The WNICC regularly pointed out that one of the chief obstacles in ministering to agricultural labourers was that so many of them were "single men with few roots anywhere."[80] In 1968, the *United Church Observer* described the mining community of Tasu as a place made up mainly of men who had "stranded a wife, or burned a draft card." Church services in Tasu attracted the community's few families, but held little appeal to the single miners who had all but "repudiated" religion.[81] Focusing on the spiritual lives of the Northwest's working classes, church leaders confirmed their assumptions about who was typically irreligious.

Like their nineteenth-century counterparts, postwar church leaders were bothered, not only by the absence of men from the church pews, but also by the feminized nature of Christianity itself.[82] The *Canadian Churchman* complained that men "consciously or unconsciously think that the Christian faith is for sissies and old ladies," while the *Presbyterian Record* reluctantly acknowledged that "the church presents a female image in the average Canadian's mind."[83] In 1965, the *BC Catholic* reported that it was the experience of many pastors that "men's clubs organized like service clubs attract more men. They feel that many men are reluctant to join a confraternity for the piously inclined."[84] An American Episcopalian journal noted the "overemphasis on feminine values" in the Christian churches, and called for a "more manly interpretation of the personality of Jesus."[85] Christianity's feminine image was often blamed for the limited appeal of the churches in the manly Pacific Northwest. In the postwar era, as in earlier times, cultural commentators characterized the Northwest as masculine, highlighting the tough and rugged character of the region's geography and its inhabitants. Church leaders also masculinized the region. As one Anglican minister remarked: "This is a land that does not tolerate weaklings."[86]

For church leaders, the masculine character of the Northwest made the feminized nature of the church both more obvious and more problematic. In 1966, a United Church student minister reflected on his encounter with lumber workers and construction crews in the British Columbia interior: "The role of the minister ... has to be reinterpreted to suit the area. It is a typical attitude of the men on this field that the ministry is made up of human beings who belong to a different sex – half way between man and weakling. This criticism is aimed at anyone who studies – teachers, doctors, and ministers alike."[87] On both sides of the border, ministers felt compelled to reinvent themselves and their profession to find acceptance within the Northwest's masculine frontier culture. According to Elizabeth Furniss, British Columbia's regional, frontier identity has been characterized by "anti-intellectualism, the value of manual over mental labour, and the general suspicion of and hostility toward academics, bureaucrats, and professionals."[88] Sensing that they, too, engendered suspicion and hostility in the frontier Northwest, clergy, missionaries, and church workers set out to redefine themselves and their work as rough, manly, and adventurous. This masculine re-imagining is evident in a 1968 *United Church Observer* article titled "A Man's Man in a Man's Town." The article reflected upon the work of one United Church minister in the community of Terrace, British Columbia: "When he sees a job to be done, he does it – like pounding a hammer, or driving a bulldozer, or becoming a minister."[89] In bringing together manual and spiritual labour, this author sought to masculinize, and thereby legitimize, the work of the minister.

In 1962, the Greater Seattle Council of Churches printed the following profile of a Northwest Methodist lay leader: "If he had been born in another era, it would be easy to picture him on horseback, with a rifle in one hand, a Bible in the other ... and his eyes on the far horizon."[90] In the postwar era, church leaders in the Northwest anxiously reproduced narratives and images of a frontier past, a past in which preachers were just as "robust" and "rugged" as other manly pioneers. One such narrative, penned by an American Presbyterian minister, described the missionary work of "husky, two-fisted Frank Higgins ... Higgins preached his first sermon to the lumberjacks in 1895. Much to his surprise, they who seemed to be so profane and godless welcomed his preaching."[91] Masculine metaphors also figured centrally in a Christian frontier narrative that appeared in a 1954 edition of the *Canadian Churchman*. The story related the "Christian adventure" of Father Pat, an Anglican missionary in British Columbia who, while on his way to visit an ailing prospector, encountered a rough and angry group of miners who would not let him pass: "Quicker than lightning, he jerked one of the miners off his horse, struck a blow at another, and having cleared the trail, drove quickly on his errand."[92] This story invests the Christian missionary with the rugged individualism and physical strength typical of more common frontier heroes such as the "virile sheriff" or "itinerant gunslinger."[93] In redefining mission work as manly, this narrative and others like it sought to resolve the gender tensions inherent in, and generated by, Christianity's tenuous place in the frontier Northwest.

Race and the Secular Northwest

Church discourse on the secular Northwest reflected and reproduced deep assumptions not only about gender, class, and family, but also about race. In 1945, the Department of Minority Relations of the WNICC reported on church work in the state: "Outside of the white American group who constitute our chief problem, the Japanese, Negro, and Mexican groups are the major groups for consideration."[94] As this excerpt implies, the churches usually identified whites as the "chief problem" in the region. White Northwesterners drew particular attention, in part because in rejecting religion they contravened dominant expectations of respectable whiteness. That white people bore most of the blame for Northwest irreligion also had to do with the fact that whites made up more than 90 percent of the region's population.[95] While it remained predominantly white, the Northwest became more diverse during the postwar decades. The region's Asian population experienced particular growth during this era, as did the African-American population of Washington State.[96] Although rarely ascribed responsibility for the distinct irreligion of this region, Indigenous, Black, and Asian populations nevertheless elicited much anxious discussion in church circles. By the 1960s, the Christian churches encountered and contributed to the emerging focus on racial inclusion and equality that found eventual expression in the civil rights movement. In 1964, the Canadian *Presbyterian Record* reported on efforts to nurture "a new appreciation of the worth and dignity of people of all races and ethnic groups, regardless of colour or accent."[97] South of the border, Methodist leaders urged church members to accept all persons, "regardless of race, color or national origin," and Presbyterian ministers distributed a booklet titled "Everyone Welcome" in order to encourage racial inclusion in their congregations.[98] In 1966, the *Catholic Northwest Progress* detailed efforts of the Archbishop of Seattle to establish "Project Equality," a program to "fight discriminatory hiring procedures."[99]

In 1962, a woman wrote to the *United Church Observer* to protest the racial biases evident in the children's literature produced by the church: "I am suddenly struck by their underlying assumption that all Canadian United Church children have fair faces and British names. The only reference to modern children of other races is in stories about Africa (from which my child deduced that all Negroes must belong in Africa!)."[100] As this comment suggests, racial prejudices and stereotypes persisted in the Christian churches despite the growing rhetoric of ethnic diversity and acceptance. Several scholars have noted an uneasy tension between older and emerging perspectives on race in the churches and other dominant institutions during the postwar era. According to Mariana Valverde, Canada's Anglo-white social reform community embraced newer discourses on racial equality but continued to harbour ingrained assumptions of white dominance. Informed by competing perspectives on race, reformers endeavoured in this period to at once "respect and yet regulate" certain immigrant and racialized groups.[101]

My research also points to ambiguous views on race in postwar church circles. The gap between the rhetoric of racial inclusion and the reality of race relations was wide in the Pacific Northwest, a region that was often imagined as especially tolerant and accepting of difference. In 1969, the United Church reported on the "multi-racial worshippers" in the British Columbia town of Steveston: "Many of the frontier areas of Canada lead in demonstrating that people of different races and religious backgrounds can be unified in their worship of God and care for each other."[102] This commentator joined in the broader idealization of race relations in the Northwest. The Bishop of the Diocese of Olympia similarly remarked: "We are, and I rejoice to say it, blessedly free from racial tension or racial discrimination in our congregations and, in large measure, in our society as a whole. I am thankful that this is so, and that we are spared the anguish and division which so many communities, both in the South and North, are now facing."[103] The Seattle Council of Churches noted that discrimination in that city was "not as open as in the South or in some places in the North."[104] Although widely disseminated, such regional constructions of race did not go unchallenged. In 1966, a writer for the *Catholic Northwest Progress* concluded that Northwesterners "salve their misguided consciences with the theory of racial relativity: 'Well, at least they're not as bad off here as they are in the South,'" but "are simply less frank and less vehement in their racial prejudices."[105]

The limits of racial tolerance in Washington were starkly apparent in the years during and following the Second World War. In the 1940s, thousands of Blacks moved to the American Northwest seeking work in the defence factories of the region, causing the African-American population of Washington to increase by more than 300 percent.[106] African-Americans continued to make up a far smaller proportion of Washington than of the nation. Nonetheless, as historian Quintard Taylor argues, the dramatic growth of the African-American population in the region "made black-white relations the focal point of far more discussion and anxiety than ever before."[107] The Christian churches joined in the discussion, much of which centred on the enduring issue of segregation. The racial harmony associated with the Northwest did not mesh with the actual discrimination encountered by African-Americans in housing, schooling, and other realms. A Seattle interfaith group noted the persistence of prejudice in its city: "Seattle has many fairylands with beauty beyond description, with lake and mountain views, winding avenues, cultivated gardens, etc. But when the question is asked very definitely the answer is given 'No,' Negroes may not live here."[108] In 1967, a writer for the *Seattle Post-Intelligencer* observed the "de facto segregation" of the city's churches: "the most compelling evidence indicates that coldness pervades the hearts of the congregation when the subject of open housing is broached."[109] Christian leaders regularly spoke out against racial segregation, but racism persisted within the churches themselves. The complex approach of the churches to race relations in postwar Washington defies easy summation. It is evident, however, that the growing African-American community was not assigned responsibility for the secular Northwest. The contested nature of Black-white relations was constructed as a national, urban issue rather than one particular to the Pacific Northwest.

Asian immigration to both Washington and British Columbia increased after the war: people of Asian origin made up 1.2 percent of Washington's population by 1970, and 3.5 percent of British Columbia's population by 1971.[110] In the postwar years, the growing Japanese and Chinese communities on both sides of the border drew particular attention from the churches. For these communities, the war's end ushered in a period of adjustment. With the repeal of Chinese exclusion legislation in Washington and British Columbia immediately after the war, the children and wives of citizens were permitted to emigrate. As Chinese communities in the region adjusted to new family circumstances, Japanese Northwesterners who had been interned during the war began the difficult process of reintegration.[111] The Christian churches worked to counter anti-Asian prejudice following the war, but they were also complicit in entrenching what cultural geographer Kay Anderson calls the "we/they distinctions" that continued to inform Northwest culture.[112] Chinese Northwesterners were alternately praised for their good citizenship and condemned for their resistance to Christianity. "For most Chinese," observed one United Church commentator, "there is nothing beyond the sky, the trees, and their being."[113] Japanese people were understood to be somewhat more receptive to Christianity; nevertheless, church discussions on Japanese people reaffirmed the we/they distinction in the Northwest.[114] Often, Japanese and Chinese populations were conflated, as in a 1963 article in the *Canadian Churchman* that referred to both as "cultures still so bound to pagan beliefs as to make Christianity a novelty."[115] Discourse on the growing Japanese and Chinese populations in the Northwest fluctuated between acceptance and exclusion, revealing ambiguous perspectives on race. The resistance of these populations to Christianity was defined as a global rather than regionally distinct phenomenon. While they drew much anxious discussion in the churches, Japanese and Chinese Northwesterners were not shouldered with the blame for the region's distinctly secular character.

In church discourse on irreligion among Indigenous and Asian populations, a resistance to Christianity tended to be essentialized as an issue of race rather than region. In her study of Canadian Protestant mission work among Aboriginal peoples at the turn of the twentieth century, historian Myra Rutherdale argues that "even when aboriginal peoples imitated [missionary] behaviours and rituals, their attempts were criticized. Inevitably, they were still viewed as inferior somehow." Drawing on the work of postcolonial theorist Homi Bhabha, Rutherdale concludes that deep-seated racial perceptions ensured that even those Aboriginal individuals who accepted Christianity were seen as "almost the same, but not quite."[116] Such ingrained notions of racial difference lingered in postwar churches, tempered but not supplanted by the growing emphasis on racial inclusion and respect. Church commentators often described Japanese people as "great imitators" and questioned their sincerity as Christians.[117] They also regularly depicted Indigenous peoples as innately superstitious. As one American Presbyterian minister wrote: "Superstitions die slowly, and sometimes paganism among the American Indians fights back."[118] Assumptions about racial difference were not confined to the churches – the wider media also reproduced the idea that some groups, by virtue of their race, might become "almost the same, but not quite." In 1966, an article on the Chinese community in the *Prince George Progress* posited that, "despite years of close contact with the western way of life," the "inner recesses of their minds ... still hold true to the Chinese dogmas born from teachings that were old long before Christianity was born."[119] In the postwar imaginary, race defined and delimited religious potential. The irreligion or superstition of certain immigrant and racialized groups tended to be viewed as innate, essential, and distinct from the specifically regional construction of Northwest secularity.

Northwest irreligion was, in fact, actively constructed as an issue particular to whites. Christian and other cultural observers bemoaned Northwest secularity, but they also saw this secularity as a product of the region's quintessential identity. Regions are imaginatively constituted, in part, by race. As the historian John Findlay notes, the "American Northwest has been heavily white, and the prevailing constructions of regional consciousness there have been the product of American whites, and for the most part, males."[120] Like the American Northwest, British Columbia has long been construed as a "white man's province."[121] Non-white populations were regularly ignored, excluded, or depicted as passive objects in dominant images of the Pacific Northwest. Their relative exclusion from regional constructions required, as Catherine Hall aptly puts it in a different context, "the active silencing of the disruptive relations" of ethnicity and race.[122] Certainly, the idea of the region as an untouched religious wilderness was contingent on the "active silencing" of Indigenous spiritual traditions and histories. Through such silencing, the Northwest has come to be seen as a place of whiteness. The region's story is most often told as a frontier narrative, a European invention with white males as the central actors. Perhaps not surprisingly, white males also emerged as the central actors in the story of Northwest secularity.

Although not deemed responsible for creating the secular Northwest, so-called "foreign" populations occasionally figured as metaphors for irreligion in church writings. In a 1961 address to his diocese, the Episcopalian bishop of Olympia expressed alarm at the low levels of church involvement in Washington: "This is not Communist China, this is not darkest Africa – this is the sovereign State of Washington and the Christian nation of America! In spite of the many spires and steeples that dot our skylines the fact remains that less than 50% of the population of this jurisdiction know the first thing about God in any terms at all relative to modern life."[123] This passage illustrates the significance of race to commonsense meanings of religion in the postwar era. "Communist China" and "darkest Africa" were used by the bishop as shorthand to mean irreligion or "heathenism." As the historian Judith Weisenfeld argues, "whether or not African Americans were physically present at the 'center' of the story at any given time or place, white Americans have often made black bodies and 'blackness' present as a trope and put them to various uses."[124] In constructing the problem of Northwest secularity, church leaders invoked well-understood racial tropes and likened the region to "foreign" mission areas. In 1952, a Canadian Presbyterian leader reported on the unchurched character of British Columbia: "one need not leave Canada to be a missionary; here is a field of service no less important and seldom less difficult than British Guiana or India."[125] In church discussions, certain racialized populations appeared not as secularizing agents in the region, but rather as metaphors for what the region might, without Christian intervention, ultimately become. In appropriating racial categories in this way, the churches actively made Northwest secularity a white issue. This secularity, although cause for great concern, was also understood to be a chief characteristic of the Northwest's frontier culture – a culture that was, in the dominant imaginary, made by and for whites.

To the consternation of church leaders, Sunday was – for many Northwesterners – "not much different from any other day." To make sense of this "problem," the churches regularly appealed to the myths, metaphors, and images associated with that most resilient and recognizable of western regional constructs: the frontier. Religion was inevitably weak, so the explanation went, in a region as new and rugged, as isolated and resource-dependent as the Northwest. Regional stereotypes intersected with gender, race, and class to shape, in the wider postwar world, commonsense ideas about who was likely to be religious and who was not. The powerful and enduring stereotype of the rough, transient, and irreligious miner or logger captured the attention of postwar church leaders, causing them to miss much. The churches rendered invisible or irrelevant some important aspects of the region's secular culture. As we will see in the following chapters, this culture was not isolated to any particular area of the Northwest, nor was it the product of white, working-class men alone. We will also encounter far broader ideas of what it meant to be religious. In the opening of this chapter we met Margaret, who, despite remaining a Christian, started "skipping church on Sunday" in the postwar years. Margaret explained why she and her husband stopped attending: "We both got to the point where we just felt that we could be ... that we could live our lives, and our beliefs, without going to church on Sunday. That we could be just as good of a person during the week."[126] As we step outside of the churches, we will meet many other Northwesterners who challenged the assumption that church involvement was an important aspect of true piety.

This chapter has traced some of the wider race, gender, family, class, and regional assumptions that underscored church discourse on the "problem" of the secular Northwest. It has focused more on representations of Northwest secularity than on the material and demographic constitution of this regional phenomenon. This does not mean that this secularity was mere fabrication; measurable levels of formal religious attachment and involvement *were* much lower in the Pacific Northwest than in other regions through the postwar years. In an effort to historicize postwar interpretations of the secular Northwest, I have highlighted the ways in which such interpretations were contingent on the shifting meanings of race, gender, region, and class. The constructed nature of these interpretations does not mean that they say nothing about what was going on in the real world. Indeed, it is a central contention of this study that to understand Northwest irreligion we must unravel how this irreligion was perceived and imagined. In discussing the "godless" Northwest, church commentators drew on what they saw and experienced but also on what they already knew about the region and its people. Such discussions not only reflected but also helped to make and entrench religious expectations, norms, and possibilities. How the secular Northwest was imagined mattered in everyday life. Church leaders were not alone in their rather narrow assessment of irreligion in the Pacific Northwest. They may have been more preoccupied than most with the religious life of the region, but the wider cultural media also shared in reproducing generally accepted ideas about the frontier character of the Northwest, the irreverence of the working classes, the spiritual aspects of nature, and the innate piety of women. Many such normative ideas about religion and region were also widely viewed as commonsense. Unlike church leaders, however, ordinary Northwesterners were apt to affirm and celebrate, rather than lament, the unchurched character of their region. In the next chapter, we will begin to look more closely at why so many in the region chose to "skip church on Sunday."

2

A "mounting tide of criticism"
The Challenge to Organized Religion

GROWING UP DURING THE 1940s and early 1950s in Richland, Washington, Larry was actively involved in a local Protestant church. He attended weekly services with his family, sang in the choir, participated in Sunday evening fellowship, and took part in many church-based activities. His childhood Sundays were "really full and rich." "Sunday was really my social day, my main social life," he recalled fondly. He reasoned: "When you're a child, you believe what you hear. I had a very good childhood, good parents, so no reason to disavow what I heard at church." Through the postwar decades Larry attended university sporadically, completed a stint in the military, and worked in the construction industry. But despite his involvement with the church as a child, Larry never joined or attended church as an adult "because it was intellectually uninteresting. And because I saw so much hypocrisy in the Christian church – people that just go through the motions." Larry was also turned off by the church's "conservative way of looking at the world," particularly regarding issues of sexuality. He attributed the guilt he felt following his first sexual encounter in the 1950s to his Christian upbringing. Although he rejected the church, he admitted that Christianity continued to have some influence in his life: "I guess I would say that I absorbed some Christian principles, that I still believe in, that are okay, like the ten commandments – some of the ten commandments – treat others as you would have them treat you, honour your father and mother and that sort of thing."[1]

By the 1960s, levels of religious adherence and involvement had started to decline in both Canada and the United States, and such levels remained markedly low in the Pacific Northwest. As the quantitative material makes clear, Northwesterners were far less apt than their national counterparts to join, attend, or otherwise actively participate in organized religion in the postwar years. This chapter not only situates the secular Northwest in statistical and comparative context but also begins to explore why formal religious connections were unimportant to so many in the region. While it is uniquely his own, Larry's story reflects some common themes in the oral interviews. Despite their varied backgrounds, most of my interviewees echoed Larry's disdain for the churches as hypocritical, controlling, and conservative. Many also shared his belief in certain Christian principles and a sense that such principles were separable from churchgoing. In their move away from organized religion, my interviewees were part of secularizing trends that were international in scope.[2] Grounded in time and place, their stories are reflective of a region in which to eschew formal religious connections was the norm. Although their perspectives on religious institutions ranged from indifference to hostility, my interviewees shared in entrenching non-involvement in such institutions as an accepted part of Northwest life.

The Secular Northwest in Comparative Context

Northwest secularity is most evident in the region's strikingly low levels of involvement in, and attachment to, formal or organized religion. Today, as in the past, many more people claim a religious identification than actually become involved in the religion of their choice. While the figures on religious identification are not a clear window on religious involvement, such figures are useful for revealing levels of attachment, however tangential, to religious groupings. The chief source for examining religious identification in Canada, the census, reveals that throughout the postwar years British Columbians were much more likely to claim that they had no religion than residents of other provinces (see Table 1).

TABLE 1

Number and percentage of those of "no religion," British Columbia and Canada, 1951–2001

	British Columbia			Canada		
	No religion	Total population	% of population	No religion	Total population	% of population
1951	25,396	1,165,210	2.2	59,679	14,009,429	0.4
1961	27,477	1,629,082	1.7	94,763	18,238,247	0.5
1971	287,115	2,184,620	13.1	929,580	21,568,316	4.3
1981	566,905	2,713,615	20.9	1,783,530	24,083,495	7.4
1991	987,985	3,247,505	30.4	3,386,365	26,994,045	12.5
2001	1,356,600	3,868,875	35.1	4,796,325	29,639,030	16.2

Notes and sources: "No religion" was not included as a separate category in the 1961 census; the figures for 1961 are estimates provided by the Census of Canada. *Census of Canada,* 1951, 10: Table 36; 1961, Table 43; 1971, Table 10–2; 1981, 92–912, Table 1; and 1991, 93–319, Table 1.

In 1951, 2.2 percent of the BC population claimed that they had no religion, compared to 0.4 percent of Canadians nation-wide. By 1971, the percentage of the population professing no religion had risen to 13.1 percent in British Columbia but to only 4.3 percent in the nation. In both 1951 and 1971, close to 80 percent of the population claiming no religion in Canada resided in three provinces: British Columbia, Alberta, and Ontario (see Table 2). However, British Columbia contributed a greater proportion of its population to the no religion category than Alberta, and a far greater proportion than Ontario. Census data on rates of no religion highlight the significance of region to patterns

TABLE 2

Percentage distribution of the "no religion" population by provinces, Canada, 1951 and 1971

	Total population	% of Canadian population	No religion (#)	% of Canadian no religion population
1951				
British Columbia	1,165,210	8.3	25,396	42.6
Ontario	4,597,542	32.8	13,943	23.4
Alberta	939,501	6.7	7,314	12.3
Saskatchewan	831,728	5.9	4,652	7.8
Manitoba	776,541	5.5	3,374	5.7
Quebec	4,055,681	28.9	3,066	5.1
Nova Scotia	642,584	4.6	883	1.5
New Brunswick	515,697	3.7	580	1.0
Yukon	9,096	0.06	236	0.4
Newfoundland	361,416	2.6	113	0.2
NW Territories	16,004	0.1	39	0.1
PEI	98,429	0.7	83	0.1
Canada	**14,009,429**	**100.00**	**59,679**	**100.00**
1971				
Ontario	7,703,105	35.7	343,685	37.0
British Columbia	2,184,620	10.1	287,115	30.9
Alberta	1,627,875	7.5	108,410	11.7
Quebec	6,027,760	28.0	76,685	8.2
Manitoba	988,250	4.6	42,490	4.6
Saskatchewan	926,245	4.3	34,090	3.7
Nova Scotia	788,960	3.7	19,185	2.1
New Brunswick	634,555	2.9	11,885	1.3
Yukon	18,390	0.09	1,625	0.2
Newfoundland	522,105	2.4	2,280	0.2
NW Territories	34,810	0.2	1,025	0.1
PEI	111,640	0.5	1,095	0.1
Canada	**21,568,310**	**100.00**	**929,580**	**100.00**

Source: Census of Canada, Vol. 10, Table 5, 1951; Vol. 5, Part 1, Table 5, 1971.

of religion in postwar Canada. Such rates follow a clear east-to-west trajectory, reaching their highest levels in British Columbia and the Yukon Territory and their lowest levels in Newfoundland and Prince Edward Island (see Table 3).

The statistical evidence south of the border also suggests a unique detachment from organized religion in the West, and particularly the Northwest. Several studies that examine religious trends in more recent years identify Washington and Oregon as together comprising the region with the highest percentage of religious "nones" in the United States.[3] A question on religious preference was included in a nation-wide survey administered in 1952 by a private research group, and replicated in 1965

TABLE 3

Number and percentage of those of "no religion," Canada, provinces, and territories, 1951 and 1971

	No religion (#)	Total population	Percentage
1951			
Yukon	236	9,096	2.59
British Columbia	25,396	1,165,210	2.18
Alberta	7,314	939,501	0.78
Saskatchewan	4,652	831,728	0.56
Manitoba	3,374	776,541	0.43
Ontario	13,943	4,597,542	0.30
NW Territories	39	16,004	0.24
Nova Scotia	883	642,584	0.14
New Brunswick	580	515,697	0.11
Quebec	3,066	4,055,681	0.08
PEI	83	98,429	0.08
Newfoundland	113	361,416	0.03
Canada	**59,679**	**14,009,429**	**0.43**
1971			
British Columbia	287,115	2,184,620	13.1
Yukon	1,625	18,390	8.8
Alberta	108,410	1,627,875	6.7
Ontario	343,685	7,703,105	4.5
Manitoba	42,490	988,250	4.3
Saskatchewan	34,090	926,245	3.7
NW Territories	1,025	34,810	2.9
Nova Scotia	19,185	788,960	2.4
New Brunswick	11,885	634,555	1.9
Quebec	76,685	6,027,760	1.3
PEI	1,095	111,640	1.0
Newfoundland	2,280	522,105	0.4
Canada	**929,580**	**21,568,310**	**4.3**

Source: Census of Canada, Vol. 1, Table 38, 1951; Series 5, Special Bulletin, Table 1, 1971.

by the *Catholic Digest*. In 1952, the regional variations were not dramatic, but the Pacific region contributed a greater portion of its population to America's "no religious preference" population than most other regions. Clearer regional distinctions emerge in the 1965 survey, which found an unusually large proportion of West Coast residents claiming no religious preference.[4] Regional variations in religious preference are also evident in Gallup reports on religion in America. A Gallup survey of America's religious life in 1970 reported that only 3 percent of people in the East, Midwest, and South claimed to have had no religious preference, compared to 7 percent in the West. In the same year, 32 percent of the population in America's West claimed no religious preference, a far greater proportion than any other region.[5] Due to the absence of state-level figures on religious identification in America, it is not possible to identify the number of people in postwar Washington State who claimed no religion or no religious preference. The distinct regional geography of religion in the United States is nevertheless apparent in national surveys, which show that residents of the western states, and especially those on the West Coast, were uniquely detached from organized religion. In this regard, people in the Pacific states shared more in common with British Columbians than with people in other regions of the United States. Examined together, a 1970 American Gallup report and the 1971 Canadian census reveal very similar levels of no religion in these two countries: 4.3 percent in Canada and 4 percent in the United States. In contrast, 13.7 percent of British Columbians, and 7 percent of people in the American West, claimed no religion.[6] Based on data from the *Catholic Digest* survey, and from postwar studies that consistently placed Washington and Oregon at the bottom in terms of church membership, it is very likely that levels of no religious preference in the Pacific Northwest were, in fact, greater than in the West as a whole. The parallels between British Columbia and the American Pacific Northwest continued through 2001, when 16 percent of Canadians and 14.1 percent of Americans claimed to have no religion, compared to a striking 35 percent of British Columbians and 25 percent of people in the American Northwest.[7]

Much to the frustration of church leaders, figures on religious preference in both countries far exceeded those on membership. In 1956, a Methodist pastor in Kent, Washington, commented on the results of a local religious census conducted in his town: "with an active membership of 350 we turned up over 1400 Methodists in this area. What a job! What an opportunity!"[8] This pastor's surprise at the deep gap between religious membership and identification in his community was echoed in church circles across Canada and the United States. Postwar clergymen, noting the wide discrepancy between membership and preference, complained about the growth of "churchless Christianity" and struggled to reaffirm the importance of church involvement to true piety. Religious leaders across both countries warned people not to confuse religion with "mere kindness," and stressed the importance of regular worship in a religious sanctuary, not under "the dome of the sky, or on the golf links."[9] The gap between religious preference and membership was especially wide in the Pacific Northwest. British Columbia's religious institutions have uniquely low levels of membership today, as in the past.[10] A 1977 national survey commissioned by *Weekend Magazine* found that only 36.3 percent of British Columbians claimed to be members of a religious group, compared to 58.9 percent nationwide.[11] Similar regional distinctions are apparent in membership figures provided by religious groups themselves. For example, in the United Church of Canada, the gap between the census figures on affiliation and the number of those under pastoral oversight was much wider in British Columbia than in the rest of Canada. In 1951, only 53 percent of the total British Columbia population claiming United Church affiliation in the census was actually under pastoral oversight, compared to 70 percent in the nation. In 1961, only 58 percent of British Columbians who claimed United Church adherence were under pastoral oversight, compared to 72 percent nationwide. This trend continued in 1971, when only 41 percent of British Columbians claiming United Church affiliation were listed under pastoral oversight – the lowest of all regions in Canada.[12] As we have seen, postwar British Columbians were much more likely than other Canadians to indicate that they had no religion. It is apparent that even those British Columbians who claimed affiliation with the United Church were far less likely than people in other parts of Canada to become involved in the church of their choice.[13]

In the American context, figures from church membership studies reveal comparatively low levels of religious membership and adherence in the Pacific Northwest through the postwar era. Unlike the data on religious preference in the United States, certain church membership studies offer a rare look at state and county-level religious patterns. Two church membership studies conducted for the years 1952 and 1971 offer a useful, albeit partial, window on the geography of American religion in this period.[14] The 1952 membership study was conducted by the National Council of Churches of Christ and includes figures collected, and estimated, from 112 religious bodies between 1952 and 1954.[15] When adjusted for certain omissions, this study points to very striking regional variations in church membership in the United States. Only 45.7 percent of people in the West are shown to be members of the participating religious bodies, compared to 59.1 percent of people in the North Central region, 65.6 percent in the South, and 66.9 percent in the Northeast.[16] When narrower regional categories are used, an even more dramatic variation in the American religious landscape emerges. The Pacific region (Washington, Oregon, and California) had the lowest membership levels in the country, at only 42.4 percent compared to a national average of 61.1 percent. The distinctiveness of Washington and Oregon is apparent in the state-level data. California had a membership rate of 45.7 percent compared to only 34.6 percent in Washington and 32.2 percent in Oregon. In Washington, not a single county reached the national membership average.[17]

In 1971, the Pacific Northwest continued to stand out as the region with the fewest church members in the United States.[18] Despite limitations, the 1971 study points to a distinct regional geography of religion in America that is very consistent with the results of the earlier study. At the state level, Washington was at the bottom with a membership count of 32.5 percent compared to a national average of 49.6 percent.[19] Several scholars have shown that, even when accounting for various gaps and inconsistencies in the data, both the 1952 and 1971 studies reveal a distinct "membership trough" in the West, particularly the Pacific Northwest.[20] Many other national, regional, and local surveys confirm the persistence of unusually low levels of church membership in the American Northwest. Through the postwar years, the Washington and Northern Idaho Council of Churches (WNICC) conducted ongoing research into the religious membership of Washington and the nation. The resulting studies, which span from the 1940s through the 1960s, consistently placed Washington and Oregon at the bottom of the membership scale by a wide margin. For instance, a 1945 survey reported a membership rate of only 21 percent for Washington State, compared to 27 percent in California, 42 percent in Ohio, and 53 percent in New York.[21] In 1952, WNICC researchers revealed a membership rate of 27 percent for Washington and 59 percent for the nation; in 1963, they identified a rate of 30 percent for the state and 64 percent for the nation.[22] Various local studies, including one conducted by sociologists at Whitworth College in Spokane County in 1956, further demonstrated the unusually unchurched character of this region. The Whitworth researchers found that only 32 percent of the Spokane population claimed membership in any religious body, compared to 62 percent of the nation.[23] The 1952 and 1971 membership studies, and the reports produced by the WNICC, are based primarily on figures submitted by religious bodies themselves. Striking regional variations in religious membership are also born out in wider, national polls based on individual rather than institutional responses. The 1965 *Catholic Digest* survey found that people in the Pacific region were much less likely than those in other regions to say that they belonged to any religious group. A 1954 Gallup poll similarly pointed to the unchurched character of the American West.[24] The American Northwest continues to maintain strikingly low levels of religious adherence. "In 2000," note the authors of a recent study, "the Pacific Northwest reached the institutional religious adherence rate of the nation at 1890."[25]

Just as statistics on religious preference must not be taken as a clear window on religious membership, figures on membership should not be equated with those on attendance. Postwar commentators were well aware that on any given Sunday, most church members were not, in fact, present in the pews. In 1965, the Greater Seattle Council of Churches reported on the absence of church members from the pews: "There are approximately 300,000 church members in the Greater Seattle area. If all these people attended church worship services next Sunday morning, then the ministers would agree it was phenomenal [sic], after they recovered from shock."[26] The persistent gap between church membership and attendance was considered a problem across the United States, not just in the Northwest. However, in the Pacific region rates of church attendance fell far below the national average.[27] Gallup polls confirm the persistence of uniquely low attendance levels in the American West through the postwar era (see Table 4). In Canada, attendance problems were especially acute in British Columbia's churches. As one pastor remarked in 1960: "the fact remains that BC people give less proportionately, and attend church less proportionately, than the people in the rest of Canada."[28] A 1960 Canadian Gallup poll reported significant regional differences in regular church and synagogue attendance: only 30.1 percent of people in British Columbia claimed that they attended regularly, compared to 79.6 percent of people in Quebec, 58 percent in the Atlantic region, 49.4 percent in Ontario, and 44.7 percent in the Prairie provinces.[29] A 1977 survey found that only 19.1 percent of British Columbia residents

TABLE 4

Percentage of the population claiming church attendance, United States and regions, selected years

	1954	1955*	1957	1961	1963	1965*	1967	1968*	1970*
US	47	49	51	47	46	44	45	43	42
East	52	52	52	49	52	49	46	46	43
Midwest	45	49	51	47	48	44	48	45	47
South	48	51	53	47	46	44	47	44	44
West	37	38	42	36	35	34	34	32	33

* Figures represent an average for the surveys conducted throughout the year.

Sources: George H. Gallup, *The Gallup Poll: Public Opinion, 1935–1971* (New York: Random House, 1972), 1222, 1389, 1479, 1746, 1856, 1978, 2095, 2173, 2276.

attended religious services once each week, compared to 29.2 percent nationwide.[30] The relatively unchurched character of British Columbia is further revealed in several local surveys, indicating that approximately one out of five people in the province regularly attended worship services in the postwar years.[31]

Dechristianization and the 1960s

At the opening of this chapter we met Larry, whose attachment to the church as a child did not last into adulthood. Larry's turn away from the church was certainly not unique, particularly in the Northwest context. As we have seen, residents of British Columbia and Washington were more likely to reject, avoid, or ignore organized religion than were their counterparts in other regions. Although the border was not irrelevant, this secularity was a distinctly cross-border, regional phenomenon. The Pacific Northwest was uniquely unchurched, but it was also very much a part of the national and global dechristianizing currents at work in the postwar years, particularly during the 1960s. At both the national and regional levels, rates of religious preference, membership, and attendance significantly declined in the 1960s.[32] Gallup polls indicate that while Canadians were more likely than Americans to attend worship services through most of these years, a sharp decline in Canadian churchgoing in the late 1960s significantly narrowed the gap. When asked in 1955 if they had attended church or synagogue in the past week, 58 percent of Canadians said they had, compared to 49 percent of Americans; by 1970, that figure had dropped to 44 percent for Canadians and 42 percent for Americans.[33] While the American figures on religious preference do not allow for a fine-grained analysis, the Canadian figures are revealing. British Columbia's religious picture remained distinct, but the gap between region and nation narrowed somewhat during the post-war years. According to the census, British Columbians were five times more likely than the average Canadian to say that they had no religion in 1951, and by 1971 they were three times more likely to do so (see Table 1). In both region and nation, church involvement declined and Christian privilege weakened during the 1960s; such developments may have seemed less jarring in the Pacific Northwest, with its deeply entrenched culture of religious detachment.

Despite ongoing debates about causes and timelines, scholars generally agree that North America and Britain underwent decisive religious change during the 1960s. As the historian Callum Brown notes, for "organised Christianity the sixties constituted the most concentrated period of crisis since the Reformation."[34] In the 1960s, Christian churches across North America and Britain came under increasing critical scrutiny, as commentators from both within and outside the institutions questioned their relevance. As early as 1961, *Maclean's* magazine printed an article titled "The Hidden Failure of Our Churches," which outlined the declining importance of the Christian churches in Canadian life.[35] Criticism of the churches grew through the 1960s, becoming a virtual torrent by the latter half of the decade. In 1968, an American Methodist commentator observed: "I suppose there has rarely been a time in history when the church has been under more criticism than it is today."[36] In 1966, the United Church of Canada reported: "Here in the North American continent the Church is on the defensive. Even though the vast majority of our people are nominally Christian, a mounting tide of criticism is directed at the organized Church, charging it with being outdated, hypocritical, irrelevant."[37] This "mounting tide of criticism" came, in part, from within the churches themselves. An Anglican priest became the focus of controversy in 1968 when, after declaring that the "really loving, sensitive and concerned people are outside the church," he left his Vancouver church to "seek Christ of the streets."[38] Despite their varied journeys, most of my interviewees contributed in some measure to the growing challenge to organized religion in the 1960s.

Like popular religious cultures, the Northwest's secular culture is not reducible to any single behaviour, habit, or convention. Most people in the region did not adhere to any formal doctrine of secularism. This does not mean, however, that being secular was simply a default position, an identity people unwittingly assumed in religion's absence. Although they ignored organized religion much of the time, many Northwestern-ers were deeply critical of the churches. The criticisms of organized religion that filled the oral interviews echoed those reproduced in the wider postwar media, especially during the 1960s. In many cases, such criticisms were not regionally specific, but they were voiced widely in the relatively secular Northwest. In conversations with the interviewees, dis-cussions about the churches often shifted from indifference to hostility, revealing the existence of deep resentment towards organized religion.

While my interviewees may have been more fervent in their critique of organized religion than others, their complaints were echoed widely in the cultural media of the time. In the 1960s and early 1970s, newspa-pers across British Columbia and Washington reported on the growing disdain for mainline Christianity; as one letter-writer observed: "Young people are turning from the seemingly hypocritical teachings of the established churches."[39] Several scholars have shown that young people were especially likely to doubt, deny, or drift away from organized reli-gion in the postwar era.[40] In the Canadian context, the proportion of the population claiming no religion in the census tends to be smaller among older age groups. In 1971 for instance, Canadians between the ages of 20 and 34 were the most likely to claim no religion, whereas those over 70 years of age were the least likely. It should be noted that regardless of age group, British Columbians were far more likely than their counterparts in other provinces to claim that they had no religion.[41] Age does not account for the Northwest's distinct secularity, but it was significant to religious adherence and involvement. According to Nancy Christie and Michael Gauvreau, the youth revolt of the sixties helped to usher in the "spirit of individualism" that came to characterize the modern world.[42] Few of my interviewees considered themselves to be part of the youth counterculture. This likely had to do with the fact that most were born in 1940 or earlier and thus came of age prior to the 1960s. Nancy, who was born in 1940, reflected on the experience of her generation:

> We preceded the hippie generation, but not by a whole lot. You know, they kind of came in about ten years after us. Our ... our group, you know, the students that we went through university with, I would say were doing the intellectual analyzing of, you know, societal values and politics and all of those kinds of things, and then the generation that followed us were the ones who became the activists. They're the ones that actually got out and did something and demonstrated and, you know, kind of put their life on the line, where we didn't, our generation.[43]

As Nancy's comments suggest, the cultural questioning that erupted during the sixties had been simmering for some time. Though the interviewees may not have fashioned themselves as counterculturalists, many admitted to being, in the words of Thomas, "very sympathetic with the philosophies of the time."[44] A few were especially sympathetic to the countercultural loosening of moral and sexual codes. Sandra rejected the Christian church, in large part, because of its conservative views on sexuality: "I started really breaking with Christianity around [the age of] 14 or 15, when I started realizing that I had a very strong sexual drive, and saw that Christianity is extremely uneasy with the body, hates the body, in fact."[45] Larry, whom we met earlier, attributed his drift from the church in part to his sense of guilt following his first sexual relationship – a guilt that he blamed on his Christian upbringing.[46]

Although only a few interviewees spoke explicitly of their rejection of Christian moral and sexual codes, most shared a general disdain for the authority of the churches. Several factors underlay the dechristianizing trends of the sixties, including the "broader cultural questioning of authority" that characterized the era.[47] Such questioning does indeed emerge as a central theme in the oral interviews. Larry explained his drift from the church: "Well, I saw that guilt was a big part of Christian authority. I saw that people wanted to control you. Some people need to control. Quite often it's the social structure, business, corporate business, police, military, you know, they're all part of that control system. I was always a maverick, you know. It wasn't conscious, but I was always anti-authoritarian."[48] Many interviewees echoed Larry in attributing their rejection of the church in part to their contempt for authority more generally. Such contempt must be situated in relation to broader postwar trends. As Nancy Christie and Michael Gauvreau aptly note,

> perhaps the most potent explanation for the difficulties of organized Christianity in the postwar era on both sides of the Atlantic was the growing centrality of precepts of individualism, involving a broader rejection of external authorities including churches among many other institutions, and an emphasis on choice, in which the terrain of the personal remained a paramount cultural objective of an ever larger proportion of people, both male and female.[49]

In shunning the churches as overly authoritarian, my interviewees shared in the wider challenge to organized religion that emerged in the postwar years. George related the main reason that church never appealed to him: "I don't like being told what to do, I don't like being told what to think."[50] Unlike George, who had no history of church involvement, several interviewees told stories of leaving churches they saw as too controlling. Helen turned away from the Catholic church of her childhood when she discovered that "there were other choices" and had grown tired of being "told what to think, what to do, and how to feel, that sort of thing."[51] Margaret and Patricia similarly described their growing resentment towards the churches. Both women were active in a Nanaimo Anglican church as young mothers. Margaret reflected upon her journey from the church: "I guess after working so many years in the church, I kind of thought, you know, there must be a different way of believing the same thing, without sitting there on a Sunday and getting lectured at." Likewise, Patricia described "finally" coming to her senses when she discovered "that you didn't need to be a sheep, and sit there, and listen to somebody's theories, and not have an opportunity to question."[52] While they may not have been part of the youth counterculture, the interviewees shared in the broader questioning of authority – particularly religious authority – that took root during the sixties.

The Charge of Hypocrisy

In Larry's view, not only was the Christian church controlling and conservative but its members were hypocritical: "the more I began to look around me, I saw that there weren't too many people living the Christian life – there was a lot of hypocrisy."[53] Several of the interviewees echoed Larry in condemning the hypocrisy of churchgoers. While Mary's social life as a teenager centred on Protestant church groups, she drifted away from the church as an adult. Born in 1919, she moved from Montana to Olympia in 1942. According to her, the churches were "over-organized, and over-hypocritical, and the women in the Ladies' Aid even, they couldn't decide whether they're going to have cream chicken or cream tuna. I mean it's ... Religion had nothing to do with it! Ladies' Aid didn't even mean religion!"[54] Mary's detachment from the church was active and concerted rather than incidental, underscored as it was by a deep resentment towards organized religion. Although she expressed her resentment in personal and emotional terms, such sentiment reflected a wider and growing antagonism towards the churches in the postwar era and conveyed a central theme of Northwest irreligion. As scholars continue to unveil the common myths, symbols, and "languages of belief" that have constituted popular religious cultures across time and place, the shared meanings of popular secularism have gone largely unnoticed.[55] Oral history is an especially useful tool for exploring such shared meanings. As the historian Robert Rutherdale argues, "personal pasts are simultaneously embedded in social pasts": ideas, beliefs, and memories that appear idiosyncratic within a single life story take on wider cultural significance when they recur across several narratives.[56] Criticisms of religious hypocrisy appeared in most, though not all, of the oral interviews in this study. Given that my interviewees were asked to reflect upon their journeys away from religion, the issue of hypocrisy likely took on significance in the very process of remembering. In levelling the charge of hypocrisy on religious persons and institutions, my interviewees explained and made sense of their own drift away from organized religion.

Northwest secularity was not a formal system of meaning, but it did embody certain shared meanings and practices. Criticisms of church hypocrisy were widely circulated, not only among ordinary people, but in the cultural media of the day. In 1971, the author of a letter to the editor of the *Seattle Post-Intelligencer* exclaimed:

> What I saw of churches, church members, church dignitaries, and church charities during my early years of church attendance caused me to forever leave any and all established churches. I do not believe that belief in a God or a Jesus is at all based upon any relationship to any church on this Earth. In fact, it is my opinion that if Jesus were to walk the streets of this Earth today he would not regard "churches" as temples or sanctuaries, but as dens of thieves.[57]

A few years earlier, in 1967, a letter in the *Canadian Churchman* similarly chided the "irrelevance, hypocrisy and archaism of the church."[58] In 1986, an article in Seattle's weekly paper reflected on the disenchantment that emerged during the 1960s: "Post-war babies now grown up left the church armed with criticisms, not the least of which was that ministers didn't practice what they preached and gave sermons that didn't relate to real life, and congregants practiced Sunday hypocrisy."[59]

Denunciations of religious hypocrisy weave their way through the oral narratives, taking on a personal and occasionally emotional tone in some memories. Nancy, the daughter of missionary parents, explained why she left the church as an adult:

> A real issue for me became – and I'll just spell it out real clear – the hypocrisy, okay, that I saw amongst people who call themselves Christians, and conducted

what one could call, I guess, a life of religious commitment where there was attending church on a regular basis, being a very involved member in the church, etcetera, etcetera. And, it's very, very sad to say, but I even saw it in my own family. The lack of consistency. I have trouble with people who say one thing, and do another. I just, to this day, I have difficulty digesting it.[60]

Nancy left the church in part because of the hypocrisy that she encountered within her Christian family. Like Nancy, Susan also experienced deep hurts around religion within her family, which caused her to abandon the Mormon faith of her childhood. She complained that people "think if they go to church on Sundays, it doesn't matter what they do during the week [laughs]. You know, they can be SOBs and thieves, as long as they go to church on Sundays."[61] Similarly, Anne related the painful personal encounters that sparked her disassociation from the church:

[A]fter I left home I could see that people who were supposedly religious were not as Christian as a lot of people that I was acquainted with. I mean, Christianity, what do you call that? My interpretation of a Christian is somebody that is kind, and good, and I didn't see that at all. [Sister] and I lived in foster-type homes for a while, they weren't foster homes but, because my father was in the services, they were friends of his, friends of friends. They weren't friends, believe me, they weren't friends. They weren't friends at all. They were supposedly good people, they took us in because we had nowhere else to go, my father was worried about us, but it turned out that there was abuse, it was not good at all. Not bad, but bad enough for a young kid ... And all the while we went to church. All the while, all those people, you always went to church with everybody. It kind of soured me ... [trails off].[62]

Anne rejected the church for personal reasons, but she was not alone in identifying a disjuncture between the ideal of Christian goodness and the behaviour of churchgoers.

While some people framed their discussions of religious hypocrisy in very personal terms, most of my interviewees – including those who had never entered a church – voiced more general complaints, directing much of their antipathy towards people who filled the pews. They described the churchgoers in their communities as "mean and grovelling," "unkind," "two-faced," and "the crookedest people in town."[63] Patrick, who worked as a bartender in Nanaimo through the postwar decades, reflected on his impression of church people: "I think even at a young age I realized that these people were not interested in helping people as much as they were interested in their own self-betterment."[64] Many attributed their own detachment from the church in part to the hypocrisy of church-goers. Margaret grew disenchanted with the church partly because of the hypocrisy of those in attendance: "So often people that would sit there, pious as could be on a Sunday, weren't so pious during the week ... There they are sitting on Sunday like butter wouldn't melt in their mouth, and then in the rest of the week just not being too – what we felt – was Chris-tian."[65] Deborah was likewise turned off by the "behaviour of people who were supposedly devout. The more I saw," she recalled, "the less enam-oured I became." Her experiences with religious hypocrisy in a small east-ern Washington town caused her to abandon religion altogether: "living in that small town and seeing the hypocrites that were lined up at the church door on Sunday, and were out with somebody else's wife on Sat-urday night, or were mistreating their employees. My experiences were more negative than positive, with the people who lived in the town."[66] Others similarly remarked upon certain "scoundrels," "bandits," "swin-dlers," and "conmen" who occupied the church pews.[67]

Historian Sarah Williams points to the ingrained idea in nineteenth-century working-class London that the "non-church attender could in fact live more closely to an ideal of true Christianity than a regular attender."[68] According to Williams, regular churchgoers were frequently charged with hypocrisy, their behaviour judged according to a far higher standard than that of people who stayed away from the churches. Similar ideas informed denunciations of religious hypocrisy in the postwar Northwest. As a Univer-sity of Victoria professor observed in 1962, people were "much more con-temptuous of non-religious churchgoers than of agnostics or atheists."[69] Regardless of their social class or religious identity, my interviewees were indeed contemptuous of churchgoers whose behaviour did not conform to well-understood standards of "true" religion. To them, it was better to reject organized religion altogether than to be superficially or insincerely religious. The prevalence of this idea incited anxiety among church lead-ers, who struggled to affirm the importance of regular churchgoing to true religion. Much to the dismay of church officials, a 1969 survey con-ducted in Victoria, British Columbia, found that most residents of that city believed that a "truly religious person" should be more concerned with "good works" than church attendance or prayer. Such results confirmed the clergy's longstanding suspicions that most people were "seriously mis-taken" about what it meant to be truly religious.[70] Despite the efforts of church leaders to define for the people what it meant to be truly religious, ordinary Northwesterners continued to make up their own minds about how, or indeed whether, to be religious.

"Going to church just never even occurred to me": Religious Indifference

Drawing on dominant discourses and their own personal histories with the churches, the interviewees complained that organized religion inspired and embodied elitism, greed, hypocrisy, and various other evils. The greatest challenge to the postwar churches was not, however, criticism or unbelief, but rather comfortable indifference.[71] Religious indifference seems to have been especially comfortable in the Pacific Northwest. While they were eager to share their criticism of the churches, the people with whom I spoke also emphasized the unimportance and irrelevance of organized religion in their own lives, and in the life of the Northwest generally. That this regional culture assigned relatively little importance to churchgoing is revealed in the low levels of institutional involvement, as well as in wider discourses on the church in the Northwest. Commentators on both sides of the border noted the absence of "cultural Christians" in the region and observed that "casual, social churchgoing of the type seen elsewhere ... isn't a major part of Northwest living."[72] Ministers who came to the region from elsewhere were surprised to come across towns where local residents avoided or disdained the churches without risk of social consequence. In a regional setting where there seemed to be "no social stigma ... attached to non-attendance," people could avoid the churches without fear of social exclusion.[73]

My interviewees widely affirmed that church involvement was irrelevant to social acceptance in the postwar Northwest. Richard, a long-time Olympia resident, commented that church involvement "may have made a difference in some communities, but certainly not here."[74] William likewise recalled the insignificance of the church in his postwar community: "Nobody went to church that I'm aware of ... There was absolutely no religion in my neighbourhood, or among my friends, or among my family acquaintances."[75] Many other interviewees reflected upon the invisibility of the churches in their Northwest neighbourhoods. The oral interviews suggest that this invisibility was, at least in part, regionally specific. Seattle resident Charles remarked: "I haven't really been cognizant of the church since we moved out here. Just never have been. But back East I was."[76] Although often overlooked, place matters to religious practice and experience. As sociologist Rhys Williams writes, "everyday, lived religion – religion as the myriad cultural expressions of people as they move, grow, marry, die, and try to make sense of it all – depends crucially on place to constitute what it is."[77] Stories about the insignificance of churchgoing were very clearly grounded in a sense of place. Reflecting upon her childhood in Montana, Sandra remarked: "We didn't go to church, and I'm sure it cost us. We were weirdos in Montana." When she moved to Seattle, Sandra discovered that non-attendance at church, while culturally subversive in Montana, was normative in her new city: "I think it's very easy to ignore religion living in Seattle."[78] It was also easy to ignore organized religion in Port Angeles, Olympia, Nanaimo, and other regional centres. In the 1960s, John left Ottawa for Nanaimo and was struck by his new town's indifference towards organized religion. When asked whether the church was important to social life and status in the postwar decades, John replied: "In Ottawa yes, in Nanaimo not that I know of."[79] Sharon similarly recalled that she "was really amazed" at the lack of churchgoing in British Columbia, after moving to Victoria from Edmonton in the 1940s: "I was quite surprised when I got here, because people, where I had come from in Edmonton, the people that we knew were – other than my grandmother – most of them belonged to some religion, and went to church. So, when we came out here it was quite surprising that so many people didn't go to church."[80]

Deborah reflected upon the irrelevance of the church in her postwar Seattle neighbourhood:

> I knew the people that lived here, I mean in this neighbourhood, most of whom are still here, and none of us went to church. There was a Mormon couple who lived across the way for a few years, but other than that, no one in this block that I knew went to church. And I had met many of [daughter's] friends' parents, but I was never friendly with them. I was the first single woman who owned a house in this development, and that was at a time when, you know, people wouldn't associate with a single parent. And, so, I wasn't invited to people's homes or anything like that.[81]

Deborah identified single motherhood, rather than irreligion, as the basis for her marginalization. Isolated as a divorced, single parent among married couples, she suffered little social disapprobation for being part of the approximately 70 percent of Northwest residents who stayed away from worship services each week. Like Deborah, Frank reflected that his social exclusion in postwar Seattle had nothing to do with his detachment from church: "No, I don't think there was any feeling about that. I felt I may have been left out for other reasons, I may have been ignored for other reasons, it may have been my evident financial status, rather than for anything I'd say about religion."[82] Joanne also recalled feeling "othered" in her Seattle neighbourhood on the basis of class rather than religious reasons: "everybody had cashmere sweaters, and they, you know, dressed to the hilt. And we couldn't afford it."[83] A range of factors, including class and single parenthood, seem to have been more significant determinants of acceptance in Northwest communities than church involvement.

In 1980, a journalist reported that "organized religion does not have the kind of reflexive backing in Washington and the Far West that it does elsewhere. The 'non-adherers' apparently do not feel social constraints here to pretend otherwise and are openly indifferent."[84] As this comment suggests, Northwesterners knew that not attending church fulfilled rather than contravened social expectations. Decisions regarding their personal church involvement inspired little uncertainty or anxiety among my interviewees, regardless of their social location. Comfortably indifferent to organized religion in Seattle, Joanne speculated about how her relationship with the church may have differed had she lived elsewhere: "If I had lived in a place where the church was the dominant thing ... I can't believe I would've become religious. I might've been involved in a social aspect of the church, but I don't believe I ever would've intellectually embraced it."[85] Edna, who moved from Oklahoma to Washington in the 1940s, recalled the deep apathy about churchgoing in the latter state: "I don't think anybody really thought about it. Go or not go, whatever you wanted to do." This wider indifference to the churches underscored Edna's own decision to stay home on Sundays: "I was reinforced in my not going to church because nobody around me did." Edna admitted that had she stayed in Oklahoma, where there was "more pressure to conform," she might not have become an avid churchgoer but she "would've probably made more of an effort to pretend."[86] Edna and Joanne echoed many of their contemporaries in attributing their detachment from the church, in part, to regionally specific social conditions. In choosing to avoid the churches, these women drew on and also helped to reinforce and perpetuate the secular culture of the Northwest.

Northwest habits of indifference to organized religion were and are more nebulous than customs pertaining to faith and worship, but no less important to understanding this regional culture. Charles assured me that in Seattle his friends and neighbours "couldn't have cared less" about his relationship, or lack thereof, with the church; likewise, Edward recalled that the church "never seemed to come up at all" among his friends and neighbours in Nanaimo.[87] In telling their stories, the interviewees not only reflected upon the secular Northwest but also helped to construct it. As Robert Rutherdale suggests, in approaching oral histories we should "treat individual memories as subjective products of social relations rather than as objective records of personal pasts."[88] The interviewees situated their own religious detachment within a wider, shared Northwest culture. They assured me that by ignoring the churches they risked neither isolation nor discrimination. Through their language and behaviour – through the very process of remembering – the interviewees constructed an indifference to formal religion as a normal and accepted part of Northwest life. They spoke a common rather than idiosyncratic language of religious detachment, echoing each other in describing organized religion as "unimportant," "irrelevant," "unnecessary," and a "non-event."[89] Many would recognize themselves in the following remark of a Vancouver woman: "going to church just never even occurred to me."[90] This quotidian expression of disinterest nicely captures the comfortable indifference to organized religion in the postwar Northwest.

In the opening of this chapter we learned that, despite his nostalgia for the church-centred Sundays of his childhood, Larry came to view the Christian church with a mix of aversion and disinterest. Although he may not have seen it as such, Larry's drift from the church was part of a larger challenge to organized religion. His story hints at broader dechristianizing currents that emerged in the postwar era, particularly during the 1960s. Such currents included a decline in religious involvement, a rejection of Christian moral and sexual codes, and a growing critique of church authority. In challenging the hypocrisy and conservatism of the churches, and relating "true" religion to individuals rather than institutions, the interviewees joined and furthered trends that were international in scope. Shaped not only by time but also by place, their stories are in certain ways uniquely Northwestern. Whether they were criticizing the churches or, as was more often the case, ignoring them, they did so in a comparatively secular region, in communities where to be comfortably indifferent to organized religion was the norm. Interviewees were part of a shared regional culture, but they were from diverse social locations. Their secular journeys varied by class and gender, as we shall see in the following chapter.

3

Class, Gender, and Religious Involvement

A LONG-TIME NANAIMO RESIDENT, Sylvia attended a local United Church as a child, a practice she continued into young adulthood. Through the early years of her marriage in the 1950s, as she and her husband started a family, she remained a churchgoer. Sylvia's husband never attended church, partly out of indifference and partly due to the demands of his work at a local pulp mill. As Sylvia remarked, "Pulp mill work was 7 days a week, 24 hours a day." Sylvia stopped attending church in the 1960s, in part due to a change in church policy. Although she had never been a formal member of the church, Sylvia had her first three children baptized in the church. When it came time to baptize her fourth child, the church refused until Sylvia became a full member. Turned off by a church that was, in her view, becoming too rule-bound, Sylvia also became disenchanted with a congregation that seemed increasingly "cliquey" and status-conscious. When I asked why she did not seek out a different church, she responded: "I guess I just probably didn't have the time, or the finances, raising four kids. And especially when our last one was born, we were in the process of probably moving at the time, my husband was working at Harmac, and you never knew when they were going to be on strike, and I didn't know whether I was going to go back to work."[1] Like Sylvia, Patricia stopped attending church during the sixties. Patricia invested much of her time and energy in a local Nanaimo Anglican church in the years following the Second World War. At one point during the 1960s, she faced exclusion, by virtue of her sex, from a church financial committee: "I thought, well, if that's the way they like it, I suppose I shan't bother to raise any more money for them ... I just thought, well that's all the cakes I bake for them! [laughs]." When she learned that she was being restricted because she was a woman, Patricia left the church. Her husband, a mechanic, also stopped attending because "he wasn't all that fired up about it anyway."[2]

While Sylvia and Patricia were part of the much broader postwar challenge to the churches, their stories also hint at some of the ways this challenge varied by class and gender. Despite the focus of the clergy on male
resource workers, Northwest irreligion was not exclusively isolated to any
group or area in the region. Church leaders observed that the Northwest's
working classes were especially secular. However, they often overlooked,
or perhaps tried to ignore, the extent to which irreligion permeated the
more respectable elements of Northwest society. Class did not determine
Northwest irreligion, but there was, as religious leaders feared, a clear
strand of working-class antipathy to the churches in the region. Several
of the working-class interviewees shared Sylvia's disdain for the churches
as overly "status-conscious." Many also saw certain material barriers to
church involvement, such as financial uncertainty and the irregularity of
shift work. Like class, gender shaped perspectives on organized religion
in the postwar Northwest. During the turbulent sixties, more and more
women began to question, and sometimes to abandon, the churches.
Some were turned off by the patriarchy of church governance; others
ignored or gradually drifted away from churches that seemed out of step
with changing gender ideals. While Sylvia and Patricia negotiated persistent (though waning) expectations of womanly piety, their husbands
fulfilled masculine norms of religious indifference. Class and gender
shaped not only individual experiences but the broader regional identity of the Pacific Northwest. Middle-class and feminine religious ideals exerted comparatively less force in the Northwest, a region that was
often essentialized as a male resource frontier.

Religion and Demography

Northwest secularity cannot be attributed to a peculiar demography of
race, class, or gender, as all residents of the region, regardless of social
location, were less likely to have formal religious connections than their
counterparts in other areas across Canada and the United States. That
Northwest irreligion was and remains a cultural rather than exclusively
demographic phenomenon is well established in the existing literature.
As Patricia Killen and Mark Shibley note, American Northwesterners
with no religious preference are so "demographically conventional" that
"not to identify with established religion is an ordinary rather than a
countercultural practice in the Northwest."[3] A rather ordinary part of
postwar Northwest life, religious non-involvement cut across lines of
race, ethnicity, class, and gender.

TABLE 5
Percentage distribution of the "no religion" population by ethnicity, British Columbia and Canada, 1971

	Canada		British Columbia	
	Total population	No religion	Total population	No religion
British Isles	44.6	56.0	57.9	55.6
French	28.7	7.5	4.4	3.7
German	6.1	7.9	9.1	7.8
Italian	3.4	1.0	2.5	1.0
Jewish	1.4	1.1	0.6	0.5
Netherlands	2.0	3.7	3.2	3.6
Polish	1.5	1.5	1.4	1.3
Scandinavian	1.8	3.5	5.1	5.4
Ukrainian	2.7	3.2	2.6	2.8
Asian	1.3	6.9	3.7	10.4
Native/Inuit	1.5	0.9	2.4	0.8
Other and unknown	5.2	6.8	7.0	7.4

Source: Census of Canada, Vol. 1, Part 4, Bulletin 7, Introduction and Table 19, 1971.

The racial and ethnic makeup of British Columbia differed in some notable ways from the nation generally. The province contained more residents of British, Asian, and Scandinavian origin, and fewer of Italian and French descent, than Canada as a whole (see Table 5). The number of persons claiming no religion in the census was highest among British, Asian, and Scandinavian groups, and lowest among Italian and French populations. We might suspect, then, that a distinct racial and ethnic demography accounts for British Columbia secularity. Yet while race and ethnicity shaped religious behaviour, these categories do not explain the peculiar secularity of Canada's westernmost province. The ethnic and racial distribution of British Columbia's non-religious population was very similar to that of the nation. Generally, groups that were over-represented in Canada's non-religious population, such as those of Asian origin, were also over-represented in British Columbia's non-religious population. Conversely, Italian, French, and Aboriginal peoples were under-represented among the non-religious in both British Columbia and Canada. The fact that groups with traditionally high levels of no religion were over-represented in British Columbia likely contributed to the province's secular culture. However, BC secularity cannot be reduced to a distinct ethnic demography. All ethnic and racial groups in the province were uniquely non-religious (see Table 6). Even ethnic groups with the highest rates of religious affiliation nationally more readily claimed

TABLE 6

Percentage of the population claiming "no religion" by ethnicity, British Columbia, Ontario, and Canada, 1971

	British Columbia	Ontario	Canada
British Isles	12.6	4.8	5.4
French	11.0	2.2	1.1
German	11.2	4.9	5.6
Italian	5.2	1.0	1.3
Jewish	11.2	3.4	3.3
Netherlands	14.7	6.5	8.2
Polish	12.0	3.5	4.3
Scandinavian	13.7	7.4	8.5
Ukrainian	13.1	4.9	5.1
Asian	37.4	17.0	22.5
Native/Inuit	4.3	3.8	2.7
Other	13.7	4.0	5.7
Total	**13.1**	**4.5**	**4.3**

Source: Census of Canada, Vol. 1, Bulletin 7, Introduction and Table 19.

no religious affiliation in British Columbia: people of French descent were a striking 10.2 times more likely to claim that they had no religion than their national counterparts, and those of Italian descent were 4 times more likely.[4]

The 1970 United States census indicates that Washington State contained proportionately more people of Swedish, Danish, British, Chinese, and Japanese backgrounds, and fewer of Italian, Mexican, and Polish descent, than the nation as a whole. Apart from these variances, the ethnic distribution of Washington's foreign-born population, which made up only 4.6 percent of the state's total population, mirrored that of the nation. American surveys from the postwar era provide a general view of religious affiliation by race. Washington's population was whiter than that of the nation as a whole: in 1970, the nation was 87.5 percent white and the state was 95.4 percent white. African-Americans made up only 2.1 percent of Washington's population but 11.1 percent of the nation's population.[5] Several studies have confirmed that Washington's secularity was not determined by a distinct racial makeup. For instance, sociologist Kevin Welch found that controlling for race did little to disturb what he calls the West Coast "membership trough."[6] In a series of Gallup polls conducted in 1970, the racial breakdown of the "no formal religion" population mirrored the wider population in both the West and the nation.[7] Further surveys indicate that all racial and ethnic groups in the West rejected formal religion in greater numbers than did their counterparts elsewhere: nationally, 4 percent of whites and 3 percent of "non-whites" claimed no formal religion compared to 7 percent of both groups in the West.[8] While the crude categories of "white" and "non-white" clearly do not capture the complexities of race in postwar America, the available figures suggest that western irreligion is not explained by a unique racial demography.

Race and ethnicity did not determine the secular Northwest, but they influenced religious discourse and practice in the region and beyond. In the literature on ethnicity and religion, much debate has centred on whether or not immigrant groups preserved or abandoned their religious traditions in the North American context.[9] Increasingly, scholars are revealing the relationship between ethnicity and religion to be multi-dimensional. Ethnic groups retained aspects of their spiritual heritage and shed others, reacted to the dominant religious culture and actively shaped it, creatively refashioned the sacred and used it to make sense of themselves and the world around them.[10] Our knowledge of the interplay between ethnic and religious identity is deepening, but we know little about how ethnicity figured in the creation of secular cultures. The Northwest's distinct secularity was more than a demographic effect, but persons originating from countries with comparatively secular traditions, such as Scandinavians, were over-represented in the region. The over-representation of certain ethnic groups likely reinforced the Northwest's secular social world, but this world exerted powerful influences of its own. In Canada, people with roots in France, Italy, and other conventionally religious countries were apt to shed their religious affiliation in British Columbia. While French and Italian Canadians may have felt culturally compelled on the West Coast to abandon their formal religious connections, it is also possible that those with secular leanings were particularly attracted to the region. In either case, it is clear that very considerable regional forces were at work here, as even the most typically devout of ethnic groups were over-represented among the religiously uninvolved.

Surveys suggest that race did not determine the secularity of the American West, but they offer little insight into the religious behaviour of specific groups within Washington State. In the Canadian context, census figures partially illuminate the religious affiliation of British Columbia's Asian and Aboriginal populations. In both British Columbia and Canada generally, people of Asian origin were over-represented among those with no religion, and Aboriginal peoples were under-represented (see Table 5). As this was both a national and regional pattern, it conveys little about the distinct religious culture of Canada's westernmost province. It does, however, point to the significance of race to religious practice and identity more generally. The importance of race to Northwest social relations became clear in the oral narratives. My interviewees alerted me to the deep divisions of race that existed in the postwar world. For instance, an Olympia man reflected on what it was like to grow up with atheist parents: "we knew that there was this gulf between us that we just didn't speak about. But it wasn't like being black."[11] As this remark suggests, race outweighed religion as a marker of difference in Olympia, as in other Northwest communities. This study draws mainly on the recollections of white individuals, statistics based in European categories, and materials written by those in positions of power. Such sources reveal something of how Indigenous, Black, and Asian populations were represented by the dominant culture, but less about the actual religious lives of these populations. Several scholars have pointed out that the Euro-Christian concept of religion, as reproduced in North American quantitative and printed materials, is fundamentally alien to Indigenous and Asian worldviews. In many Asian and Indigenous cultures, religion is understood as inseparable from the whole of life, rather than something practised in discrete circumstances.[12] In many Indigenous spiritual traditions and Eastern religions, such as Buddhism and Confucianism, priority is not given to regular worship in public settings.[13] Indigenous and Asian conceptions of religion defy easy summary, but it is clear that such conceptions departed from dominant, Christian views of religion. The histories of Canada and the United States further complicate perceptions of the sacred. In the postwar Northwest, a long history of anti-Asian racism, in which the churches were complicit, ensured that many Asian-Northwesterners would see Christianity as, irrevocably, a "white man's religion."[14] Also, as Judith Weisenfeld contends, given the American experience of slavery, "the meaning of Christianity for blacks and whites could not be anything but disparate."[15] Cognizant of such disparate meanings, I focus my attention on the Northwest's dominant white culture. Although Northwest secularity seems to have crossed the boundaries of race, it awaits future researchers to explore the making and meaning of this secularity among those who were marginalized by the region's dominant culture.

On the relationship between class and irreligion, the demographic evidence is fragmentary but suggestive. The "no religion" population of Canada spanned all occupations but was slightly over-represented in certain professional fields such as engineering, social sciences, and teaching.[16] Although the published census reports do not cross-tabulate religion with occupation at the provincial level, there was nothing obviously exceptional about British Columbia's occupational distribution that might explain the province's secularity. British Columbians were employed in all fields, including those that were characteristically secular, such as the natural sciences, in approximately the same proportion as workers nationwide.[17] British Columbia dedicated less of its labour force to farming (3.0 percent in British Columbia, 5.9 percent in Canada as a whole), and more to forestry and logging (2.1 percent in British Columbia, 0.8 percent in Canada), than did the nation generally. Apart from these discrepancies, however, British Columbia's occupational distribution reflected that of the nation. The data on income point to an intriguing regional variance: irreligion was more evenly dispersed across all income groups in British Columbia than elsewhere in the nation. In 1971, people with no religion in British Columbia and Canada were in the second highest income bracket of all religious groups.[18] Although British Columbia partly reflected the national pattern, non-religious residents of that province were less concentrated in the upper income category than their counterparts in other regions (see Table 7). The income results are complicated by gender: of all people claiming no religion across Canada, British Columbian males were the only group to report an annual income that was lower than the average. Although the income statistics do not fully account for the striking irreligion of British Columbia, they suggest that the clergy's focus on working-class men was not entirely misplaced.[19] Northwest secularity crossed class lines but drew particular strength from the region's deep-rooted, and largely male, working-class culture.

Quantitative sources south of the border also suggest that while Northwest secularity was not bound to a single class, it was less prevalent among the elite, professional classes. In the postwar decades, Washington's occupational structure was very similar to that of the nation.[20] While surveys from the era do not reveal the class demography of religion at the state level, such surveys do indicate that people with no formal religion in the American West were distributed across all fields in approximately the same proportion as in the wider population.[21] Those with no formal religion in the West were, however, less concentrated in business and the professions than elsewhere. Professionals in the American West rejected formal

TABLE 7
Average income of the "no religion" population by sex, Canada and regions, 1971

	Average income	Average income of the "no religion" population
Canada	5,033	5,931
Male	6,538	7,033
Female	2,883	3,330
British Columbia	5,255	5,628
Male	6,967	6,769
Female	2,843	3,025
Prairie Provinces	4,556	5,320
Male	5,884	6,231
Female	2,602	2,958
Ontario	5,459	6,485
Male	7,250	7,717
Female	3,079	3,641
Quebec	4,969	6,272
Male	6,288	7,352
Female	2,971	3,959
Atlantic Provinces	3,993	4,947
Male	5,085	5,692
Female	2,274	2,689

Notes and sources: Based on persons over 15 years of age reporting an income. *Census of Canada,* Vol. 5, Part 1, Table 16, 1971, 49–50.

religion more than those in the South and Midwest, but slightly less than those in the East. Other surveys indicate that irreligion was especially concentrated among professional groups in the East.[22] Gallup surveys show that manual labourers, farmers, and clerical and sales workers in the West were far less attached to formal religion than their regional counterparts. Such surveys also reveal that those without formal religion in the West had slightly lower incomes than their counterparts in other regions. At the same time, people across all income categories in the American West were less committed to formal religion than were their national counterparts.[23] Sociologists have confirmed that neither income nor occupation accounts for the irreligion of the Pacific states.[24] In the American West, irreligion was a cross-class phenomenon that was somewhat less tied to the professional classes than in the East and other regions.

Further evidence reveals that Northwest irreligion was not, as the clergy so often supposed, concentrated in mining and mill towns. Canadian census figures reveal that those who claimed to have no religion were more urbanized than the general population. In 1961, 30.4 percent of Canadians lived in rural areas, compared to only 21.5 percent of the no religion population. By 1971, the no religion group was still more urbanized than the general population: 23.8 percent of Canada's population lived in rural areas, compared to 19.3 percent of the no religion population.[25] While religious non-involvement was more characteristic of urban than rural areas, this does not explain the distinct secularity of British Columbia. In 1971, urban and rural residents of British Columbia were both far more likely to claim no religion than their counterparts elsewhere: 3.5 percent of rural Canadians claimed no religion compared to a striking 12.9 percent of rural British Columbians. Urban centres in British Columbia were also more secular than urban centres in other provinces. In 1971, 13.2 percent of urbanites in British Columbia, and only 4.6 percent or urbanites nationally, claimed to have no religion.[26] All thirty-seven towns, cities, and municipal subdivisions with populations of 10,000 or more in British Columbia contained proportionately larger no religion groups than the nation.[27] Preoccupied with British Columbia's "godless" resource frontier, Canadian church leaders failed to recognize that religious non-involvement was in fact more prevalent in Vancouver than in Port Moody, in Victoria than in Powell River, and in Oak Bay than in Kitimat. A distinct secularity reached beyond the province's mining and logging towns and into its respectable, middle-class communities.

Although they do not offer a view of religion at the state level, American surveys point to the geographically dispersed rather than localized character of irreligion in the American West. Americans with no religion, like their Canadian counterparts, were more urbanized than the general population.[28] At the same time, regardless of whether they lived in small or large communities, or in urban or rural districts, inhabitants of the American West were less attached to formal religion than residents of other regions. Approximately 5 percent of residents of the nation's largest cities rejected formal religion, compared to 9 percent of those in western cities. Regional discrepancies emerged across all urban and rural centres: nationally, only 2 percent of residents in small towns and rural areas claimed no formal religion, compared to 5 percent in the West.[29] The secularity of the American West, then, was not solely a product of the urban environment. Studies of church membership also point to the broadly dispersed character of this regional secularity.[30] In 1952, church membership levels in all of Washington's 39 counties were much lower than the American average. By 1971, all but 3 counties in the state had distinctly low rates of membership.[31] The churches fared somewhat better in the eastern part of the state. In both 1952 and 1971, those counties with the most church members were concentrated in eastern Washington. My interviewees acknowledged the existence of cultural, and often religious, differences between eastern and western Washington. Having lived in Spokane, Seattle, and Olympia, Alice found eastern Washington to be far more socially and religiously conservative than the western part of the state: "east of the Cascade Mountains," she remarked, "it's a different state over there."[32] Alice's comment reminds us that the Pacific Northwest, and Washington itself, was internally diverse. Despite such diversity, residents of eastern and western Washington shared much. Staying away from the churches was the norm for most Washingtonians, regardless of which side of the Cascades they called home.

Northwest secularity was not determined by race, ethnicity, class, or location – it was also not determined by gender. In North America, women are and historically have been more likely to claim religious beliefs and to engage in religious practices than men. This gender gap has remained remarkably consistent across time and space, and was certainly evident in the postwar Pacific Northwest.[33] While this fascinating phenomenon has captured the attention of researchers, it has also drawn focus away from women who had little to do with religion and religious institutions. Although men greatly outnumbered women in the nineteenth-century West, in the years following the Second World War this gender imbalance largely disappeared in both Washington and British Columbia.[34] The relative secularity of the postwar Northwest, then, cannot be attributed to a preponderance of men in the region. In the absence of census or other cross-tabulated data on religion in postwar America, it is not possible to precisely calculate the sex-ratio of the religiously affiliated in Washington State. At the national level, it is clear that despite broader fluctuations in religious practice, women have consistently outnumbered men among the religiously involved.[35] This does not mean, however, that men were solely responsible for the secularity of Washington State. In many cases, those counties with the lowest proportion of women also had the highest rates of church membership.[36] A 1945 WNICC survey in King County found that women made up approximately 60 percent of church membership in this sub-region.[37] Given that many men were away in the armed forces in 1945, it is likely that the difference between male and female membership rates lessened over time. However, with such strikingly low levels of religious involvement in Washington State, even if women continued to make up 60 percent of total church membership in this district through the postwar era, they were still much less likely to join churches than women in other regions. National polls on religious preference also point to the significance of both women and men to religious non-involvement in the American West. An analysis of 10 Gallup surveys conducted in 1970 revealed little variation in the sex-ratio of the "no formal religion" population across the United States. The "no formal religion" population was 70 percent male and 30 percent female in the West, and 69 percent male and 31 percent female across the United States. The same analysis found that both women and men in the West were twice as likely as their counterparts elsewhere to profess no formal religion.[38] Such evidence suggests that men alone did not determine Northwest secularity.

Males consistently outnumbered females in the census "no religion" population in Canada and British Columbia through the twentieth century. National surveys also reveal a persistent gender division in other areas of religious involvement in Canada, including church membership and attendance.[39] While British Columbian females were more religiously involved than their male counterparts, they were far less so than their national female counterparts. The census reveals uniquely high levels of no religion among both females and males in Canada's westernmost province. For instance, in 1971, males *and* females in British Columbia were approximately three times more likely to claim no religion than their counterparts nationwide (see Table 8). Clearly, the relative

TABLE 8

Number and percentage of those claiming "no religion" by sex, British Columbia, Ontario, and Canada, 1951 and 1971

	Male		*Female*		*Total*	
1951						
BC	17,991	3.0%	7,405	1.3%	25,396	2.2%
Ontario	9,532	0.4%	4,411	0.2%	13,943	0.3%
Canada	41,330	0.6%	18,349	0.3%	59,679	0.4%
1971						
BC	169,240	15.4%	117,875	11.0%	287,115	13.1%
Ontario	209,265	5.4%	134,420	3.5%	343,685	4.5%
Canada	561,250	5.2%	368,325	3.4%	929,580	4.3%

Source: Census of Canada, Vol. 1, Table 38, 1951; Vol. 1, Table 10, 1971.

secularity of postwar British Columbia cannot be treated as an exclusively male phenomenon. The Canadian census indicates that the sex ratio of the no religion population was remarkably similar in both British Columbia and Canada through the postwar era.[40] Interestingly, the gender gap in Canada's no religion population narrowed over this period. In all parts of the country, the female proportion of the no religion group, which was approximately 30 percent in 1951, increased to about 40 percent in 1971. In 1951, males in British Columbia were 2.3 times more likely than females to claim that they had no religion, and by 1971 they were only 1.4 times as likely. The national pattern is similar: in 1951, males in Canada were 2 times more apt to claim they had no religion than females, and by 1971 they were about 1.5 times more likely to do so. During the postwar decades, the female non-religious population grew at a greater rate than the male non-religious population, lessening the gender imbalance among secular Canadians. As Callum Brown has shown in the British context, countercultural and feminist currents of the 1960s helped to erode the longstanding association between femininity and piety.[41] Despite such changes, the unique secularity of the Northwest persisted.

"Shift work had no respect for Sundays":
Class, Work, and Churchgoing

Susan reflected on her experience growing up in a working-class family in the mining communities of Washington and northern Idaho. She contrasted her own childhood with a more idealized, well-dressed, churchgoing version:

> Sunday morning was, you have to get up and prepare a meal for the day, put something together, figure out how you were going to get your meals, you know, whatever. So, it wasn't about church. And survival, I think with that class of people, was the main concern. And, I know that we saw pictures of people going to church, and they got all dressed up on Sunday, and all of that, you know, and it was the smiling happy family kind of thing. Well, we never knew that, because we lived in a place that wasn't like that.

Susan noted the existence of real material barriers to church involvement: "What little we had went for the basic necessities. There wasn't money for new shoes. There wasn't money for dresses to go to church, or anything like that."[42] Susan became disenchanted with organized religion in childhood, as she became aware of certain differences between middle-class, churchgoing families and her own. She was not alone in offering a class-based critique of religious institutions. Northwest secularity crossed class boundaries, but hostility towards the churches was especially widespread among the region's working classes. In 1961, Canada's *Maclean's* magazine reported that the church was "holding its farmer and small shopkeeper, as well as its professional and successful and even rich business members ... [but] it [was] losing labor."[43] Concerns about the "indifference and suspicion of labor toward the church" echoed through the cultural and religious media of both nations.[44] Such concerns were not without basis in the postwar Northwest, a place where regional norms of non-involvement reinforced working-class indifference and hostility to the churches.

Although there was a significant working-class component to Northwest secularity, class did not determine religious participation here to the same extent that it did in regions where churchgoing was more central to middle-class status and respectability. Scholars have debated about the meanings of the revival of churchgoing in North America following the Second World War, but most agree that church involvement was central to middle-class ideals of the era.[45] My research suggests the importance of accounting for regional distinctions, as the normative association between church involvement and middle-class respectability did not seem to obtain in the postwar Northwest. The author of an article in *Seattle Magazine* puzzled about the widespread indifference to the churches in his city: "The most surprising aspect of low church membership here is that it seems to contradict Seattle's definition of itself – a city of staid, self-satisfied middle-class virtues." The churches, the author noted, were considered irrelevant by Seattle's "decision-makers" and "movers and shakers."[46] To the confusion of this observer, churchgoing did not confer social acceptance among Seattle's middle classes. Another writer concluded that churchgoing sometimes acted as a "social disadvantage" in Washington. According to this author, "Some professional people say privately that religion is a career burden here."[47] North of the border, British Columbia commentators also noted that affiliation with organized religion was not central to acceptance in the province. In 1962, a Victoria reporter remarked that Canadians "on the west coast – can get along in society without putting [their] religious affiliation on a platter for everyone to see."[48] The churches continued to be seen as middle-class institutions, but church involvement was not as central to middle-class respectability in the Northwest as it was elsewhere.

In his commentary on the 1851 religious census in England and Wales, Horace Mann described the working classes as "unconscious secularists – engrossed by the demands, the trials or the pleasures of the passing hour, and ignorant or careless of the future."[49] This image of the working classes as "unconscious secularists" is echoed in mid-twentieth-century church writings on the Pacific Northwest. One clergyman of the era complained that British Columbia's lumber workers were "careless about regarding [Sunday] in any sense as a day for worship and indeed rest. They work on their homes, their cars, and other personal concerns."[50] In recent years, scholars have challenged the notion that the working classes were "unconscious secularists." Focusing mainly on the nineteenth century, they have uncovered thriving working-class religious cultures that existed outside of the churches, beyond the purview of religious statistics.[51] My findings also undermine the image of the working classes as "unconscious secularists." However, rather than focusing on popular, often hidden, religious practices, I identify a strand of willful, deliberate secularism among the Northwest's working classes. Material circumstances influenced, but did not dictate, working-class detachment from the churches. Such circumstances intersected with more concerted, deeply held objections to organized religion to shape working-class secularity in the region.

Some interviewees acknowledged that the everyday realities of work limited the possibilities for church involvement. For Sylvia, whom we met at the opening of this chapter, decisions about voluntary activities, including churchgoing, hinged on her husband's irregular work schedule at the pulp mill; "whatever we did," she remarked, "depended on what shift he was on."[52] Anne, whose husband was a firefighter, voiced similar sentiments: "Well, my husband worked shift work so, you know, that tells you something all by itself. So, Sunday didn't make that much difference one way or the other."[53] Like Sylvia and Anne, Larry identified shift work as an impediment to regular church involvement: "Shift work had no respect for Sundays. Everybody worked all the shifts."[54] Bill recalled that working as a miner left him little time for church: "Nobody went to church. How the hell could they go to church when they were over the mountain or something, and they worked every day. We all worked every day! We had a big crew of men ... I worked twelve hours a day, every day. I never gave church a thought. We were always too tired."[55] As such comments suggest, the material conditions of work could at least partially limit religious practice. In British Columbia, Lord's Day Alliance officials complained that in the lumber fields "love of time and one-half seems to predominate. Rare cases of men known to request Sunday off."[56] The clergy's suspicions that resource workers regularly chose work over church on Sundays were not without basis. Their assumption, however, that the working classes were simply drawn away from the churches by work – that had they had no material demands, they would be filling the pews – obscures the existence of a strand of purposeful working-class secularity in the region. Frank, a Seattle longshoreman, explained that he had always sought out Sunday work: "Yes, no problem. I was always at work on Sunday. And you get paid extra, so I probably worked on Sundays more often than any other day of the week [laughs] ... Except for one or two religious people, I don't think that anybody would feel obligated not to work on Sunday."[57] For Frank, an atheist since childhood, Sunday work was the result rather than the cause of his very conscious secularity. Material conditions, such as the requirements of shift work and Sunday labour, could clearly delimit religious practice; working-class secularity in the region is not, however, reducible to such conditions. The everyday irreligion of the Northwest's working classes took shape on ideological as well as material terrain, a product of both economic circumstances and a conscious disdain for the churches.

Several interviewees recalled struggling to reconcile the economic needs of their families with those of the church. Many found that they were unable to manage the financial demands of churchgoing, particularly at the stage of life when they were starting their careers and families. Margaret and her husband left their Vancouver church in part because they were "struggling financially" and found that "the church [was] never ... satisfied with what they were getting." She reflected: "And, as I say, I understand that it gives them a thing that they can count on for the year, but on the other hand if you can't do it, you can't do it. I don't think it should mean that you can't go to church! [laughs] Which is the way it comes across."[58] Sylvia also recalled the difficulties of fulfilling the economic requirements of both family and church:

Used to get letters with envelopes in to put my donation in, but no way [laughs]. Make your pledge for the year, and I thought no, I'm not doing it. And another thing too, in the '60s, although my husband was making fair wages, but raising four children, we didn't have the extra money to put in as a ... you know, so much a month. So, when I went to church I would take a donation, you know, something to put on the plate, but when they started sending the envelopes to fill out for the year, you know, I thought well, what's more important the family or the church? And at that time the family was.[59]

For Sylvia, as for most others, family survival came before the needs of the church. For many, family economic priorities, particularly at that critical intersection of life when careers were beginning and children were being born, could push church involvement to the wayside. Although this was mainly a working-class issue, the financial demands of church involvement also kept some middle-class people away. David attributed his drift away from an Olympia church partly to financial reasons:

> I started in church, the first year or two I was out here. This is a secret I've never told anybody [laughs]. Because I was a doctor they were asking me for money right away. Here I was trying to start a practice, and not married, so there's that thing happening called girls [laughs]. And late nights and sleeping in on Sunday mornings. So, I went to church expecting to want to keep it up, continue – but it gradually petered out as I socialized more with girls. Plus the practice did develop, but I wasn't making as much money as they thought I was. They wanted me to give a lot more money than I was prepared to give. I wanted to build up a reserve first. Anyway, I was turned off a little by that.[60]

As David's story suggests, even some middle-class individuals struggled with the material demands of church involvement. These personal stories reveal that secular behaviour in the Northwest could, at times, have much to do with economic circumstances.

Criticisms of organized religion often centred on economic concerns. John, a salesman in postwar Nanaimo, reflected on his disdain for the churches: "To me, they're money-grubbers. They're only interested in supporting the system on the backs of the population, and keeping themselves in relative comfort."[61] Interviewees from all social classes echoed John in complaining about the financial excesses of organized religion. They referred to the churches as "big money-making businesses" and organized religion itself as "a cover for greed and business." Complaints about the monetary obsessions of the churches and "the wealth of priests and ministers" peppered the interviews.[62] Most interviewees, regardless of social class, would concur with Anne's simple assertion: "Most of the churches are rich. I don't like any of them."[63] This common criticism was at least partly grounded in widely held assumptions about the meanings of "true" religion. As Robert Orsi suggests, because religion has typically been understood as something disconnected from, and untainted by, "material things," it is often upsetting to people when "money makes an appearance in the space of the sacred."[64] The idea that money taints "true" religion underscored criticisms of organized religion. Recalling the many financial ventures of a priest he had known in British Columbia, Patrick questioned whether such a man could be considered truly religious: "was he really a religious person, was he a man of God or whatever? Or was he just a businessman?" He continued: "How can a guy sitting in that booth say I forgive you of your sins, just put ten bucks in the collection plate at the door. I can't look at it any differently, that's the way it is. So, once again, it's business, it's not religion. It's not religion, it's not comforting to anybody, it's just straight business."[65] Similarly, Richard saw the emphasis on financial contributions within the churches as "one more manifestation that god couldn't have set this up. But then god wasn't counting on contributions."[66] Like Richard and Patrick, many Northwesterners saw money-making as antithetical to true religion.

The irreligion of working-class Northwesterners was influenced by material circumstances but also by the region's very strong tradition of working-class secularism and socialism. Several interviewees articulated specifically class-based critiques of organized religion. Gary, a long-time socialist, described the church as "an arm of the capitalist establishment." He reflected on the reasons for his disassociation from organized religion:

> Well, it goes back to my early ... I wouldn't say early childhood, but by the time of my adolescence, anyway, just becoming disabused of the doctrines of organized religion. And probably not being overly impressed by the holiness of most people I knew who were churchgoers. In other words, I didn't see anything so sublime about them. And, of course, later on, as I became more aware politically, and so on, and became more aware of the fact that organized religion, as Marx said, is a tool of the ruling class, which it is. Still is, to a great extent.[67]

Some interviewees joined Gary in describing the churches as instruments of the ruling classes and employers. Edward, a Nanaimo socialist, recounted an argument he had with a minister about the class privilege embedded in the churches: "I said, why is it that the best Christians are the ones that have the most money, and who have donated to the church?

He said, well now, I don't think that's quite right. And I said, well, let me put it this way, and I named a few names, they're pillars of the church, aren't they? Well, yes. One's a lawyer, the other's an industrialist, one had donated the organ." Edward's views were influenced by his father: "I think dad felt that if Christ were alive today, he'd be a socialist. That he would want to help people, as he did – if you believe the bible – he went out of his way to help people who were poor. Dad had no difficulty with that."[68] Like Edward, Alice described the impact of her father – a "card-carrying member of the Wobblies" – on her disdain for organized religion:

> he figured at that time that religion was just a way to bilk the poor of their money, and he never changed his opinion on the subject [laughs]. He did remember the old hymns, some of them. "At the Cross," which was one, "where I first saw the light, and the burdens of my heart rolled away, rolled away, rolled away." He would sing "and the nickels and the dimes rolled away, rolled away, rolled away" [laughs].[69]

Such stories suggest that in some cases working-class opposition to the churches was nurtured within Northwest households, passed on from parents to children.

Committed socialists were not alone in articulating economic criticisms of organized religion; many Northwesterners, regardless of their politics, voiced similar concerns. Although Anne was not a socialist, her critique of the churches reflected the politics of class: "all the money that the church has, and all the poor people that go grovelling, and it's the people in the church, that work for the church, that make the church all that money. And the poorest of the poor don't get much, I'll tell you that."[70] When asked to comment on when and why he became a non-believer, Charles responded: "I lived on the wrong side of the tracks, so there was a lot of, relatively speaking, poverty. And the ones who had money, and so forth … I can remember, and this is as a kid, well how come these people have a big car, and all the great things, and my father, who's a wonderful man, can't find a job? So, what's all this stuff that god takes care of you? So, I really questioned that, I thought that it was … [trails off]."[71] Although Charles later became a university professor, his early economic experiences planted the seed for his eventual rejection of religion.

Northwest secularity crossed class lines, but irreligion among the working classes was fuelled and facilitated by the material and imaginative conditions of the region. In the 1930s, the American Postmaster General made the now-famous reference to the "forty-seven states and the 'Soviet of Washington.'" As this comment implies, Washington has been home to a relatively well-developed socialist movement. Historically socialism has had even wider appeal in British Columbia, once disparagingly referred to as "Canada's Communist Fortress."[72] In the postwar decades, uniquely high rates of unionization also distinguished British Columbia and Washington from their respective nations as a whole. In the 1950s, approximately 40 percent of non-farm workers in British Columbia and Washington were unionized.[73] Although scholars no longer depict the Northwest's working classes as exceptionally radical, few would debate the existence of a strong working-class culture and consciousness in the region. Of course, as several studies have shown, a well-developed working-class culture does not preclude religion. However, the oral, printed, and quantitative evidence suggests that hostility to organized religion was a significant part of the Northwest's working-class culture. Such evidence also indicates that middle-class ideals of religiosity held comparatively little influence here. The reasons for this are complex, but part of the answer rests in how the region has been imagined. Historian Laurie Mercier notes the widespread tendency to see loggers as representing "'a way of life' symbolic of the rugged Northwest."[74] Mercier's observation, which is confirmed by several other researchers, hints at the extent to which working-class values and ideals have permeated and defined this regional culture. The Northwest's quintessential identity has been located in the male wageworkers frontier. The values associated with the lifestyle of a particular segment of the working classes – ruggedness, individualism, and irreligion – seemed to resonate in Northwest culture more than in other regions.[75] Seen as central to Northwest identity, such values worked to lessen the pull and prevalence of middle-class religious ideals in the region.

"A woman's thing": Norms of Feminine Impiety and Masculine Religious Indifference

Prior to the 1960s, when Margaret and her husband started "skipping church on Sunday," both were active in an Anglican church in Nanaimo. According to Margaret, having a religiously involved husband made her something of an anomaly: "Well, of course my husband was very devout, whereas I think a lot of the men weren't quite as devout as the women. I think it was more the women who saw that the children went to Sunday school. According to my friends [laughs]. You know, it seemed to be a woman's thing that you went to church."[76] Margaret was not alone in seeing churchgoing as primarily a "woman's thing." Despite varied backgrounds and family histories, the forty-four interviewees in this study reproduced shared ideas about the gendered character of religious practice. Those who had never stepped foot in a church themselves nonetheless knew the pews to be filled mainly with women. Those who had rarely discussed religion with their friends or colleagues nevertheless knew spirituality to be a female domain. Brian recalled that when he was growing up in Olympia, girls "were much more openly, usually, Christian"; James, a Vancouver resident, likewise reflected that "girls were much more religious than the boys were."[77] Sharon, a long-time non-believer, matter-of-factly stated that women were (and are) "definitely more religious than men."[78] Beverly echoed her contemporaries when she remarked that women "are more religious than men, I think. In most places the women will go to church while the men don't go."[79] While the oral histories in this study tell us something of "what happened" in the past, they also offer useful insights into the deeply ingrained ideas, beliefs, and stereotypes that resonate in the culture of the Northwest. In their narratives, my interviewees revealed the taken-for-granted notion that churchgoing was, and is, a "woman's thing."

The feminized character of religious practice was cause for concern in church circles. Through the postwar years, Christian leaders nervously contemplated questions such as: "How often do men pray?," "Is Christianity a Man's Religion?," and "Does the church present a female image?"[80] Anxious affirmations of Christianity's masculine character were common in this era. "Being a Christian," observed the guest editor of the *Nanaimo Free Press* in 1960, "is no sissy thing fit only for old women and little children, for tea meetings and Sunday school. It is a battle from day to day against fearful foes."[81] In their efforts to redefine religious practice as manly, religious and cultural observers betrayed, and paradoxically reaffirmed, the feminized connotations of Christianity in the postwar social imaginary. As in earlier eras, in the years following the Second World War, Christian leaders in the Northwest and nationwide poured a great deal of energy into the "task of interesting more men in the church."[82] In 1950, an American Congregationalist minister observed that a "few churches are noteworthy because they do have more men or as many men at church on Sunday morning as women. These churches excite the envy of visiting ministers."[83] This telling comment reflects the persistent tendency on the part of Christian leaders to privilege men's participation in the churches.[84] Church officials remained preoccupied with men's relative absence from the churches. Ongoing discussions about the "unfortunate" and "sad but true" fact of women's predominance in the churches at once devalued women's religious participation and blinded observers to those women who abjured religious practice.[85] Prior to the significant changes brought by the sixties, women's involvement in the churches was, for the most part, so deeply taken for granted as to escape notice.

Normative assumptions about male religious indifference regularly surfaced in the oral narratives. When asked to explain why he felt men were less religious than women, Charles, a retired university professor in Seattle, responded: "I think a lot of men who are non-cerebral haven't really thought about it. A lot of them are non-religious because they probably find it non-macho, and they would never, ever admit that they had help from the local minister, or the priest. And women – there is a difference, I think on the average, by and large, women are a little more sensitive."[86] Donald gave a similar explanation for male secularity:

> I think women get more out of religion, in being able to get away from whatever they were doing, it's some place they can go and be themselves, and converse with the priest, and whatever. I don't think men would necessarily take the same approach as women. A man isn't going to talk over his personal problems with a priest very well. You know, he might, but he's more likely to talk it over with a chum in a bar, or something [laughs]. Where a woman couldn't do that.[87]

Charles and Donald called upon the masculine ideal of independence to explain men's avoidance of the churches. Donald's wife Jean likewise hinted at men's discomfort with the dependent elements of religion: "priests always say, you know, you have to give yourself to God. And I think men, maybe, have a more difficult time with that."[88]

According to the interviewees, men were not only repelled by the dependent elements of religion but drawn towards a range of manly and secular business and leisure activities that left little time for the sacred. James recalled that during his childhood boys were less religiously involved than girls because they were "mostly interested in outdoor activities, in sports and things like that, you know."[89] Margaret echoed others when she placed the blame for male secularity on paid work:

"I think maybe men if they're out in the business world, aren't quite as tuned into some of the things as women are."[90] In the interviews, comments about the secular sensibilities of men usually opened up wider discussions about masculine expectations in the postwar world. For instance, Brian's insights regarding male religious indifference flowed into a discussion about pervasive gender norms in the postwar era: "I think there might very well have been much more pressure on [girls] to conform. Guys were freer to be, you know, guys – boys will be boys. A bit of hell-raising was encouraged, a bit of running about or running amok was not at all considered bad. And the girls were to be nice girls."[91] George similarly pointed out: "Men probably had more free time too. If you weren't working, you'd go out canoeing, or fishing, or hunting, you'd come home and the wife would be there looking after the kids and making dinner. So men had a lot more freedom."[92] Like Brian and George, several interviewees described a postwar gender culture that required greater conformity, religious and otherwise, from women than men. As the conventional idiom "boys will be boys" suggests, males were expected, if not subtly encouraged, to opt for profanity over piety. As one woman tellingly quipped, men were less religious "because there was so much fun going on!"[93] In the view of the interviewees, men were more likely than women to ignore or reject organized religion in the postwar decades because they were under little pressure to do otherwise.

Regardless of their own thoughts on religion, the interviewees presented men's greater secularity as part of their common-sense social knowledge. In this, they were influenced not only by wider cultural norms but also often by personal family histories. Twenty-six of the forty-four people interviewed for this study recalled their mothers as religious, whereas only thirteen used that term to describe their fathers. Only two individuals claimed to have grown up with a religious father and non-religious mother. By contrast, fifteen remembered having a religious mother and a non-religious father. In the oral interviews, people depicted their parents' religious behaviour in ways that conformed to normative gender patterns.[94] Many recalled their father's often limited religious involvement as something motivated not by personal piety but, rather, by their mothers. Larry attributed his father's occasional church-going to his mother: "[my father] was never really religious, he just went along with the program." According to Larry, his father was "religious, I think, just by default."[95] The idea that many men were religious "by default" echoed through the oral interviews. Donald reflected: "I think my dad was like me. He used to go to church on Easter, a couple of times a year, maybe, because of my mother – because of her. But, I think he felt the same way I did that this was it, right here, right now, today."[96] A few interviewees remembered their fathers being openly hostile towards religion, particularly in its organized forms. More often, however, the interviewees struggled to recall precisely how their fathers felt about religion. Fathers were often described as not at all "churchy" and, in contrast to (most) mothers, as rather indifferent to religion.[97] Charles echoed others when he remarked that he "never heard [his father] talk about [religion]."[98] David similarly commented: "I had never heard that [my father] was enthusiastic about religious attendance or indulgence"; another woman reflected: "I can't remember my father going to church."[99] In these life stories, memories of fathers' religious feelings appear more hazy and indistinct than those of mothers. This is not surprising, as my interviewees grew up during a time when mothers were largely responsible for the religious lives of children.

In postwar culture, masculine indifference to the churches was seen as typical, and often served as a source of humour. Even the churches themselves played upon the comic nature of masculine irreverence. Jean, a Nanaimo resident, recalled that in the postwar decades, there "were always jokes about people falling asleep in church."[100] Such jokes were distinctly gendered. In a 1964 edition of the *Canadian Churchman*, a cartoon portrayed a congregation in which wives glared at their impassive, yawning husbands; the cartoon depicted a woman rebuking her husband: "It's bad enough snoozing, but yelling out 'Fore!' in your sleep ... well!!!"[101] Cartoons such as these that were meant to admonish men for their impiety also helped to convey and entrench cultural perceptions of male religious disinterest as both normative and humorous. Such perceptions were not isolated to official or elite sources but, rather, were reproduced by ordinary people. Personal, humorous memories of irreligious fathers wove their way through many of the narratives in this study. While anecdotal, taken together such memories hint at the taken-for-granted, even comic, nature of male religious apathy in the wider postwar world. Shirley, who lived in Olympia in the postwar years, reflected: "I think that my dad didn't believe in anything. He'd go to church with her because she liked to go to church, and she liked to sing – she had a lovely voice. But dad would sleep all through the sermon. And I thought that was great [laughs]!"[102] Bill similarly found humour in his father's tendency to fall asleep during worship services: "Well, my old man, he wouldn't go to church because my mother said that he went to sleep, and my mother had to poke him [laughs]."[103] Several interviewees adopted a distinctly humorous tone when telling stories of religiously indifferent fathers. Edna laughed as she described her father's role in her religious upbringing: "My father would take us to church. He would not go, I mean he would not go inside, he'd stay outside ... There were lots of men waiting outside, he wasn't the only one [laughs]!They probably had a craps game going [laughs]!"[104] The historian Sarah Williams notes that oral history is useful in giving "access to the ephemeral world of the joke, the rumour, and gossip which are valuable in revealing the attitudes of the observed."[105] Playful, humorous memories of religiously indifferent fathers recur in the oral interviews of Northwesterners. Such memories suggest that male secularity was seen as predictable, and not to be taken too seriously.

The notion that churchgoing was a "woman's thing," and that men were naturally indifferent to religion, formed part of the common-sense social imaginary of the postwar world. Such gender norms were learned and disseminated at both official and everyday levels, within ordinary families and the broader culture. Although they were subject to national gender norms, Northwesterners also lived in a region that did not privilege religious involvement. Regional and gender norms inter-sected to shape, in complex and sometimes unexpected ways, everyday approaches to organized religion. Northwest women encountered gen-der ideals that assigned them primary responsibility for the sacred, but they also inhabited a region that attached relatively little value to reli-gious involvement. Faced with such contradictions, most women in the region marked out complex, and often shifting, identities in the middle ground between piety and indifference. Men faced clearer expectations in the postwar Northwest. Manly ideals of independence and rational-ism reinforced regional norms of religious detachment, making this a place where men's indifference towards the churches was expected. The region itself was defined not only as working class but also as a manly frontier. The gendering of the Pacific Northwest as masculine served to further reinforce its secularity.

Gender and Church Involvement

Although they were subject to competing gender norms, both men and women were responsible for the distinct secularity of British Columbia and Washington State. Northwest women and men shared in criticizing organized religion, and in perpetuating a regional indifference towards church involvement. Attitudes towards the churches, however, had a gendered dimension. Historian Lynne Marks reveals that in late-nineteenth-century Ontario, women outnumbered men in the pews in part because they had few alternative social outlets.[106] Women enjoyed access to a far greater range of leisure options in the 1950s than in the 1890s. With the emergence of the feminist movement of the 1960s, many women began to view the churches not as spaces for rare social interaction but as bastions of sexism. Muriel reflected on her disdain for the churches:

> I definitely am quite anti-church, and I base that on some of my friends who have had bad experiences with churches, who have had church leaders tell them terrible things, who go to ministers for help and they give them very bad advice. I think you're better off going to your friends, who will give you good advice. And, I think I'm the first generation of women to be somewhat of a feminist ... And I think I find churches to be male-dominated, which bothers me a great deal. I think in a lot of churches, the women do all the work, the women do all the volunteer work, and the men come and sit down and say "where's the tea?" [laughs].[107]

Several women echoed Muriel's complaints, and identified patriarchy as one of the chief reasons that they avoided the churches.[108] Joanne and Sandra of Seattle never joined churches, in part, because they viewed institutional religion as irredeemably sexist. Joanne remarked: "I think very early I decided that the Christian religion is a very sexist, patriarchal religion." Sandra similarly observed: "Organized religions were incredibly sexist. They were incredibly sexist. They had a place for women that involved doing an enormous amount of the work, and having none of the say."[109] While Joanne and Sandra had never attended church, several other women rejected the churches of their childhoods partly for feminist reasons. Edna, who had attended a Baptist church with her family as a child, refused to join as an adult: "I resented the fact that the church teaches you to obey your husband. And I had a husband that couldn't keep a job. I lost respect for him, and there was no way I was going to obey him, you know!"[110] Susan rejected the Mormon church as a teenager in part because "the treatment of women was as a third, fourth, fifth class person." Susan, who assured me that she had never "burned her bra" or considered herself a feminist, deeply resented the church's treatment of women: "I wanted more than that. I knew I was as smart as some of those men! [laughs] ... I was tired of the church telling me I wasn't worth anything. You're a female, you need to do what you're told."[111] Sharon, who had left the Catholic church of her youth, simply quipped: "I'll belong to the Catholic church again when they make a woman the pope."[112] Repelled by patriarchy, and influenced by the growing feminism of the day, many women chose to leave, or stay away from, the churches.

In the 1960s and 1970s, North American mainline church leaders began to lament the decline of women's church work, which they attributed to an expanding female labour force and the emergent feminist movement.[113] Some women, such as Patricia, whom we met at the outset of this chapter, left their congregations during this time period due to a lack of recognition for their church work. Patricia reflected on her decision: "Having spent lots of my energy and time, ever since I was young, into these church things, I felt that I was being used. And I didn't wish to continue with that, and figured that you have to sort out your own beliefs, and way of living, without having to conform to what some people have made up."[114] Margaret similarly recalled the growing sense that women's church work was undervalued and taken for granted: "I think in some ways, they got kind of used to us doing things. You know, we always seemed to be there. And I don't think, I can't recall the women's groups being asked to do something that they didn't come up and do it. Definitely. We did what we thought was necessary."[115] Beverly related the story of a friend who, having devoted much of her time to a Protestant congregation over the years, left quite abruptly in the 1960s: "all of a sudden she decided that she was working her butt off for nothing for this outfit, so she quit! She never went back to church!"[116] Although not framed in explicitly feminist terms, such stories nevertheless reflect the growing postwar resistance to the patriarchy of organized religion. In 1970, an article in the *United Church Observer* anxiously assessed the feminist movement: "although this is primarily a secular revolution, it is a particularly challenging one for the church ... Although in the past the church has led in seeking freedom for the individual – male or female – the feminists today see the Church as one of the last bastions of male superiority."[117] During the 1960s, many women began to view the churches as "bastions of male superiority." While most of the female interviewees did not call themselves feminists, they were nevertheless influenced by the burgeoning feminist movement and increasingly turned off by the sexism of the churches. Many Northwest women responded to this sexism by avoiding or leaving the churches, and by participating in the critique of organized religion that grew through the postwar years.[118] This response was not regionally specific, but Northwest women did voice their criticisms with little risk of social ostracism, from within communities that were comparatively indifferent to the churches.

Women and men described their relationship with the churches in distinctly gendered ways. As Callum Brown has observed in the British context, the link between piety and femininity was severed during the 1960s, which opened the way for women's exodus from the churches.[119] Such changes were more evolutionary than revolutionary in Canada and the United States, but the feminist currents of the 1960s also affected women's relationship with the churches in these countries. Although the secularizing currents of the 1960s did not pass them over, men were subject to more longstanding masculine norms of religious indifference. Northwest men certainly shared in criticizing the hypocrisy, and sometimes the sexism, of organized religion. Generally, however, men described the churches in more detached terms than women did. For a striking number of men in this study, reference to the churches called up memories of heterosexual, rather than spiritual, relations. Charles admitted that his brief attendance at church was inspired by less than sacred reasons: "I went to church, primarily because the minister – I think it was Presbyterian – because I liked his daughter, she was a pretty girl. And then they brought in a new Presbyterian minister from Scotland, Reverend [name withheld], and I told my mother I didn't like him."[120] For Richard, the church gradually became "irrelevant" as he acquired new means of meeting women: "I still did things with the church, because it was still a good place to meet girls – and one never throws that out. So, I went to church things until, I think until I got into high school, and then I had jobs that caused me to work on weekends, so church just didn't fit in anymore. And I had a car, so I had other bait to troll for girls."[121] Bill playfully described the churchgoing habits of a childhood friend in Dawson, Yukon Territory: "He tried to date pretty near every girl in Dawson. If he was trying to get friendly with a girl in the Church of England, St. Paul's, he would go there. If he was trying to get friendly with a girl in the Presbyterian Church, he'd go there [laughs]."[122] Patrick similarly established a brief relationship with the church for the purposes of heterosexual courtship: "I went to church one time when I was about 13 because the Smith sisters both were going to church, and I had a crush on one of them and so I went, so I had an ulterior motive [laughs]. Church had nothing to do with it!"[123] Patrick's assertion that "church had nothing to do with it" captures the nature of many men's relationship with the churches in the postwar era. As scholars have shown, both women and men have sought and found opportunities for heterosexual courtship in the churches and other religious venues throughout history.[124] The narratives in this study reveal a clear gendered discrepancy in this regard: the subject of heterosexual relations predominated in men's, but not women's, memories of the churches. In focusing on courtship, men conveyed both their deep detachment from the churches and their understanding of the churches as feminine spaces.

Several of my male interviewees attributed their sporadic church involvement to their relationships with women in the context not only of courtship but of marriage. Gary, an agnostic who long ago married a devout Catholic, reflected that he had occasionally attended worship services over the years because he was "dragged there" by his wife.[125] James admitted that when it came to churchgoing, he was a "bit of a lazy bugger." He did attend sometimes, however, to keep the peace in his marriage:

> my wife was up at 8 o'clock every morning, and she'd make me breakfast or make me coffee or something, and a lot of times I would argue with her, she'd ask me if I'm going to church with her, and I'd say no, because I was a little lazy myself, I wanted to sleep in. So I said no. But there was a lot of times I did go to church with her, rather than have an argument, I kept the peace around the house. My wife wanted to drag me to church and make a good boy out of me. So I went to church with her on some Sundays … But I don't think I went to church to pray, it was just part of the scene, I just stood there like the rest of the people. I don't think I said any prayers, or anything like that.[126]

Richard also endured the occasional worship service to please his wife: "every so often my wife would get all excited, 'we ought to go to church because it's Easter or Christmas' … I'd say, 'okay sure.' Or, once in awhile, she'd get spun up, spring-time, spring-cleaning, let's go to church. But it never stuck, so I just had to be patient, and it would go away."[127] Many men also described fathers who attended church just to please mothers. As Larry recalled, "My dad just went because mother went." Thomas similarly remarked: "My father was not a churchy person. He would go occasionally, I think, to please my mother."[128] In their narratives, men imparted and entrenched wider cultural assumptions of churchgoing as, fundamentally, a "woman's thing." In constructing the churches as female spaces, these men called upon gender meanings that were national rather than regional in focus. However, in the Northwest context, male indifference towards the churches was further buttressed by regional norms of religious detachment.

The Pacific Northwest's distinct secularity cannot be explained by the region's particular class, ethnic, or gender demography. Partly the product of single, working-class men in the logging camps and resource communities of this region, this secularity was also made in unexpected spaces, such as middle-class neighbourhoods, and by people from all social locations. It was made by working-class women like Sylvia and Patricia, who abandoned churches they saw as overly status-conscious and patriarchal. It was also made by Larry and Bill, who saw churchgoing as incompatible with shift work, and by middle-class men such as Richard and David, who drifted from the church due to financial concerns and indifference. Regardless of class or gender, postwar Northwesterners could comfortably stay away from organized religion without risk of social exclusion. However, memories of, and relationships with, the churches were classed and gendered. As church leaders feared, there was a strong strand of working-class opposition to organized religion in the region, an opposition that was shaped by material realities, a tradition of socialism, and a broader disdain for church money-making. Presumptions about male religious indifference were also not without basis. Men revealed their detachment from the churches in playful stories about heterosexual courtship and nagging wives. Through such stories, men conveyed the deeply held assumption that the churches were feminine spaces. On the other hand, many women decried the sexism of organized religion, and attributed their sometimes painful disengagements from church to the institution's patriarchy. Class and gender shaped not only personal secular journeys but also the broader identity of the Pacific Northwest. Churchgoing seemed out of place in a region so often imagined as a rugged, masculine, working-class place. Many Northwesterners were comfortably indifferent to organized religion, but their responses to religious belief were more diverse and complex, as we shall explore in the following chapter.

4

Belief and Unbelief

ALTHOUGH SHE ENJOYED GOING to Sunday school during her childhood in Ontario, Anne never became a churchgoer as an adult. She moved with her family to Victoria, British Columbia, during the 1940s, was married in 1950, and had four children. Anne wed in a church and sent her children to Sunday school, but she disdained organized religion as hypocritical and money-centred. During our conversation, she described herself as "very spiritual" and also as an "agnostic who loves people." When I asked her to describe her spirituality, she said: "It's hard to put into words without sounding corny. I love going and looking at the mountains, because they're so majestic, and so much bigger than I could ever be or you and anybody else. And trees, and flowers, and just everything. Just beauty. Seeing happy children playing. It does something to you. Lifts your spirit, whatever your spirit is. It lifts you. I don't know."[1] Anne's somewhat eclectic approach to religion was not unusual. My interviewees embraced and rebuffed religion in multiple, and sometimes seemingly contradictory, ways. I interviewed an economics professor who considered himself to be both unbelieving and spiritual, a middle-class homemaker who drifted away from the church but remained Christian, an agnostic railway worker who derided organized religion but occasionally attended worship services with his Catholic wife, and a nurse who defined herself as an atheist yet turned to prayer in times of crisis. As such stories suggest, neither the narrow assessments of church leaders nor the discrete categories of statisticians fully capture the complexity of religion and irreligion in the postwar Northwest.

In approaching the secular Northwest, we must be alert to the "ambivalence and ironies" that so often characterize human experience in the realm of religion.[2] Unlike other regional religious cultures, such as Catholicism in Quebec or evangelicalism in the American South, Northwest secularity had no theological or institutional centre. Nonetheless, it was loosely structured according to certain well-understood norms and practices. It was characterized, on the one hand, by a generalized indifference and antagonism towards organized religion and, on the other hand, by flexible, intermittent, and sometimes ambivalent approaches to the sacred. This chapter turns from a focus on organized religion to look more closely at belief and unbelief in the postwar Northwest. In a region where non-involvement was the norm, many people went extended periods without ever encountering or engaging the churches or other religious institutions. They may have comfortably eschewed organized religion, but few in the region rejected religious belief entirely. Scholars have shown that in the postwar era, and particularly during the sixties, it became increasingly common for North Americans to describe themselves as "spiritual but not religious." This was especially the case in the Northwest, with its longstanding tradition of religious non-involvement. There was also a significant though less often acknowledged minority in the region who considered themselves neither unbelieving nor spiritual, and for whom religion was simply unimportant. As we shall see, although Northwesterners were more likely than those in other regions to be indifferent to religious belief, many feared the social consequences of openly identifying as non-believers. Public admissions of unbelief were widely known to cross the boundary of social acceptance in the Northwest, as elsewhere. Such admissions were also deeply shaped by gender, class, and other categories of social identity. Many in the region approached religion in ways that balanced on but did not cross this boundary.

A Godless Place?

Most residents of the Northwest were uninvolved in organized religion, and a significant minority claimed no religious identification. Was this, then, a "godless" place? The historian Sarah Williams reminds us that we must be careful to avoid the "simplistic identification of religion with institutional church practice."[3] Statistics on religious preference and involvement should not be taken as clear measures of personal piety and spiritual practice. As I learned in my conversations with Northwesterners, personal piety and organized religious involvement are not mutually dependent. Like Anne, who described herself as agnostic, spiritual, and anti-church, many in the region approached religion in ways that are not easily quantified. Some interviewees, like James, became increasingly disinterested in the churches but continued to define themselves as Christian. Others, like Patricia, drifted from both the church and Christianity but still considered themselves spiritual. When asked if she had no religion, Patricia replied: "No, I'd say I have no churchman-ship [laughs]. No, because I feel connected to these birds, and growing things, and there is a force, so the thing is to try and keep in touch with the harmony in the world."[4] Like Anne, James, and Patricia, an increasing number of people in the Northwest and beyond drifted from the churches and shed their formal religious connections, but few eschewed religious belief entirely. Even in the secular Northwest, the global secularizing currents of the 1960s did not turn "believers into atheists."[5]

Unfortunately, there is a paucity of data on regional patterns of religious belief in the postwar decades.[6] In Canadian surveys conducted since the Second World War, British Columbia is identified as the least believing province in the country. An Angus Reid survey conducted in 2000 reported that British Columbians were less likely to believe in a God than were residents of other provinces: only 75 percent of British Columbia residents professed belief in a God, compared to 84 percent of their counterparts nationwide.[7] Sociologist Reginald Bibby surveyed religious beliefs across Canada in 1985, and found that British Columbians were less apt than other Canadians to believe: while 83 percent of Canadians claimed to believe in a God, only 73 percent of BC respondents did so.[8] A 1977 national survey also found British Columbia to have the lowest levels of belief of all regions in Canada: 83.5 percent of British Columbians, and 88 percent of Canadians, claimed to believe in a supreme being.[9] While limited, Canadian surveys on religious belief have consistently identified British Columbia as the least believing province.

The few American surveys of religious belief offer broad regional, rather than state-level, data. Although certain surveys point to distinctive levels of unbelief in the American West, the results of these surveys are less consistent than those in Canada. A 1944 Gallup poll indicated that residents of the Pacific region were somewhat less likely than others to believe in a God: 93 percent of people in this region professed such a belief, compared to 96 percent nationwide.[10] In contrast, in 1968 Gallup reported that residents of the American West were on par with the national average: 98 percent professed a belief in a God.[11] Consistent regional variations in belief are also not readily apparent in a national survey undertaken in 1952 by a private research group, and replicated in 1965 by the *Catholic Digest*. These surveys show high rates of belief across the United States. They do indicate that residents of the Pacific states were among those who were "least certain" about their beliefs. In 1952, 84 percent of people in the Pacific region were "absolutely certain" about their belief in a God, compared to 87 percent nationally; in 1965, those who were "absolutely certain" made up 81 percent of America's total population but only 74 percent of the population of the Pacific states.[12] Drawing on a study of the National Opinion Research Center (NORC) in 1972, sociologists Rodney Stark and William Bainbridge reveal regional variations in religious belief in the United States. Their research indicates that residents of the Pacific and East South Central regions were relatively, though not dramatically, less believing than their counterparts in other regions: 81 percent of people in these regions claimed to "believe in the existence of God as I define Him," compared to 84 percent nationwide.[13] While some surveys suggest that people in the Pacific region were less likely than other Americans to believe in a God (or to be certain about that belief), the results are certainly not as conclusive as those regarding institutional adherence. Inconsistencies also emerge in American surveys with regards to other dimensions of personal piety. In response to a 1944 Gallup poll, only 63 percent of people in the Pacific region claimed to believe in life after death, compared to 76 percent nationally. This regional discrepancy is not reproduced in a 1968 Gallup poll, which shows rates of belief in life after death to be lowest in the East. Other surveys from the period show that West Coast residents were among the most likely to reject the idea of life after death, and the least likely to pray, but the regional contrasts are not stark.[14]

Although certain surveys suggest that West Coast residents were less believing than others, the regional differences are neither as conclusive nor as deep as those pertaining to organized religion. Turning to a comparison of religious belief in Canada and the United States, certain distinctions emerge. Survey data suggest that levels of unbelief were somewhat greater in Canada than in the United States and greater in British Columbia than in the American West. In a 1972 NORC survey, 6 percent of American respondents said that they did not believe in a God, compared to 11 percent of people in the Pacific region.[15] North of the border, a national survey conducted in 1977 found that 13.6 percent of British Columbians, and only 8.7 percent of Canadians more generally, denied the existence of any God.[16] A 1947 Gallup poll reported little difference between Canada and the United States with respect to belief: 95 percent of Canadians, and 94 percent of Americans, claimed to believe in a God. By the mid-1970s, Gallup reported that the level of professed belief in Canada had dropped to 89 percent but remained stable in the United States at 94 percent.[17]

Like statistics on church involvement, those on belief should not be taken as a transparent lens on religiosity. Survey questions about religious beliefs generally solicit a yes or no answer, revealing little about the importance or role of such beliefs in the lives of respondents. In the few surveys that sought to capture not only whether or not people believed but also how religion actually figured in individual lives, the regional differences are telling. A 1977 Canadian survey did not reveal dramatic regional variations in belief, but it did find that only 62.7 percent of British Columbians held "very or somewhat strong religious beliefs," compared to 73.1 percent of the national population.[18] The 1952 and 1965 surveys conducted by a private research group and the *Catholic Digest* revealed only slight regional variations in belief in the American context, but they did indicate that residents of the Pacific region were much less likely than their counterparts elsewhere to claim that religion was "very important" to them; in 1952, 64 percent of Pacific region residents claimed religion was very important, compared to 75 percent nationally; in 1965, only 61 percent of Pacific residents did so, compared to 70 percent nationwide.[19] These surveys, together with evidence on religious identification, membership, and attendance, suggest that although levels of belief were not strikingly low in the Pacific Northwest, religion in all of its forms was comparatively less significant to the people who lived there. The Northwest was certainly not a godless place, but it was also not uniformly or uncomplicatedly religious.

"You didn't have to go to church on Sunday to do good": Popular Religion and the Golden Rule Ideal

Although Northwesterners were more indifferent to religion, in all of its forms, than their counterparts nationally, most were not professed unbelievers. What part, then, did religious belief play in the lives of people in the region? It is difficult to answer this question precisely due to the fluid, shifting, and contextual nature of religious identity. No matter how inclusive they are, statistics on religion confine and contain identities that are often changeable and uncertain. They rely on neat categories that inadequately capture the complicated and indeterminate ways that religion is experienced in everyday life. This inadequacy was revealed in my interviews, as people struggled to answer when I asked how, in the postwar years, they defined themselves in terms of religion. For many, the answer was neither settled nor singular. David described his (public) religious identity thus: "I would say Christian, but only with a certain crowd. If I was out with a crowd of agnostics or a mixture of religions I couldn't ... I wouldn't be able to defend why I was a Christian, and wouldn't say I was definitely a Christian."[20] Larry also described his religious identity as shifting and contextual: "I'd probably say I was a Methodist. But, it depends on the social situation. I might say I was a Buddhist. Occasionally I put down Methodist and Democrat, and occasionally I put down Zen Buddhist and Democrat."[21] Patricia pondered my question: "Well, I don't know. I don't think I'd say agnostic. I just ... [pause] ... I don't know."[22] Like David, Larry, and Patricia, several people resisted my impulse to religiously categorize them. They described religious and secular identities that were uncertain, dynamic, and incapable of being wholly summed up in a single census or survey response.

Like statistics, church-based definitions of religiosity are too narrow to fully capture the popular religion of Northwesterners. As many scholars have shown, to understand the religious lives of ordinary people we must extend our analyses beyond organized forms of religion.[23] For growing numbers in the Northwest and beyond, religious institutions were seen as unnecessary to spiritual growth and understanding. This was a constant source of worry for church leaders through the postwar years. In 1951, the *BC Catholic* advertised a discussion on the issue titled: "Can There Be Salvation Outside the Church?"; a decade later, in 1961, the *Catholic Northwest Progress* announced an upcoming television panel: "The three religious leaders taking part in the program will explain why the spiritual feelings derived from listening to a symphony, a walk in the woods, reading inspirational books, or private meditation, are not sufficient for complete religious understanding."[24] Despite the concerns of religious leaders, my interviews indicate that many ordinary people saw churchgoing as irrelevant, and sometimes even as an impediment, to religious understanding. Robert, who drifted away from the church as an adult but remained a believer, commented: "I don't think that attending church necessarily increases your elevation, or whatever, towards religion. I think, quite frankly, it's how one lives one's life."[25] Thomas, an atheist, likewise distinguished religiosity from churchgoing in a comment about his mother: "I don't think of her as being deeply religious, but I think of her as being churchy."[26] Regardless of their own religious or secular identities, most interviewees echoed Thomas and Robert in viewing institutions as unnecessary to true religion; as one woman pointed out, "God lives with us every day, he's not in a building."[27]

Several interviewees made a distinction between religion, which they associated with institutions and creeds, and spirituality, which they saw as more affective and personal. As Susan remarked: "Spiritual is the way you live your life, and religion is a creed." Richard likewise observed: "spirituality can be an individual exercise, whereas for religion, you've got to have a church, you've got to have administration – all the baggage that goes with it."[28] Similar comments were made throughout the interviews, and suggest that for many the term "religion" *meant* organized religion. Jean, like growing numbers in the postwar years, described herself as "spiritual but non-religious." In her view, religion is a "man-made thing," whereas spirituality is "something you feel in your soul or your gut or whatever." She further reflected: "I'm looking at a hummingbird sitting on this little feeder, and to me that gives me much more joy, and much more feeling, than going to church would. Because it's right there, and it moves me, and quite frankly, I have never ever been to a church service that has moved me."[29] Some scholars have described the Pacific Northwest as a "secular but spiritual" region – a place where most people hold some religious beliefs, or define themselves as spiritual, but are relatively indifferent to formal religious involvement.[30] The "secular but spiritual" label aptly applies to many of my interviewees. While some held to beliefs evolving out of established religions, such as Christianity, others defined their spirituality in terms that were more fluid and imprecise. Mary, an Olympia resident, reflected on her beliefs:

No, I've never been an atheist. Uh-uh, uh-uh. That means people who believe there's no god of any kind, anywhere, any shape, any form. Something created us, and whatever that something is is what I consider [pause] where my blessings go. Whether I came out of the sea as an amoeba, or whether some huge something or other was responsible for all of this wonderful, wonderful, wonderful world that's going, shall we say, to hell in a handbasket [laughs].

When asked whether she had ever identified as Christian, Mary responded: "I might have before I realized there were other things, and that you could have none of the above."[31] Religious "nones" like Mary are beginning to attract the attention of scholars. According to Robert Putnam and David Campbell, most "nones" "reject conventional religious affiliations, while not entirely giving up their religious feelings." Most are those who, to borrow Grace Davie's phrase, "believe without belonging."[32] Long the region with the largest proportion of "nones," the Pacific Northwest was at the forefront of this increasingly popular way of engaging religion in the modern world.

The interviews reveal that even nonbelievers encountered, and sometimes engaged, the sacred in the context of their personal lives. For these highly secular people, such encounters often occurred in times of crisis, particularly those relating to illness and death. Edward, an agnostic who had never prayed, felt compelled to do so for his dying wife: "there was one bit of funny thing happened before [wife] died. She wanted me to pray for her. And I said, 'well, I think you know how I feel about this.' And she said 'yes, but would you do that for me?' And so, I did." Praying for his wife did little to change Edward's views on religion: "I would say that, personally, religion had little appeal to me. And the more I see of it, the less it appeals to me. I know that a lot of people keep saying that, well you know when you die you'll be with [wife], and I don't see that."[33] For many interviewees, extended periods of detachment from religion were punctuated by moments of prayer for ailing family members. For Robert, prayer was something broached only in relation to family crises: "Obviously when my mother was ill, I said silent prayers for her. Same with my brother, when he died in '49."[34] Likewise, Sylvia's efforts to come to terms with family illnesses had spurred sporadic prayers through her life: "My husband was very ill, and you wonder why is this happening and what am I supposed to do. And when my mother was ill, it was a very painful cancer, and then she got shingles on top of it, and for her last two years she was in pain every day, and I prayed for her to die."[35] Some, though certainly not all, of the interviewees intermittently engaged in prayer during times of crisis. While James considered himself to be non-spiritual, he admitted that he reflexively fell back on prayer in certain moments: "when there's danger on the road, for example. If we get into a car accident, the first thing we say is 'oh good Lord.' Or God save me from this, or save me from that. We all utter those same words, even though we're not religious."[36] When asked if he had ever prayed on a regular basis, David, a non-churchgoing Christian, responded: "No, in an irregular way. There were spurts when you feel like you're reminded that you'd better get in touch with any unknown power that might be able to help you."[37] Reflexive, sporadic moments of prayer, usually tied to crises, punctuate many of the narratives in this study. Such moments remind us that the boundary between sacred and secular is often blurred in ordinary human experience.

That nonbelievers sometimes prayed does not negate the existence of a clear strand of indifference and indecisiveness towards religious belief in the postwar Northwest. Perspectives on religion in the region are only partly captured by the "secular but spiritual" – or "belief without belonging" – interpretation. There were many people in the region who rejected organized religion but were spiritual, religious, or believing. There was also a smaller but still significant, and typically overlooked, group of people who rejected organized religion and were deeply ambivalent about belief or disinterested in it. For instance, take this excerpt from my conversation with Beverly:

Interviewer: Would you consider yourself to be spiritual at all?
Beverly: No, I don't think I would consider myself spiritual in any way.
Interviewer: Would you consider yourself an atheist?
Beverly: Well, no, I wouldn't probably say I was an atheist but I'm just …
I'm not religious, you know.
Interviewer: Do you believe there's a god?
Beverly: Well, I suppose I do, but at the same time I can't see that there
is … [trails off].[38]

Such mixed reflections on personal religious beliefs echoed through many of the narratives. Unwilling to call themselves atheists, yet ambivalent about their religious beliefs and disinterested in the spiritual, people such as Beverly tend to slip through the theoretical cracks in studies of postwar religion. British historian Callum Brown breaks new ground in his work on the "no religionism" of the 1960s, a phenomenon that he suggests had "less to do with principled atheism, freethinking, or secularism, and more to do with disinterest in religion." In Brown's view, "unbelief can be at the heart of somebody's no religionism, but equally it may not be; no religionism can be the product of non-speculative atheism – that is, an absence of reflection on the issue of belief in a god."[39] Evidence from the oral interviews and statistics that show comparatively high levels of indifference to religious belief in the region suggest that a "non-speculative atheism" was a significant part of the Northwest's secular culture. When asked whether she considered herself an atheist, Joanne replied: "I just think it's irrelevant, it's just not part of my life. Atheist implies to me, the word implies to me, that you are actually thinking about religion, and rejecting religion, you know. It's really an involvement in anti-religious thought, and I would not put myself in that category."[40] Joanne's comment suggests that we must widen our analytic framework to capture not only the atheistic and the spiritual but also those who considered themselves neither. Such a framework would make room for the indecision of people like Donna, who claimed: "I'm not exactly an atheist. I don't believe in organized religions. But, I don't know, sometimes I think there's something, and sometimes not."[41] It would make room for the many people who carved out secular identities that balanced on but did not cross the social boundary of atheism. Although the secular culture of the Northwest remains elusive and resistant to categorization, religious ambivalence, indifference, and indecision were central to its character.

Though the interviewees' perspectives on religion varied, most expressed a belief in the "golden rule" ideal or, more simply, goodness. Sociologist Nancy Ammerman suggests that "Golden Rule Christianity" is pervasive in America. Golden rule Christians are those who subscribe to ideals of Christian goodness but not to any firm doctrine, and who place less importance on churchgoing than on "care for relationships, doing good deeds, and looking for opportunities to provide care and comfort for people in need."[42] Golden rule Christianity aptly characterizes the spiritual lives of many Northwesterners. One of the interviewees insisted that leaving the church had made her a "better Christian than ever." She explained: "I don't want to talk the talk, I just want to walk the walk, and let my life exemplify my convictions."[43] This woman joined many others in defining good works rather than churchgoing as the mark of a true Christian. When asked to describe his understanding of religion, Patrick remarked: "My own personal view on religion is people helping people. If you need a hand I'll help you, and if I need a hand you help me ... But to go into a building and throw money into a silver tray after some guy has stood up there and shot his mouth off for an hour and a half and made you completely bedsore on the rump, I don't buy it, you know."[44] According to Ammerman, golden rule Christians are not secular, as they "have not given up on transcendence."[45] The golden rule ideal was not the exclusive domain of Christians in the Northwest. Although many people outside of the churches adhered loosely to Christianity, a significant minority favoured an ideal of goodness that was decidedly non-transcendent. Like Ammerman's "Golden Rule Christians," these people emphasized the importance of caring for others and living a good life. Donald, a Nanaimo resident and atheist, reflected on what it meant to live a good life:

This idea that you have to be a Christian in order to be good does not appeal to me at all. I remember, I wrote a thing when I was younger, a creed for

myself. I can't remember where it is. I know that the creed by which I live is
like the ten commandments, but I don't think the religious aspect has ever
had any effect on me.[46]

Henry, also an atheist, affirmed that "treating other people the way you
expect them to treat you, that's all you have to know."[47] Henry and Donald
were not alone in their insistence that living a good life had little to do with
transcendence. Muriel, who considered herself non-religious, remarked: "I
think that the best thing you can do is be nice to other people, treat other
people well, and be honest. And the chances of me going to church are
probably somewhere between slim and none."[48] Charles, who described
himself as both spiritual and as "an atheist with a small 'a,'" reflected on
what he considered to be spiritual values instilled by his father:

> Through your life you treat people the way that you like to be treated. And
> he didn't have to go through the whole New Testament to instill that in me.
> And also, in other things as well, being your own man, and things of that
> nature. Which is a spiritual thing. You answer to yourself, fundamentally. And,
> so that's, I would say, spirituality. The church, the organized churches, they
> don't stress that as much. They're very, very materialistic. So that would be
> my view on it.[49]

Whether they were believers or non-believers, all of the interviewees
would have agreed with Margaret's assertion that "you didn't have to go
to church on Sunday to do good."[50]

"I didn't have any ground beneath me": Journeys to Unbelief

Born in 1930, Thomas lived in various cities in Washington and Idaho
as a child and young adult. He settled in Port Angeles during the 1960s.
As a child, Thomas was a regular churchgoer, involved in church activities, and a believer in Christianity. This changed in the summer of 1948,
when Thomas went to work in a forest service camp in northern Idaho:

> In 1948, in this mix of people, was a guy, his name was [name withheld], he
> was attending MIT – Massachussetts Institute of Technology – and he and
> I clicked. He was an atheist, and I brought into this my philosophical religious
> position, my having come out of church. At least philosophically I was …
> I didn't have any questioning, I would have argued with anybody the validity
> of my church background. [He] and I virtually spent the summer, and he

was more of an intellectual than I was, and ... you might say we debated. We were pushing each other, we were defending, we were arguing back and forth. And I admired him greatly, I admired his intellect. We talked easily. And by the end of the summer, I didn't have any ground beneath me.[51]

After that summer, Thomas became an atheist. While many Northwesterners drifted from religious belief due to apathy and indecision, some, like Thomas, rejected religion more actively, choosing non-belief or atheism. Frank abruptly shed his beliefs when, as a child, he learned that there was no Santa Claus:

I was a believer for the first four years of my life, and my belief was centred on Santa Claus, and god was on the periphery. And then my dad comes up to me one time when I was about four and a half years old, and told me that there was no Santa Claus. And the first thing I asked him was 'is there a god?' And he said, 'oh yes there is a god' [laughs]. But, I decided in my mind that next year he was going to come around and tell me there was no god, so I was going to beat him to it in that respect.[52]

While Frank and Thomas described fairly sudden departures from belief, most of the non-believing interviewees recalled losing their religious convictions more gradually. Karen described being slowly drawn to atheism during her teenage years: "I think when I came to the point of recognizing that this was an imaginary being that somebody had invented, we were told this, we must have faith, we must not ever argue or question, and I couldn't accept that."[53]

Whether they were gradual or sudden, postwar journeys to unbelief unfolded during a time when to publicly deny the existence of God marked a significant departure from dominant norms. While staying away from the churches educed few social consequences in the postwar Northwest, there was far more at stake in decisions about what (and whether) to believe. The available statistics show that levels of professed unbelief were relatively low in postwar Canada and, especially, the United States. That there were fewer declared nonbelievers in the United States reflects in part the fact that atheism was especially vilified in that country. In the years following the Second World War, atheism and communism became virtually inseparable in the social imaginary of both countries. In the United States more than Canada, however, religious belief was further intertwined with national identity in the 1950s, a decade that saw the addition of "under God" to the Pledge of Allegiance, and the creation of "In God We Trust" as the country's official motto.[54] Both Canadians and Americans lived in countries where to believe in a God was normative. However, while the postwar decades saw a gradual softening of the link between belief and social acceptance in Canada, God and nation became even more tightly knit in the United States. Robert Putnam and David Campbell observe that even today, atheism remains an "alien ideology" in America, and "not so much a description of people who happen to be nonreligious, but a symbol of cultural rejection."[55] The cultural emphasis on Christianity in the United States partly explains why levels of professed belief in God remained high in the postwar decades in the Pacific states and throughout the nation.[56] This is not to suggest that American beliefs were in some way inauthentic but, rather, that such beliefs, like all elements of religion, were shaped by the imperatives and expectations of the wider world.

Although national ideals of piety mattered in the Pacific Northwest, the religious differences between British Columbia and Washington State should not be overstated. My research suggests that these two places shared much in the religious realm. In the past and present, cultural commentators have made much of the persistently high levels of belief in God in the United States. While few researchers today would equate churchgoing with religiosity, the association between belief in God and religiosity is regularly taken for granted.[57] As scholars are increasingly recognizing, statistics on church involvement do not by themselves reveal all that religion meant to ordinary people. Statistics on religious belief must be approached with the same critical scrutiny. In the postwar era, people who denied the existence of God or called themselves atheists often encountered incredulity. In 1956, the WNICC reported on a religious survey of the town of Kent: "One lone atheist appeared in the census, and that might have been a prank."[58] In not taking this atheist seriously, the authors revealed just how far public atheism fell outside the bounds of social convention. Similarly, British Columbia atheist activist Marian Sherman found that, because she was not a "moral degenerate," people often did not believe that she was an atheist.[59]

Those who called themselves atheists or unbelievers in the postwar era risked not being taken seriously; they also risked social ostracism. While there is evidence to suggest that unbelief was at least somewhat more accepted in the Pacific Northwest than elsewhere, and in Canada more than the United States, it is clear that professions of atheism crossed the boundary of social acceptance in both nations.[60] This boundary marked the well-understood parameter of Northwest secularity. In public discourse in the region and beyond, atheists were defined as unreliable and deviant. Those who admitted to their atheism risked being denied the right to act as witnesses in court, to adopt children, or even to become citizens.[61] Within this context, it is not surprising that atheism was a boundary that some broached, but few crossed. In 1963, a journalist for the Victoria *Daily Colonist* discovered that most atheists did not want their unbelief made public, for fear of discrimination.[62] I likewise found that many people on both sides of the border kept silent about their unbelief. One of the Seattle interviewees noted that, in the postwar decades, she publicly claimed to believe in a deity so as not to draw attention to her unbelief: "I spent no time on it, I just didn't want to deal with the response of being an atheist."[63] A Nanaimo man remarked that, even in a place as secular as British Columbia, "some people would be afraid to say they were atheist, even to the census-taker."[64] People who identified as atheists or unbelievers in the postwar era risked much. That many kept silent suggests that levels of atheism and unbelief may have been greater than the numbers and reports indicate.

The interviewees were well aware that atheism carried with it significant social consequences. Karen recalled that, while she refused to hide her atheism in the postwar years, she did "learn that you can't just be as blatant with atheism as you can be with Catholicism or something." She went on to complain: "In our culture, we get nagged at. You must believe, you must believe, you must believe, or else you're lost, or you're not going to be saved, or some of these things."[65] Gary acknowledged that calling yourself an atheist in the postwar years "wouldn't get you any brownie points with the establishment."[66] People well understood that to identify oneself as an atheist was to risk social exclusion. As Thomas acknowledged:

> I mean, you didn't go out in the world and announce yourself as an atheist
> if you wanted to mingle with people, and work with people, because atheists,
> in many circles, are pariahs. So, you pick and choose. I would never deny it,
> I don't care what my audience was. But I would not announce it, on the other
> hand, either, unless there was some advantage. Unless there was some integrity
> issue that was involved.[67]

When asked if it would have been acceptable to call oneself an atheist or agnostic in the fifties and sixties, Helen replied: "No, no, I don't think they would have understood it. And if I did that, why then they would've called me a heretic or a heathen or said 'we'll beat some sense into you,' that sort of thing. No, you wouldn't say that to anyone. And a lot of people didn't discuss it either."[68] Some of the British Columbia interviewees confirmed that people in that province were "afraid" to publicly identify as atheists in the postwar decades. Although the social constraints around atheism crossed national borders, such constraints were particularly evident in the American context. Atheism was especially vilified south of the border, in part because of its association with communism. The anti-communist hysteria of the Cold War era crossed the border, but had a more profound effect in Washington than in British Columbia.[69] Seattle resident Alice remarked: "in those days, all communists were atheists, therefore all atheists were communists."[70] Frank, also of Seattle, recalled: "Anybody who called themselves a communist would almost automatically be considered an atheist."[71] Unlike simply not attending church services, atheism was clearly a marker of social difference in the postwar Northwest – one that most, though not all, avoided. Even many committed unbelievers refused to publicly call themselves atheists.

Historian Laurie Maffly-Kipp notes that few studies "see material discrepancies as having some direct bearing on religious faith or practice."[72] Although it is not possible to chart in any fixed or stable way the relationship between class and religious belief in the postwar era, it is clear that material circumstances had a direct bearing on the possibilities for public atheism through these years. That this was a national rather than specifically regional phenomenon is evident in the following excerpt from a letter written by an Edmonton man to British Columbia atheist activist Marian Sherman: "Thank you, Madam, for using your financial freedom to be honest. I, along with several millions, have the same thoughts but our living depends so much on how we express ourselves in the presence of our superiors. We live a life of almost continual lies."[73] Sherman's financial independence allowed her to be open about her unbelief. Those who depended for their livelihoods on the goodwill of their "superiors" generally felt compelled to keep silent. As one British Columbia atheist confessed in a letter to Sherman: "I must admit that my husband would likely be out of work, should I make myn [sic] believe [sic] too much known around town."[74]

Class made a difference to the social expectations and consequences of unbelief. Middle-class religious ideals may have compelled few to attend church in the Northwest, but such ideals exerted considerable force in the realm of religious belief. Deborah, a public school teacher in postwar Washington, reflected on why she kept her atheism under wraps in the 1950s:

> you couldn't be a communist safely in the 50s, and you couldn't be an atheist as a public school teacher, safely, either. I think it would have been very possible that if you announced you were an atheist, particularly east of the mountains, your next evaluation would have found fault in your teaching or in your evaluation of student performance or something, and then put on probation and fired. I wasn't courageous enough at the time to risk anything like that [laughs]. But by the mid-60s, I would have been. But again, I didn't go around announcing it.[75]

As Deborah's story suggests, atheist school teachers were considered especially abhorrent in the postwar years, although things had started to change by the sixties. Public school teachers encountered similar constraints north of the border. In 1962, a Victoria journalist reported on the opposition towards atheist school teachers who, it was believed, might "unconsciously sow a grain of doubt in religious faith in the receptive minds of their pupils."[76] On both sides of the border, atheist teachers drew particular concern because, like parents, they were responsible for turning children into well-adjusted citizens. Canadian historian Mona Gleason argues that teachers were the focus of concern in the postwar era because they were seen as central to reproducing the "ideals, values, and priorities of a particular Canada: white, middle class, heterosexual, and patriarchal" – and, I would add, Christian.[77] Although atheist teachers in the Northwest faced considerable pressure to keep their unbelief hidden, such pressures may have been somewhat tempered in this religiously uninvolved region. Sociologists Rodney Stark and William Bainbridge note that residents of the Pacific region were, in fact, more accepting of atheist high school teachers than their counterparts in other regions.[78]

While unbelieving school teachers were judged especially harshly, atheism carried risks for most sections of the middle class. In a 1964 article titled "No Jobs for Atheists," the *Progressive World* complained that the House of Representatives had made it legal "to refuse to hire and employ any person because of such person's atheistic practices and beliefs."[79] According to Alice, American civil servants have long felt compelled to keep silent about their atheism: "there's kind of an unwritten law in this country, no atheists need apply for a government job. Now, they have government jobs, there's no question about it, but you do keep your mouth shut."[80] The oral evidence suggests that working-class Northwest-erners were somewhat less compelled to "keep their mouth shut" when it came to atheism. Henry regularly discussed his atheist views with his colleagues at a Nanaimo pulp mill, even though most were not professed atheists. Frank, a longshoreman in Seattle, was also comfortable discuss-ing his atheism at work. Frank suspected that most of his colleagues were at least nominally Christian, but admitted, "if you were to poll longshore-men, you'd probably find a higher percentage of atheists than you would among the general population."[81] Henry, Frank, and other working-class Northwesterners were not unaffected by atheism's social stigma, but they did seem to be less at risk of losing their jobs than people in certain middle-class professions.

Despite such risks, some middle-class Northwesterners openly defied convention and publicly ascribed to atheism. Those seeking a more orga-nized outlet for their atheism could join one of the many secular human-ist organizations in the area. In these years, the American Humanist Association worried that it was projecting the image of a "very small, select and aloof intellectual club."[82] Canadian humanists expressed simi-lar concerns: "'Humanism becomes meaningless if it is held to be an elitist philosophy or understandable only by the university graduate."[83] Despite efforts to broaden their appeal, humanist associations in the Northwest and beyond drew support mainly from the middle and upper middle classes. University professors were particularly attracted to such organizations. While certain elements of the middle classes faced intense social pressures against atheism, others – such as university professors – were freer to challenge middle-class religious norms. In 1951, an Ameri-can Episcopalian journal remarked: "Many of our clergy are doing an heroic job in the face of the almost insurmountable barriers of hostility and indifference toward religion in the part of faculty and administra-tion."[84] Through these years, religious periodicals carried headlines such as "Are Our Universities Irreligious?" and "Is the Church Losing Out on Campus?"[85] One church paper affirmed that university administrators and professors were "as ignorant about religion as children."[86] A couple of the interviewees similarly remarked upon the secular character of the academic community. Linda, whose husband was a scientific researcher, commented on her husband's workplace: "The scientific community was, by and large, non-religious."[87] Charles, who worked as a professor at the University of Washington, summed up the feelings of his colleagues towards religion and the church: "University people didn't give a crap, they really didn't."[88]

Alice, once a member of the Seattle Humanist Association, reflected on the financial situation of the American humanists:

> I think the reason why they're as wealthy as they are – probably the 6000 members today of the American Humanist Association on the national level, the ones that join the national organization – I would vouch that education, income, and age, they're in the upper categories of any institution remotely similar to it. We once counted the number of PhDs and there are more than there are members. And that sort of thing. Most of them are retired. And those that aren't are making six or more figures.[89]

A 1962 survey of the American Humanist Association confirmed the primarily upper-middle-class character of this group. The survey found that close to 80 percent of association members were professionals, mainly in the fields of science, business, education, and medicine.[90] Regardless of their thoughts on religion, the working classes were certainly not drawn to organized secularism. Secular humanism seemed to hold particular appeal among upper-middle-class professionals.[91] Perhaps part of the appeal of such groups lay in their use of the more socially tolerable identity of "humanist" as opposed to the more controversial "atheist." While not representative of the Northwest's broad-based irreligion, secular humanism constituted the main organized outlet for middle-class atheism in the region.

Gendering Belief

Like class, gender shaped approaches to, and decisions about, religious belief. When our conversation turned to the subject of belief, Richard remarked: "I think women have an easier time with spirituality ... I think it's easier for them to adapt to the mystery."[92] Like Richard, many of my interviewees understood women to possess a greater capacity than men for spiritual understanding. Certainly, the available statistics reveal that women were, and are, more apt than men not only to affiliate with and participate in religious institutions but to maintain private religious practices and beliefs. A persistent gender gap is evident in American surveys of prayer, Bible reading, and the importance placed on religion in daily life.[93] In the United States, men were also more likely than women to profess unbelief: in 1968, Gallup reported that 2 percent of men and 1 percent of women claimed to not believe in a God.[94] The American statistics point to an enduring gender gap in all religious activities and across different age groups and education levels.[95] In the Canadian context, national surveys similarly reveal a persistent gender division in all areas of religion, including belief and private prayer.[96] The gender imbalance in religious belief was influenced in part by entrenched gender ideals. Normative assumptions about female religiosity and male impiety were reproduced in official and everyday circles. Such assumptions shaped how Northwesterners encountered, engaged, and resisted religion in the postwar world. Although they were subject to cultural pressure to believe, Northwest men were also influenced by manly ideals of rationalism, and by regional expectations of male religious apathy. In this context, men were more comfortable than women adopting and declaring nonbelieving identities. Formed in relation to entrenched assumptions of feminine piety, women's secular identities tended to be less stable and less certain than men's. At the same time, in turning away from religion even partially, Northwest women regularly and boldly challenged such ingrained gender expectations.

In their narratives, the interviewees revealed the gendered character of religious belief in the postwar world. Women were generally far more hesitant than men to voice their unbelief and, especially, to call themselves atheists. For women, to reject religion altogether meant to significantly transgress the bounds of both social convention and normative femininity. Although atheist men were also subject to cultural disapproval, such disapproval was subtly mitigated by the masculine ideals of rationalism and independence. Working- and middle-class men negotiated competing class ideals, but they encountered and reproduced shared norms of masculine impiety. Several male interviewees referred matter-of-factly to the more rational (and thus less religious) nature of men. David observed that men were inherently more critical and questioning than women: "I think a man is more apt to be critically analytical of all he hears about religion, and is maybe a little bolder to reject."[97] Also informed by the manly, rational ideal, Thomas, an atheist and retired lumber-worker, thoughtfully articulated how gender had informed his perspectives on religious belief:

I felt it was less to be expected that a man would be religious, and be outwardly demonstrative of his religion than a woman would be. It would be ... a man would be more apt to keep it to himself, I would expect, and if a man were outward I would be more uncomfortable with him. I could be more comfortable with a woman who was religious, than with a man who was religious, and who sort of wore it on his sleeve.

Thomas went on to admit that he expected men, but not women, to be intellectual, critical, and, ultimately, secular:

I guess I tended ... and this probably shows a little bit of sexism. I think I've always expected – I think I've experienced, until more recent times, that intellectual women were more unusual, more uncommon than intellectual men. You didn't expect a woman to not, sort of, fit the mould of the times. You wouldn't expect her to be intellectually bold enough to break new territory. And it was not uncommon, I think I felt, that a man, intellectually, would launch out on his own.[98]

For Thomas, as for many of his contemporaries, atheist women, like religious men, confounded conventional gender expectations. Contrary to such expectations, many women in the Northwest were indeed "intellectually bold enough to break new territory" when it came to religion. However, entrenched gender norms meant that public admissions of atheism constituted not only a more difficult but also a more subversive move for women than for men.

Decisions about belief and unbelief were deeply gendered. When asked about his thoughts on religion, John replied: "I'm an atheist."[99] Seattle resident Frank asserted: "I would probably have defined myself as an atheist starting at my fifth birthday."[100] Like John and Frank, several Northwest men, in letters and oral interviews, simply and confidently identified themselves as atheists. Some male interviewees related incidences in which they had insisted on being identified as atheists when asked, for official purposes, to state their religious preference. Brian recalled that when his brother Andrew joined the military, he demanded that his dog tags bear the label "atheist" as opposed to the more socially acceptable "no preference." According to Brian, Andrew's public commitment to atheism was a matter of masculine resolve: Andrew would have considered it "weakhearted" to settle for the label "no preference" or even "agnostic."[101] Both men and women in this region were well aware that public admissions of atheism crossed the boundary of social acceptance. Gender norms, however, made this boundary more passable for men than for women.

In their recollections, Northwest women criticized organized religion at length and expressed very few doubts about their decisions to eschew regular church involvement. These women were not impervious to broader cultural expectations of female piety, but regional norms of religious non-involvement held greater sway when it came to organized religion. National discourse on the "atheist evil" intersected with ideals of feminine religiosity to shape Northwest women's approaches to unbelief. Women expressed far more conflict than men around issues of unbelief, and they appeared more hesitant to call themselves atheists. Edna was an unbeliever but rejected the "cruel" and "harsh" label of "atheist": "I don't use that word – I don't like it, but maybe that's what I am, because I'm a non-believer ... I've never referred to myself as an atheist, although I suppose some of my friends have."[102] When asked if she considered herself an atheist, Beverly cautiously replied: "Well, no, I wouldn't probably say I was an atheist but I'm just ... I'm not religious, you know."[103] Many female interviewees described their lack of belief in faltering, uncertain terms. Sharon admitted that, as a homemaker and part-time public servant in the postwar decades, she evaded discussing her atheism publicly: "I think that was a word that people didn't like. I probably didn't ... I really didn't discuss it, you know, with anyone, except to say 'no, I don't believe anything.'"[104] In a letter to atheist activist Marian Sherman, a British Columbia woman expressed her aversion to the term "atheist": "After many years of religious faith-inquiry, and a feeling of being led around like a puppet, I have reached the same conclusion as yourself and yet hated to say I was an atheist."[105]

In suggesting that gender mattered to decisions about belief, I do not mean to reify female religiosity. That women were more hesitant than men to call themselves atheists reflects the influence not of some pious feminine essence but of wider norms of respectable womanhood. To be sure, few Northwesterners, male or female, identified as atheists. However, masculine norms of rationalism and religious indifference ensured that men in the region were more willing and able than women to declare their unbelief. By contrast, Northwest women encountered contradictory regional and gender norms: part of a regional culture that was strikingly secular in terms of religious practice, these women were also subject to wider expectations of feminine piety. Faced with such contradictory expectations, most women marked out complex and often unstable identities in the middle ground between piety and indifference. While Northwest women regularly challenged the ideal of female religiosity by avoiding the churches, this ideal proved to be more power-ful and more entrenched in the realm of religious belief. Although to define themselves as atheists they had to travel far from the dominant, believing mainstream, some women certainly did so. Indeed, two of the most prominent atheist activists in postwar North America were women: Marian Sherman in Canada and Madalyn Murray O'Hair in the United States.[106] Women were also actively involved in forming and sustaining the secular humanist associations in postwar Seattle and Victoria.[107]

At the opening of this chapter, we learned that Anne considered her-self both an agnostic and "very spiritual." Such religious eclecticism was not unusual in the postwar Northwest. The region was characterized by a generalized indifference and antagonism towards organized reli-gion, but perspectives on religious belief were more varied and com-plex. Most Northwesterners believed without belonging, and valued the golden rule, or goodness towards others, over church involvement. With strikingly low levels of religious involvement and relatively high levels of professed belief, the region was at the forefront of the increasingly popular "spiritual but non-religious" category. The Northwest was not filled with unbelievers, but religion in all of its forms mattered compara-tively less to those who lived there. Although few people in the region identified as atheists, many more expressed ambivalence and disinterest in religious belief. Such ambivalence and disinterest is not insignificant but, rather, points to secularizing currents at work in the postwar North-west. As British historian Callum Brown argues, within a religious society, even drifting from religion due to apathy constituted "an act or jour-ney of adventurous rejection."[108] These adventurous journeys were dis-tinctly classed and gendered, unfolding during a time when non-belief was silenced – although this did start to change during the sixties. Some Northwesterners risked social exclusion and identified as atheists, but doing so did not necessarily preclude encounters with religion. Such encounters most often took place in relation to the family and the house-hold, as we shall see in the next chapter.

5

"The closest thing to me"
Religion, Irreligion, and the Family

MURIEL MOVED TO TORONTO from her hometown of London, England, in 1955 at the age of 19. She settled in Vancouver, British Columbia, the following year. Throughout her life, Muriel never attended church and understood herself as non-religious. But while she stated that religion was "unimportant" to her and that she did not "think about it very often," religious encounters and events punctuate her oral interview.[1] She recalled attending Sunday school as a child, getting married in a church, and sporadically praying for the health and safety of her children. Muriel's story echoes others in its emphasis on the family. Robert Orsi notes that all "religious ideas and impulses are of the moment, invented, taken, borrowed, and improvised at the intersections of life."[2] For Muriel, as for many others in the postwar Northwest, religion was something that came into play at those "intersections of life" involving family – at times of ritual and celebration but also in ongoing relations with parents, spouses, and children. In the interviews, references to family called up memories of religious comfort and togetherness, but also of spiritual conflict and tension. As parents, interviewees struggled with how, or indeed whether, to introduce their children to religion. At the same time, they negotiated with religious expectations placed upon them by their parents and extended family members. They often engaged the sacred in response to the needs or desires of family members, or in an effort to fulfill wider domestic ideals. However, the family could be secularizing as well as sacralizing. The distinct irreligion of the Pacific Northwest was partially reproduced within families, in everyday decisions about such things as whether to take the children to church or to say grace at the dinner table.

"The home," remarked a writer for the *Presbyterian Record* in 1961, "has been looked upon as a nursery of faith. In the home one generation has borne its witness to another. Children acquire standards of conduct and standards of faith from what they are taught in their homes."[3] Through the postwar years, the churches affirmed the religious significance of that "nursery of faith," the home. Recognizing the importance of religion to domestic life, scholars have probed the relationship between faith and family in various eras.[4] Regularly identified as the chief setting for religious nurture and socialization, the home is rarely considered in relation to the development of secular thought and practice. By analysing irreligion and the family together, this chapter offers a new perspective on each. It contributes to the growing historiography on the white, heterosexual, middle-class family ideal that predominated in the cultural narratives of postwar North America. In the popular imagination, postwar families were made up of homemaking mothers, breadwinning fathers, and happy children behaving in gender-appropriate ways, and living in affluent suburbia. Scholars have shown this to be a largely unrealizable ideal that obscured the actual complexity of postwar family relations.[5] This invented ideal was not only white, middle class, and heterosexual, but also Christian; however, its religious implications have drawn little attention. This chapter further disrupts the postwar domestic ideal by revealing the religious conflicts and ambivalences that simmered behind this ideal, in real family circumstances. Idyllic images of churchgoing families and cozy Christian domesticity obscure the tensions of gender and generation that characterized religion in many postwar homes. Pervasive, national norms shaped domestic life in the Northwest, but the region also embodied distinctive meanings of family. A regional emphasis on mobility and individualism subtly undercut the wider family ideal and, in the process, at least partially attenuated the religious obligations of family.

The Family and Religious Identity

The family has often escaped analytic attention because of the difficulties involved in finding sources that illuminate the often private world of the household. As Cynthia Comacchio suggests, oral history offers an invaluable, if partial, lens on many of the otherwise "dark corners" of family life.[6] The family is also often overlooked because it is seen as something that reflects and responds to wider forces but does not create them. According to Nancy Christie, much of the new family history challenges this notion by situating the family and household at the "nexus of broader cultural and social relationships." Recent studies show political and social hierarchies and identities flowing from, rather than imposed upon, the family.[7] In this interpretive framework, daily decisions about what to tell the children about religion or whether to send them to Sunday school are taken seriously as determinants of the main story of Northwest secularity. This distinct secularity was not, of course, created and defined solely within the home but also in the streets, schools, churches, and various other spaces where religion was encountered, engaged, resisted, or ignored. Nevertheless, the family was at the centre of the secular Northwest, and the household was a site of some of its deepest tensions.

While my focus on the family draws on theoretical innovations in the study of lived religion and family history, it is grounded in the memories of Northwesterners themselves. As the oral interviews make clear, it would be impossible to understand the religious lives and decisions of the people in this region without giving serious attention to the family. When asked to discuss where and how she developed her views on religion, Nancy responded: "Within my own family, and I can speak to that, because that's the closest thing to me, and what I lived on a regular basis."[8] Nancy's simple yet telling remark underlines the enduring connection between religion and family in the postwar world. Like Nancy, people in the region crafted their religious stories in relation to "the closest thing" to them, their families.[9] Most often, they attributed their perspectives on religion, whether positive or negative, to their parents. Echoing many of his contemporaries, Robert identified his mother as the main religious influence in his life: "Well, I suppose my mother because, you know, if it hadn't been for her I wouldn't've even gone to church to begin with. She planted the seed."[10] Typically, the most painful and joyful religious memories recounted in the oral testimonies centred on relations with family. My interviewees recalled resenting their parents for "sentencing them to church," arguing with their in-laws about religion, and worrying about the spiritual lives of their children. They also remembered the pleasures of participating in sacred family rituals, and the comforts of spending time with children and parents on religious holidays. From dramatic tales of religious estrangement to ordinary accounts of churchgoing, the family was at the nexus of religious memory.

More than simply a recurrent topic of conversation, the family figured as a common reference point for the articulation of religious identity. The oral interviews are revealing, not only for their content but for what historian Sarah Williams calls the "manner of the telling." How certain subjects were discussed or not discussed reveals much about the commonsensical idioms, norms, and habits of Northwest culture.[11] These oral histories were narratives of religion and family at once. Religion was made sense of in terms of the family, both ideal and lived. For most of the interviewees, the religious influence of family members far outweighed that of friends, neighbours, and colleagues. Nanaimo resident Jean took for granted that religion was a family matter: "you're bound to be influenced by your family, and what goes on within the family."[12] Most people, regardless of where they were on the spectrum of belief, defined themselves religiously in relation to their parents and their experience of the sacred in childhood. Many claimed the denominational affiliation of their parents as their own, regardless of personal feelings of unbelief or religious indifference. In other cases, narrators invoked the family in their stories of secular "awakening" as the starting point in their journeys away from religion. They described themselves in relational terms, as having "broken from," "left," "rejected," or "drifted from" the religion of their parents. For Joanne, the absence of religion in her childhood home mattered most to her secular identity: "Well, you know, if you really aren't raised in religion, you aren't exactly an atheist. It's irrelevant. It really is a very different thing. It just doesn't occupy my brain at all, unless somebody starts imposing upon me."[13] Richard told me that his wife is "just ambivalent, period" about religion because she "wasn't raised in a church."[14] Similarly, Charles attributed his religious apathy to a secular upbringing: "It just was not important to me. Because my parents weren't that way, so there's no environment of being involved in church, and no feeling of guilt if I didn't go, and so, I didn't really need it."[15]

The family was so widely held to be the cornerstone of religion that the absence of family provided an easy explanation for religious indifference. Patrick claimed that he was not religious because he lost both of his parents as a young child and "didn't have that parental guidance that most normal people get."[16] To Frank, an atheist who never married, being single and religiously uninvolved went hand in hand: "If I were in a church, I'd probably be married by now [laughs]. I would probably have some sort of a relationship with a woman, especially if they agreed with me in my religious principles."[17] The oral interviews in this study demonstrate the centrality of the family to religious memory and identity. That people conveyed their religious histories in relation to the "closest thing to them," their families, is not of course a startling revelation. Perhaps so taken for granted as to escape analytic notice, the family has not been given priority in studies of irreligion, which have instead looked for the roots of secularization in dominant, elite institutions. The impulse to construct one's religious and secular identity in relation to the family was widely shared across lines of class and gender. In "the manner of the telling," interviewees revealed the association between religion and family to be very much a part of their commonsense social world.

Constructing the Northwest Family

While the oral interviews convey the commingling of religion and family in the wider culture, they also hint at the existence of regionally specific meanings of family in the Pacific Northwest. Scholars have identified distinct geographies of sexuality and gender, but the relationship between place and family has drawn scant attention.[18] Constructions of the family were somewhat distinctive in the Northwest context. References to the individual rather than the family predominated in cultural representations of the region. One postwar writer described the archetypal Northwesterner as a "man of destiny on whose broad shoulders rested the future of the nation and in whose veins flowed the sterling quality of individualism which impressed itself so deeply on the American consciousness."[19] Domestic images and metaphors did not figure centrally in representations of the quintessential Northwest. When the Northwest family did come under discussion, it was often made out to be especially fragile and conflicted. On both sides of the border, religious and cultural leaders regularly cited unusually high rates of divorce in the region as evidence of the instability of the Northwest family.[20] As one observer anxiously noted in 1957, in both Canada and the United States the divorce rate "rises rapidly as we go west."[21] A religious commentator reflected on the unusually troubled and secular character of the West Coast family: "Especially in our western city life have the weapons of paganism and secularism taken their tragic toll in the family."[22]

Such commentaries hint at place-specific meanings of family. Sometimes seen as exceptionally fragile, the Northwest family was also superseded by individualism in constructions of regional identity. Place-specific notions of family were evident not only in the printed sources but in the memories and perceptions of Northwesterners themselves. George grew up in Ontario, lived for a time in Montreal, and settled in Vancouver, British Columbia, in 1949. He described his initial impressions of British Columbia:

> When I came to the coast it was a totally different atmosphere, I believe, as far as religion was concerned. Those people I met in Montreal were all ...

had been brought up in Montreal, and still lived in Montreal, their parents were still there. And when I came to BC, people were alone here, their families were back east or somewhere else or they didn't have family.[23]

In his recollections, George reproduced the widely held perception of the Northwest as a rootless place, where the ties of extended family were not readily apparent. He attributed the lack of religion in his own life and in West Coast culture more generally to the region's less family-centred culture. In constructing the Northwest as an individualistic, restless region, George echoed several of his contemporaries. In the oral narratives, the Northwest was imagined as a place of adventure and newness, rather than of tradition and family. The wider ideal of Christian family togetherness competed with, and was subtly undercut by, a powerful regional identity premised on individualism and mobility. Articulated by cultural leaders and residents, this identity was evident not only in the social imaginary but in the demography of this region, a place where, as George noted, "just about everybody had been born elsewhere."[24]

British Columbians and Washingtonians did indeed live in an especially transient part of North America. The highly mobile character of the West Coast population, historically and at present, is well established in the existing literature. Through the postwar decades, people who lived in the Pacific region moved more often than their counterparts elsewhere. This was also a region that attracted large numbers of people from other places in North America. More people moved, and desired to move, to the West Coast than to other regions through the twentieth century.[25] Population instability is a long-standing characteristic of the region. A number of scholars have argued that mobility contributed to irreligion in the West.[26] Sociologists have shown that high rates of mobility at least partly contributed to the large "no religion" population in British Columbia, and to the unchurched character of the American Pacific states. There is no general agreement on the nature and meaning of this relationship, however. Some studies contend that moving causes people to abandon their religious ties, while others suggest that non-religious individuals are more apt to move. Few scholars, however, have asked the people themselves. While the precise connection between mobility and secularity remains somewhat elusive, the oral interviews in this study suggest the importance of bringing family into the analytic mix. For several interviewees, moving did indeed prompt a turning away from religious practice. It did so, however, primarily when it involved a separation from family.

Moving was not invariably secularizing, as church leaders so often supposed. Nor was "rootedness" a clear predictor of religiosity: several decidedly non-religious interviewees had resided in the same community throughout their lives. While the relationship between mobility and secularity is neither transparent nor predictable, moving away from family constituted a central turning point in many personal journeys away from religion. Through his teenage years, Thomas lived in Tacoma with his father and "churchy" mother, and spent much of his time involved in Protestant youth organizations. Following a summer of discussion and debate with a newfound atheist friend, Thomas shed his religious beliefs at the age of eighteen. He recalled feeling anguished about his turn to atheism:

> One of the biggest agonies that I had was keeping all of this secret from my family. I mean, my interest in sex, of course, was somewhat comparable. But religion was bigger ... There was so much, I don't know, trauma associated with my taking this position, and living at home, you know. I felt like ... I used to say, if my mother learned I was an atheist, it would kill her. I felt so strongly about it ... So, I had to live a double life.[27]

Compelled to lead a "double life" while living with his parents, Thomas felt comfortable abandoning his religious façade only after he moved away from his family. Several other interviewees recalled that moving away from their parents had "liberated" them from religious practice. Robert stopped attending church after he moved away from his mother; although his experience was not characterized by anxiety, Robert based his own religious participation on the proximity of family.[28] David shared a similar inclination, confessing that he left home "to have a damn good time, where a church or a mother wouldn't be looking at me [laughs]."[29] There was a distinct gender dimension to these stories: men were far more likely than women to describe their experience of moving away from family in terms of liberation, freedom, and individualism. George told me that he left his Ontario home, and the church of his childhood, because of his "sense of adventure": "It was sort of the 'go west, young man,'" he admitted.[30] Gary similarly reflected on his decision to move west: "I guess just reading about things. You know, you read novels, and you read this kind of stuff, the West is where it's at, you know [laughs]."[31] Calling upon the central myths and images of Northwest culture, Gary and George joined other men in framing the experience of moving as a narrative of frontier adventure and liberation. The myths and images associated with the frontier appear less frequently in women's testimonies. This is not surprising, as women have long been excluded from, or marginalized within, the masculine narrative of the frontier.

In 1965, a Seattle journalist hinted at the connection between mobility and irreligion in the Northwest: "People who, at best, went through the motions of going to church back home are hardly likely to maintain the practice here, since no social stigma is attached to non-attendance."[32] Apart from one Catholic man who deliberately moved to the West Coast to escape the religious gaze of his anti-Catholic in-laws, the interviewees did not move for reasons explicitly related to religion.[33] However, several speculated that had they not moved, they likely would have continued attending church. Margaret, for instance, attributed her disengagement from the church in part to her move from Manitoba to British Columbia: "I think if we had stayed in Winnipeg at the same place, I think probably we would still have been going, but I think you do lose a certain attachment when you move around quite a bit."[34] Joe grew up in New Brunswick, joined the army, travelled extensively, and settled in Nanaimo in the sixties. In a discussion about life in his New Brunswick hometown, Joe reproduced regional stereotypes of the Canadian Atlantic region as backwards and family-oriented:

> There was nowhere else to go, nobody ever moved out of there. You married the girl next door if she was Catholic, or whatever … If I had stayed there, I'd a been as dumb as the rest of them. I don't think anybody – if they stayed there, definitely they all still went to church. Because it was something to do, in their small little own little family world, and that's it, you know.[35]

Like Joe, Susan believed separation from the church went hand in hand with separation from family; she remarked on the nature of church involvement in the Idaho town of her youth: "I think that if they lived with their extended family, they were more likely to [attend church]. Whereas if they were independent and away from their family, they didn't, they didn't."[36] The oral interviews reveal the family as the nexus between mobility and irreligion. Moving appeared to have little consequence in the religious lives and decisions of the interviewees, except when it involved departures from family. Even then, moving affected religious practice, not belief. For instance, Thomas left the church and stopped leading a "double life" after he moved away from his family, but his atheism remained unaltered. Similarly, George stopped attending church after he moved away from his family, but confessed: "no matter where I lived, I wouldn't have been religious. No, I don't think so."[37] Moving did not make unbelievers out of people, but it often disengaged them, at least temporarily, from one of the chief motives and settings for religious practice: the family.

Historian Suzanne Morton observes that in Atlantic Canada, "older and relatively stable populations fostered intense localisms and bonds of community and kinship," and women "carried an especially important burden as the arbitrators and guardians of family reputation."[38] It seems that "family reputation" was less relevant to social relations and religious practice in the Pacific Northwest. Family meant something a little different in the Northwest, a region where independence was valorized and mobility attenuated the ties of extended kin. Of course, family did not mean the same thing to all people in the region. Family ideals and realities were negotiated and lived in race-, class-, and gender-specific ways. In highlighting the significance of place to family I do not mean to reify regional stereotypes – to imply, for instance, that West Coasters were an inherently independent, transient, family-evading people. Indeed, most Northwesterners aspired to fulfill domestic ideals and gave priority to family relationships. However, certain demographic and discursive factors combined to lessen the influence of extended family in this region. This, in turn, likely moderated religious activity here, since religion was often encountered and practised within the family realm.

Religious Rites and Celebrations

The Northwest was typically imagined as a place of lone adventurers, but this was still a region where most people lived within families. Even those people who had left connections of church and kin behind in their move to the Northwest usually engaged religion anew when they formed their own families. Worship services held limited appeal in the region, but residents continued to seek out religious institutions for the family-centred ceremonies of marriage and baptism. That the churches were regularly used for family rituals but not worship frustrated religious leaders in both nations. In 1960, a writer for the *Olympia Churchman* grumbled that the "hitchhiker is a symptom of an age when all too many people are chiselers – out to get something for nothing. The Church has its hitchhikers, too; people who use it for burials, baptisms and weddings, but who do not support it and who rarely think of it at other times."[39] The *Presbyterian Record* likewise complained about "part-time" Presbyterians, adherents who avoided the church except "during that small but important part of life which is concerned with baptism, marriage or burial."[40] The Northwest was predominantly unchurched, but most people in the region continued to engage religious institutions for family rituals. Many also sporadically entered such institutions on religious holidays, usually with family members. From the perspective of the clergy, that people used the churches for family rituals and not for worship revealed the superficial character of postwar religion. A Canadian Anglican priest, concerned that the churches were being used for "festivals" and "family occasions" but not worship, remarked: "Religion, real religion, isn't too popular today ... To omit the work of worship is rather like filing off the sharp edges of the Cross, rendering Christianity into something weak and harmless, sentimental and palsy-walsy."[41] People who entered the churches occasionally for baptisms, weddings, and holidays, but not Sunday services, were, in the eyes of this Anglican priest and many of his contemporaries, not "really" religious.

Much of the texture and disorder of popular religion is missed by an exclusive focus on formal church involvement. There is a growing literature that challenges the idea, perpetuated by the clergy, that regular church involvement defines true piety. Scholars in North America and Britain have shown that popular religious cultures often take shape outside of institutions, as people engage the sacred in the streets and within households, during festivals and on family occasions.[42] This is a welcome corrective to earlier scholarship that accepted the views of the clergy and interpreted non-attendance at church as straightforward evidence of indifference. In recent studies, practices such as church weddings and baptisms are judged on their own terms rather than against a normative standard of regular church involvement. In her work on nineteenth-century London, Sarah Williams rejects the "association of irregular church attendance with religious indifference" and contends that the "passion among local families" for baptism and other church ceremonies "constituted a distinctly popular religious response."[43] I, too, consider church-based rituals and celebrations part of the popular religious culture of the postwar Northwest. It is important to recognize, however, that this culture embodied certain tensions and ambivalences. Some Northwesterners happily entered the churches for weddings and baptisms, but others did so reluctantly and against their own secular desires.

While most studies of church-based rites of passage focus on the nine-teenth century and the early twentieth, sociologist Reginald Bibby has explored the nature and meaning of such rites in more recent years in Canada. Drawing on national surveys conducted periodically since 1975, Bibby reveals that most Canadians have continued to look to the churches for marriages, baptisms, and burials. According to Bibby, such rites are not just "rote performances" but, rather, practices that "indel-ibly link individuals with religious groups and traditions."[44] He contends that, in "many cases," people engaged in religious rites of passage due to the "pressures of relatives and friends."[45] Such pressures were indeed prevalent in the postwar Northwest, and are central to understanding the nature of popular religious practice in the region. In-depth oral interviews enable us to see not only *that* people engaged in such rites and rituals but also *why* they did so. Many interviewees reluctantly bap-tized their children or were married in churches to placate their fami-lies. Such practices were not somehow superficial, as church leaders claimed, but neither do such practices indicate a passion for religious practice. In recent years, scholars have rightly objected to the correlation of churchgoing with religiosity, and have worked to illuminate those reli-gious practices, such as baptisms and church weddings, that remained widely popular. Although it would be a mistake to accept uncritically the view expounded from the pulpit that such practices, independent of regular church attendance, were superficial, we must also be careful not to attach meanings to these practices that were not understood by the practitioners themselves. Northwesterners initiated and participated in church weddings and baptisms for a range of spiritual and cultural rea-sons. It is clear that many did so reluctantly, ambivalently, and to fulfill the obligations of family.

In the postwar decades, marriage ceremonies remained firmly tied to the religious realm. Most residents of the United States, including those in Washington, opted for religious marriage ceremonies. In 1972, only 19.5 percent of people in Washington were wed in a civil ceremony, in line with 20 percent nationally.[46] While most British Columbians were married in religious ceremonies, they were more apt to choose civil cer-emonies than were their Ontario counterparts. Figures reported by the *Presbyterian Record* and the *United Church Observer* reveal that in 1959 only 4.9 percent of Ontarians were married in civil ceremonies, compared to 11.5 percent of British Columbians.[47] According to Reginald Bibby, by the 1970s, approximately 20 percent of British Columbians opted for civil ceremonies, compared to 10 percent nationally.[48] One need not be non-religious to marry in a civil ceremony, but the relative appeal of such ceremonies in BC does fit with the province's secular character. Although civil marriages were more popular in British Columbia than in other Canadian provinces, most British Columbians were wed in religious ceremonies. In the Pacific Northwest and across both nations, far more people opted for religious weddings than were found in regular attendance at church. As one Presbyterian writer noted: "Whether the wedding is simple or elaborate, the majority of couples still seek the blessing of the church upon it. This is true even though only half of those who wish to be married by a minister are church members, or attend divine service more than once a month."[49]

A few of the interviewees opted for religious wedding ceremonies because they saw such ceremonies as representing a deeper commitment. As Muriel explained, "there were some things, even if you say you're not religious, I've heard people say that if you get married at City Hall, it's like going and getting a driver's license, and getting married in a church feels like real commitment. I think a lot of people feel this way, even if they're not churchgoers."[50] Most interviewees attributed their decision to marry in a church to family pressures. Religion is inextricably bound to other facets of human experience, including those involving the family. While it is difficult to disentangle motivations based on religion from those based on family, many Northwesterners identified family as the singular basis for their religious practice. Some who participated in family-centred religious rites did so begrudgingly, and in contradiction to their own secular impulses. Torn between personal secular inclinations and family obligations, most opted to oblige those who were closest to them. Asked why she was married in a church, Jean put it quite simply: "Because it wasn't my decision, it was ... [pause] ... perhaps the thing to do. You know, girls got married in churches, and although I'd probably been a non-conformist all my life, but not to the point where I would hurt my parents. So, that was why."[51] Most of the interviewees would see themselves in Jean's response. For them, the desire not to "hurt" family members overrode personal feelings in preparation for marriage. Over and over again, respondents told me that they opted for religious weddings to appease their families. They did so to "make everybody happy," to "placate" their parents, and to avoid upsetting their in-laws. Anne, a homemaker in postwar British Columbia, recalled: "His family was very religious, which is why we got married in a church! [laughs] I think that happens to a lot of young people. The pressure is there, it was the thing that you did, it was a family thing you did, and you were respectable, and you didn't get pregnant when you weren't supposed to. You know, it was the times. Beaver Cleaver type of thing."[52] Edward likewise indicated that family dictated the religious setting of his wedding: "Well, mainly I think because both mothers [laughs] thought that we should be married in a church ... They seemed to be quite interested in how things should go [laughs]. And then we wanted my sister to come, too, and she would've been very upset if it hadn't been in a church."[53]

The oral interviews suggest that, for many Northwesterners, religious wedding ceremonies were motivated by wider norms. James reflected on such norms:

> I think it was just because it was the normal thing to do at that time. I mean today people have their own ... you know, kids in your age group, they have their own minds made up, if they decide to go to a church or not go to a church, but back then you followed the whole system, what people did before you, and you just went through the whole system. Back then I don't think anybody would walk into a City Hall and get married.[54]

David, who worked as a physician in postwar Olympia, recalled why he was married in a church: "Not because, to be perfectly honest with myself, of that great judge in the sky [laughs]. Church was the way to go, it was the proper way to have a wedding. It was part of the social milieu of marriage. So, I mean, it wasn't because of any religious connection or affiliation or feeling."[55] Like David, several others confessed that their church wedding had not been motivated by spiritual inclinations. In these oral histories, decisions to get married in churches were framed as family decisions. For many, the religious aspect of marriage "didn't mean anything" and "wasn't important." Linda echoed several interviewees in recalling her unvoiced desire for a civil marriage ceremony: "Oh, I would've loved to have [a civil ceremony], but it was kind of like pressure from ... from all sides. All sides."[56] The few interviewees who were married in civil ceremonies did so against the wishes of family members. For instance, Thomas upset the religious sensibilities of his future in-laws by insisting on a civil ceremony. He recalled a conversation with his future mother-in-law: "I said 'hey, if you want us to get married in a Catholic Church, it doesn't make any difference to me. If you want me to go to this thing before, for non-Catholics, to learn all this stuff, fine. It doesn't make any difference to me. I'm comfortable where I am, but I'll do it.' And that made her furious, that, in effect, I was scoffing at all of this."[57] Unlike most people in that era, Thomas resisted family pressures and was married in a civil ceremony.

Despite the absence of statistics on the regional distribution of baptisms in postwar America, certain printed materials suggest that the practice remained popular in postwar Washington. In 1964, the *Olympia Churchman* noted that the demand for baptisms remained high despite the difficulties involved in finding godparents in this transient region:

> So many of the persons living in the Diocese are virtually displaced persons, who have no relatives in the area and have very few friends. This is affecting the Church today. There are families in the parishes and missions of the Diocese who have adults and children to be presented for Holy Baptism. They do not know enough people to be able to find qualified persons to act as Godparents or sponsors.[58]

Baptism remained a popular practice in postwar British Columbia, although less so in that province than elsewhere in Canada. According to Bibby, in the 1970s approximately 70 percent of British Columbians desired baptism for their children, compared to 90 percent of Canadians more generally.[59] A complex mix of sacred and secular underscored the decisions of Northwesterners to baptize their children. For many, family pressures loomed large. Anne, a mother of four, recalled why her last child was not baptized:

> Oh, because the grandparents had gone by then, and I really thought it was a bunch of bull. I mean, I really did it ... oh, it was a family thing, you just did it. My husband was one of four, and he was the baby. And oh god, he was the big baby that everybody loved, and for his wife to be a miserable little bitch that won't do this and won't do that ... so I just did it. But I didn't do it for the girl because they weren't around! [laughs].

Anne shared the similar experience of her close friend: "she had all her kids done [baptized] but one too! [laughs] I don't think she got the last one done either, and that was again because his parents died. I think that's the push for it."[60] For Anne and her friend, baptism was a practice anchored to the presence of grandparents. Patrick also baptized his

children to oblige his family: "I basically think that was to accommo-
date my wife at the time. And the family, who said you should have your
children baptized or christened. So, fine and dandy, we did that."[61] The
majority of the interviewees attached little religious significance to the
ceremony of baptism. Nancy, who defined herself as a Christian, conveyed her view of baptism: "It was more that, okay, this is traditional and
customary, and we will do this. Not that we felt that, in any way, it was giving greater eternal security to the children. That was not our perspective
on it at all. And that it would give them a commitment to the church, at
large, in the future – we never had any of those feelings at all."[62] In the
oral interviews, baptism was typically described as "unimportant," "harmless," "the thing to do," and a family requirement. Like church weddings,
baptisms constituted a popular religious response of Northwesterners.
This response was sometimes reluctant, ambivalent, and motivated less
by spiritual priorities than family pressures.

Although the Northwest was a distinctly unchurched region, residents often engaged the churches for family rituals. Many otherwise
religiously uninvolved residents also entered the churches on religious
holidays. As most of my interviewees were raised in the Christian tradition, my discussion here centres on holidays that were part of this tradition. In 1959, a cartoon in an Olympia Episcopalian paper depicted a
couple attending Easter services with the caption: "Oh, Father, we look
forward so much to seeing you each year."[63] As this cartoon suggests,
Northwest churches, unfilled most of the time, drew large crowds on
the Christian holidays of Easter and Christmas. This was a phenomenon
specific to neither the Northwest nor the postwar era. Several scholars
have shown that church attendance on holidays, and not at other times
of the year, was an important part of popular religious cultures.[64] Religious holidays have always embodied both secular and sacred elements.
Regardless of their religious or secular identities, the interviewees celebrated Christmas and Easter within their homes through the postwar
decades, and a few marked such occasions by attending worship services. Even those Northwesterners who were indifferent to the churches
encountered Christian idioms and expectations ingrained in the dominant culture. One respondent reflected on the story of Christ's birth:
"it was just something I had heard and it was there, so you have to live
with it."[65] Often, like baptisms and weddings, these religious holidays
marked sporadic encounters with the sacred in otherwise comfortably
secular lives.

Through the postwar decades, the clergy in the Northwest and beyond worried that Christmas and Easter were turning into "carnivals of commercialism" and urged people to "bring Christ back in" to their celebrations of these increasingly "paganized holidays."[66] Evidence from the oral narratives suggests that the clergy had reason to worry, at least in the Pacific Northwest.[67] Most interviewees described their participation in these religious holidays in explicitly secular terms. Gary recalled what a typical Christmas was like for his Port Angeles family:

> well, my wife and children – two daughters – would go to church on Christmas. I even went once or twice, for the hell of it. And then we'd have people, often my wife's relatives, they'd come for Christmas. But there again, it had very little to do with religion, at least as far as I was concerned, it might have meant a lot to them. We didn't discuss it. For me, Christmas was like Thanksgiving or the Fourth of July.[68]

In likening Christmas to the Fourth of July, Gary echoed a widely held secular sensibility. Those who (sporadically) attended services on religious holidays often did so for cultural rather than explicitly spiritual reasons. The following comments from the oral interviews reveal the ambivalence of those who attended church on Christmas and Easter: "it wasn't significant, you didn't know why you were there"; "I went, but there was no feeling there or anything"; "I went, but there was no religion involved."[69] While some attributed their church attendance on holidays to family obligation, Sharon had a more material motivation for attending Easter services: "we went to the Catholic church one time, but it wasn't because we were religious, particularly, it was just to see what was going on, what people were wearing [laughs]."[70] Edna likewise celebrated Easter because it "was an occasion to get a new outfit."[71] Religious symbols and festivals embody multiple rather than singular or fixed meanings. In the circumstances of their everyday lives, people appropriate such symbols and festivals, making them religiously their own.[72] Although they embodied and circulated Christian idioms and images, Christmas and Easter were capable of being understood and celebrated in the most secular of ways. Interviewees repeatedly affirmed that these occasions were "good, secular holidays" celebrated as "cultural" and familial rather than spiritual festivals.[73] The continued relevance of Christian holidays further reveals the complexity of the Northwest's popular religious culture, a culture in which secular impulses intersected with the spiritual demands of family.

Parenting in the Secular Northwest

In the oral narratives, church weddings, baptisms, and religious holidays were often described in terms of ambivalence. For the most part, interviewees participated in these ceremonies and celebrations without complaint. Looking back, many acknowledged that although they had often set aside their own preferences, they were quite comfortable doing so in the name of cultural tradition, or for their families. Far greater tensions arose in the narratives when discussions turned to religion and parenting. Those who quite comfortably participated in church weddings and religious holidays experienced greater conflict and anxiety when it came to decisions about what to tell their children about religion. Even many non-believing Northwesterners worried about how or whether to religiously educate their children. That they did so reflects, in part, the immense reach of the postwar Christian family ideal. Images of family and home were not central to constructions of the Northwest's regional identity. Nonetheless, residents of this region, like their national counterparts, were subject to the pervasive ideals of family that resonated in postwar North America.

In the postwar era, a growing cadre of experts, including educators, psychologists, and social workers, weighed in on the subject of proper parenting. They did not originate in the postwar years, but calls for more effective parenting were especially fervent in this family-centred, baby-boom era. As several historians have demonstrated, the end of the Second World War ushered in a period of soaring birth-rates and heightened domesticity. According to Joy Parr, this era saw a "yearning for a settled domesticity after the disruption of depression and war."[74] The family images that crowded public discourse in these years perpetuated a white, middle-class, heterosexual version of domestic bliss that was exclusive and largely unattainable. Cultural commentators reinforced and entrenched domestic norms, but their discussions also betrayed deep concerns about all that seemed to threaten the family. Family stability was said to be "assailed" by multiple forces, including rising rates of delinquency, divorce, unwed motherhood, and wage-working wives.[75] While the postwar domestic ideal was prescriptive rather than descriptive, it served to normalize particular family behaviours and patterns and make others seem deviant. Several studies have unveiled "cracks" in the shiny, one-dimensional image of the postwar family. They have shown that few actual families conformed to the class, gender, race, and sexual norms that were embedded in the domestic ideal. Although rarely addressed, religion – or the lack thereof – could also locate real families outside of the ideal. This became sharply apparent to a Canadian couple who were denied the right to adopt a child in 1964 because of the husband's atheism.[76] Postwar observers affirmed the significance of religion to stable families, and urged parents to educate their children spiritually as a bulwark against the threat of "atheistic communism."[77] While scholars recognize that the family ideal was not only white, middle class, and heterosexual, but also Christian, few have examined the religious "cracks" in this ideal. The idealized images of cozy Christian domesticity obscure the religious tensions and conflicts that existed in some Northwest homes.

Parenting could be a realm of religious anxiety and contradiction in even the most secular of Northwest homes, particularly for mothers. Men and women shared in negotiating Christian family norms, and in constructing their religious identities in relation to family. However, gender discrepancies emerge in memories of child rearing. Women devoted far more attention than men to the subject of religion and parenting, and were also more apt to recall feeling troubled about the religious training of their children. While it may be that women were more willing and able to express such feelings, as mothers they also carried primary responsibility for the spiritual life of the family. Postwar commentators reminded women that men might casually "leave the practising of religion in the family to the mother," but women must accept "their great responsibility in the training of their boys and girls" and recognize the "paramount need to establish the Christian home."[78] Such religious norms, together with wider expectations about motherhood, could inspire uncertainty in even the most secular of women. Several studies have shown that postwar advice on parenting focused mainly on mothers, who were reminded "time and time again that errors in child rearing were their sole responsibility."[79] Subject to contradictory directives, women were warned of the dangers of over-mothering and under-mothering, of coddling their children and working outside of the home. Scholars have identified a strong current of "mother-blaming" in this era, which prompted feelings of guilt and inadequacy in women.[80] Given these wider pressures, as well as ingrained ideals of motherly piety, it is not surprising that ordinary Northwest women often felt anxious about the religious education of their children.

Family was a central priority in the oral interviews regardless of who was doing the telling. However, in the broader culture and the homes of ordinary Northwesterners, decisions about the religious lives of children fell mainly to mothers. Joanne recalled that in postwar Seattle women "generally had the responsibility for raising the kids, and so they then felt that that was part of their responsibility, teaching their children religion."[81] Gendered views of parenting echo through the oral narratives. Thomas remarked that "women in those days, as mothers, would be inclined to think that this was good form, [a] good way to raise children. Like my mother, in part, it was just that she wanted her kids to have a church background."[82] Beverly likewise speculated that "women are the ones that are bringing up the kids, and they want maybe to give them a little ... how would you say, bringing up in the proper way, or whatever, you know, in a little more of a religious attitude, more than a father would give them, I guess." She further remarked: "most fathers left everything to the mothers to teach their kids and so on."[83] My interviewees widely ascribed responsibility for the religious upbringing of children to mothers. Many matter-of-factly pointed out that men were disinterested in the spiritual training of children. As one woman remarked, "I don't think men particularly cared."[84] According to several interviewees, fathers avoided religion because they were interested in more manly pursuits. As George commented: "Men were out fishing, or they were out, you know. And women probably if they wanted to give their children religious training, it would've been them who brought the kids to church."[85] Others likewise noted that "dads want to go fishing, or watch the hockey game" or "spend their time in the beer parlor" rather than share religious time with their children.[86] As these comments indicate, mothers were assigned primary responsibility for the religious life of the family, not only by professional and popular observers but by ordinary people. Such gender expectations were difficult to ignore, even in the comparatively secular Northwest.

Female respondents worried about how or whether to introduce religion to their children. Many turned, for at least a brief period, to the Sunday schools. Levels of Sunday school enrolment were somewhat lower, and dropped more sharply in the 1960s, in the Northwest than elsewhere.[87] Nevertheless, Sunday schools remained a popular option for religious education in the region, even among those who were indifferent or hostile to the churches. Through the postwar years, church officials complained about the apparent increase in "Sunday school orphans" – children who were dropped off at the churches by their non-attending parents. Church leaders derided parents for using the Sunday school as a babysitter. A comic in the *Canadian Churchman* showed two women playing golf, with the caption: "I'm deeply perturbed by the void created when Sunday school closes ... I mean, where d'ya dump the brats every Sunday morning ..."[88] Unchurched parents who enrolled their children in Sunday school drew wide disapproval from postwar religious leaders; they have also been criticized by present-day historians. Margaret Bendroth notes the "distressingly high proportion of parents" in postwar America who dropped their children at the churches without attending themselves.[89] According to historian Doug Owram, the common practice of parents sending "their children off to Sunday school while one or both of them remained at home" reveals the "obvious superficiality" of religion in postwar Canada.[90] That many Northwest mothers sent their children to Sunday school but stayed away from the churches themselves was neither merely superficial nor uncomplicatedly religious. Neither interpretation captures the tensions, ambivalences, and feelings of guilt often evoked by decisions about the religious lives of children.

Despite the assumptions of the clergy, unchurched parents did not always arrive easily at the decision to send their children to Sunday school. For mothers with secular inclinations, this decision could cause particular anxiety. In 1967, an author for the *Victoria Humanist* noted that secular mothers encountered particular difficulties: "Those of us brought up in the Judaic-Christian tradition are sometimes puzzled as to what attitude to adopt toward teaching our children these concepts."[91] Many Northwest mothers were indeed "puzzled' about how or whether to religiously educate their children. Through the postwar decades, prominent British Columbia atheist Marian Sherman received several letters, from mothers in particular, requesting advice on secular parenting. In one letter, an atheist woman from Alberta described her struggle to reconcile a personal secular sensibility with the feeling that her "children needed a certain degree of religious instruction." She wrote: "I taught church school for one term, and this time I really tried to put my heart and soul into it, because I felt that the future spiritual welfare of my family was at stake."[92] The religious expectations associated with motherhood reached across both nations in the postwar years, affecting women even in the comparatively secular Northwest. A Nanaimo woman discussed her hesitant decision to enroll her children in Sunday school: "I had a problem with the children, I have four, and I decided against my better judgement of not wanting to bring them up believing a lot of myths and decided to send them to a Sunday school. My only reason was that they cannot defend themselves later on, against a subject they know nothing about."[93] Many women similarly recalled sending their children to Sunday school against their "better judgement." Mothers sometimes reluctantly enrolled their children in Sunday school to appease extended family members. Even in the absence of family pressures, however, secular women worried that they were not fulfilling their responsibilities as mothers. They put their children in Sunday school out of a sense of duty and responsibility and, as one woman put it, because "they didn't want that guilt."[94] Some of my interviewees removed their children from Sunday school after a very brief period due to their discomfort with the teachings or atmosphere of the church. A Seattle mother sent her children to Sunday school once, but decided not to send them again after she concluded that it was "too religious."[95]

Spiritual concerns were not always the main impulse behind the practice of sending children to Sunday school, but this is not evidence of superficiality. To presuppose that non-attending parents were casually using the Sunday school as a babysitter (as many members of the clergy presumed) misses the careful consideration and concern that often went into decisions about the religious education of children. Neither want of a daycare nor a strong commitment to religious education prompted the female interviewees to send their children to Sunday school. Rather, most were motivated by a sense that to do so was good mothering and would contribute to the well-being of their children. More specifically, secular Northwest mothers enrolled their children in Sunday school for two central reasons: to fulfill the democratic family ideal and to provide their children with a sense of belonging. Many women who had otherwise led comfortably secular lives found that the arrival of children compelled them to revisit their feelings on religion. Although she never attended church and considered herself a non-believer, Olympia homemaker Edna decided to send her children to Sunday school. Edna reflected on her decision:

> That kind of stumped me. I didn't know what to do about it, because I didn't believe myself, and my husband wasn't participating in it. But I thought they should be subjected to it, and let them make their own decisions. But I'm not sure that they made their own decisions, I think they made the same decision I did. Maybe because I did. They could see that we were not religious.[96]

Like Edna, many mothers felt they needed to introduce their children to religion so that their children were able to "make their own decisions." Anne echoed this sentiment: "I sent my kids to Sunday school. They all went to Sunday school. I wanted them to make up their own minds. I didn't want to prejudice them. But we didn't go to church as a family."[97]

Women worried that to not expose their children to religion was to deprive them of choice. In emphasizing the importance of providing choices for their children, my interviewees drew on and reproduced wider ideals of democracy within the family. As several scholars have shown, in the years following the war, parents (mothers in particular) were urged to raise their children "more democratically."[98] My respondents worried that in not exposing their children to religion they were making their minds up for them. Karen, an ardent atheist, reflected upon why she sent her children to Sunday school: "I guess I felt that … you know, some people say, I send my children to church or Sunday school so they can make up their own minds. I suppose it was something along those lines, because they didn't become rigid churchgoing people later."[99] Similarly, Ruth commented: "I thought they should have some kind of exposure to something. I just thought it was the thing to do, and then they could make up their own mind, which they did."[100] In sending their children to Sunday school, many Northwest mothers were deeply influenced by the democratic family ideal, a "powerful trope" in the years following the Second World War.[101] Few secular mothers expected or hoped that the Sunday schools would make their children religious. Rather, they were mainly concerned about allowing their children the freedom to choose.

Mothers also sought to provide their children with a sense of belonging. Through the postwar years, many secular humanist groups in North America and Britain replicated the Sunday school format in an effort to appeal to families. An American humanist observed that "the young humanist couple with children … have been known again and again to leave the humanist movement because we have made no provision for the equivalent of a 'Sunday school.'"[102] Another writer noted the benefits of a weekly program for the children of secular humanists: "In form, at least, it gives them something in common with their peers who attend traditional Sunday schools, and this goes far in counteracting the feeling of being 'left out.'"[103] Many Northwest mothers sent their children to traditional Sunday schools so that they would not be "left out." They worried that if their children knew nothing of religion or rejected it altogether they would be alienated from their peers and the wider world. Alice anxiously reflected on how her outspoken atheism in postwar Washington had affected her children: "the two older girls had an awful lot of trouble in school. The neighbours wouldn't allow their little girls to play with them, and things like that because ... First of all, because we objected to the creationist point of view, we were considered communists."[104] While few were atheists, the female interviewees were generally resistant or indifferent to organized religion. As mothers, however, these same women turned to the Sunday schools in search of acceptance for their children. They saw such involvement as a way to provide their children with a sense of belonging. A Seattle mother hoped that attending Sunday school would help her introverted children make friends and become more "connected to peers."[105] Another woman noted that she sent her children to Sunday school because that was "what was considered best for the family."[106] Concerns about doing what was "best for the family," especially the children, underscored religious practice in many Northwest homes.

In the postwar era, the religious expectations of motherhood extended into the Pacific Northwest and affected even the most secular of women. Linda was non-religious but recognized that as a mother she was expected to feel spiritually connected: "You have the babies, so you should be feeling connected, but no."[107] Sharon similarly remarked: "having children probably should've made me more religious. Maybe thinking ... wanting to guide these children, but no, it didn't."[108] While many secular mothers sent their children to Sunday school, it would be a mistake to characterize Northwest motherhood as wholly sacralizing. Sunday school enrolments were comparatively low in the region, and Northwest women were less apt than their counterparts elsewhere to see religion as an important and relevant part of their lives. While much has been made of the role of mothers as spiritual teachers, their secularizing influence has been largely ignored. The oral interviews indicate that at least some Northwest women deliberately shielded their children from religious influences. Donna, who was a homemaker in the postwar decades, affirmed that her children "never went to Sunday school, never had them brainwashed. Which is what, to me; religion is – brainwashing."[109] In a more emotional tone, Linda recalled that she had actively protected her children from religion:

I wouldn't do it to them, I just wouldn't. It's kind of like a painful thing, working through the religion thing. I don't think it is something that comes without a lot of soul-searching. For me, anyway. It means coming to terms with a lot of stuff. I just wouldn't do it to them, no. No, I wouldn't do it to them.[110]

While these women were unique in deliberately shielding their children from religion, many more mothers in the region helped to nurture, in overt and subtle ways, secular children. Although they often used the Sunday schools, few interviewees recalled bringing religion into their households. Sharon enrolled her children in Sunday school but refused to teach them religion at home: "I wouldn't want them to have to go through all that – it was a lot of mumbo jumbo, and a waste of time."[111] As the oral interviews suggest, in many Northwest homes religion was rarely discussed, prayers were not uttered at dinner or bedtime, and children were not pressured to believe. In such homes, children were not explicitly taught to be non-religious, but they did grow up in relatively secular environments. Their role has escaped notice, but mothers helped to nurture these domestic secular environments and played a key role in reproducing the distinct irreligion of the Northwest.

At the beginning of this chapter we met Muriel, a British Columbia woman who defined herself as non-religious but admitted that she had called on the sacred at certain moments in her life. For Muriel, such moments usually involved relations with family: "I think there have been times in my life where I felt a great deal like a bit of a hypocrite, when my kids are sick or something and I think 'oh please, God,' and you pray, go to bed at night and you can't sleep, and so ... something is ingrained, from way way back."[112] As Muriel's comments suggest, even the most secular of Northwesterners found that, especially when it came to family, the boundaries between sacred and secular were blurred. Like religiosity, secularity is not "a fixed dimension of one's being, the permanent attainment of a stable self."[113] People who otherwise never entered the churches did so for baptisms, weddings, and religious holidays. The persistence of such practices does not negate the existence of a distinctly secular culture in the postwar Northwest. However, it does suggest that this culture was neither discrete nor totalizing, and that it embodied tensions and ambivalences. Certain contradictions emerged when it came to the practice of religion in Northwest homes, particularly for mothers. Some mothers struggled to reconcile their own secular inclinations with the broader expectations of motherhood. In the end, most did what they felt was "best for the family," which often involved sporadic engagements with the churches. Such engagements were neither wholly superficial nor straightforwardly spiritual. In using the churches for rituals, celebrations, and Sunday school, Northwesterners carved out a popular religious culture centred on the family. At the same time, family religion was somewhat attenuated in the region by high levels of mobility and a regional valorization of individualism. As we shall see in the following chapter, regionally specific material and imaginative conditions, including an emphasis on individualism, helped to nurture a distinctive, secular sense of place in the Pacific Northwest.

6

"So much sin amid so much beauty"
Secularity and Regional Identity

DONALD WAS BORN IN the early 1930s in Prince George, British Columbia, and moved to Nanaimo with his wife in 1953. Although he attended Sunday school sporadically as a child, Donald eschewed church involvement as an adult and gradually shed his religious beliefs. During our conversation, Donald reflected upon the secularity of British Columbia:

> We are less religious because we had to stand on our own two feet from the beginning. My grandmother came from Ohio, and her husband came from Ontario, and they were pioneers in the Okanagan, there was no welfare, there was no handouts from the government, there was nothing, they had to do their own thing. Everybody who came to BC had to do their own thing. That idea of being independent stuck, I think.[1]

Donald was not alone in attributing Northwest irreligion to the region's frontier qualities. Several interviewees suggested that Northwesterners were non-religious because of their inherent self-reliance, individualism, and distrust of authority. Many described secularity as part of a distinctive Northwest identity, characteristic of a place where people did "their own thing" and stood "on their own two feet from the beginning." Although they simplified and homogenized Northwest history and culture, such ideas helped to lessen the power and appeal of organized religion in the region.

In this chapter, I explore the imaginative, demographic, historical, and material constitution of the Pacific Northwest as a secular place. As we have seen, Northwesterners were neither uniformly nor wholly secular, but they were more apt to ignore, reject, or otherwise "live against" religion than were residents of other regions. This secularity cannot be attributed to any single demographic factor. People in British Columbia and Washington, regardless of their social identity, were far less religiously involved than their national counterparts. We are left to consider what, in fact, produced and sustained this irreligion. More than just a neutral setting, the Pacific Northwest contributed to the making of this regional secularity. In addition to being gendered, raced, and classed, religion is also placed. People form attachments and give meaning to multiple places – local, regional, and national. They define themselves, and each other, in relation not only to race, gender, and class but also to place. They create places but are also situated by them, often behaving in ways that are geographically specific. Irreligion was nurtured and sustained by certain symbolic and material elements of the Pacific Northwest itself. Geography is central, not incidental, to our understanding of Northwest secularity.

In the existing literature, secularization often appears placeless, as a nationally uniform rather than regionally diverse phenomenon. My work indicates that secularity was not only more prevalent in the Pacific Northwest but it carried with it meanings specific to the region. Focused on uncovering the often elusive spiritual life of the Northwest, scholars rarely acknowledge that secularity has itself been a significant strand in the culture of this region. In his seminal work, the geographer Wilbur Zelinsky contends that the American West "has substantial numbers of members in almost all the denominational groups, but is not the major centre for any." He concludes by characterizing the West as the region with the "least recognizable religious personality."[2] In Zelinsky's study, as in many others, religiosity is approached as normative. In the postwar Northwest, secularity was not simply a lacuna, or a regional variant of a national development, but something distinctive in its own right. I draw here on theoretical innovations in the study of "place," which the geographer John Agnew defines as "how everyday life is inscribed in space and takes on meaning for specified groups of people and organizations."[3] Northwest secularity produced and reflected regional, or place-specific, sensibilities. Scholars have rarely examined regionalism and secularity together, perhaps because the former is conventionally seen as traditional and the latter as modern.[4] In the postwar Northwest, secularity and regionalism were mutually constituted. Secularity helped to define the Pacific Northwest identity and was itself produced and entrenched by regional discourses.

"We're all the same people": Border Crossings

Throughout her life, Susan lived in various communities of Washington and northern Idaho, finally settling in Port Angeles. During our conversation at a local coffee shop, she gestured out the window and said:

> You know, I think that actually this part of Washington and Canada should be one country, because we're a lot alike, a great deal alike. We can go way up in the woods, and it's people that we enjoy. But, say, if we head east, and we get to the Midwest or something, it's like we're from Mars. I think we're all the same people. It's just this piece of water out here, that's the only thing between us.[5]

Cultural leaders and ordinary people echoed Susan in representing British Columbia and Washington as a cross-border region inhabited by a similar type of people. In 1952, an American Northwest Baptist paper commented upon the British Columbia Bible Conference: "the people seem little different in crossing the national boundary line. They are a vigorous, happy, outdoor, independent breed like all the people of the great Northwest."[6] Divided by an international border, Washingtonians and British Columbians often imagined themselves, and were imagined by others, to inhabit a common place. Place, historian Katherine Morrissey reminds us, refers to an "organized world of meaning" rather than a definite location. Secularity was a significant strand in the crowded "world of meaning" that constituted the Pacific Northwest.[7]

The porosity of the border between British Columbia and Washington is well established in the existing literature. Popular and academic writers note that British Columbia and the American Northwest states are and have been bound by common trade and tourism interests, a shared commitment to environmentalism, and an historic tradition of labour activism. Some even argue that this cross-border region should form a separate nation with an alternative name, such as Cascadia or Ecotopia. Migration rates between Washington and British Columbia were high through the postwar era.[8] The majority of interviewees travelled often across the border, and many had lived in both places. Cultural media of the postwar decades, including fiction, histories, and travel books, typically conceptualized the Pacific Northwest as a cross-border region.[9] The easy movement of ideas across the border sometimes caused concern among church leaders. In 1954, the United Church introduced its new Social Service Secretary for Canada's west-coast province: "With headquarters in Vancouver, he is responsible for British Columbia, so rapidly developing; and because it is so much shut off from the east that it is affected by American mores moving up the coast – mores not always the best for Canada."[10] While British Columbia religious leaders occasionally bemoaned American influences, they also enjoyed strong connections with their counterparts south of the border. Organized secularism also crossed the national boundary. Secular humanists in British Columbia and Washington met regularly for meetings, conferences, and work-shops. In 1964, the editors of the *Victoria Humanist* considered changing the name of their journal to better capture the transborder character of Northwest secularism. One woman offered her opinion on the pro-posed name change: "From my own experience of publishing, I would not worry about changing the title to embrace a wider field. Our friends across the line consider us as part of their Pacific Northwest cultural heri-tage."[11] As this comment suggests, many Northwesterners saw themselves as sharing common ground with their "friends across the line." Literal and symbolic border crossings nurtured the distinctive culture of the Pacific Northwest, including its secularity.

This does not mean that the international boundary was irrelevant to religious practice and identity in the postwar Northwest. William New maintains that, while porous and constructed, borders configure "sepa-rate arenas of social possibility and expectation: in other words, *cultural difference*."[12] Secular humanist literature of the postwar period hints at the significance of the border to religious possibilities and expectations. Humanist commentators on both sides of the border noted that the American mainstream media was far more averse to the subject of atheism than its Canadian counterpart. As one writer remarked in 1952, "Canada permits programs on atheism even if the US does not."[13] Rates of atheism and "no religion" were higher in British Columbia than in Washington, a finding that at least partly reflects the greater stigma attached to unbe-lief in America. The interviewees readily identified religious differences between Canada and the United States. Most pointed out that religion is and was more central to public life and social acceptance south of the border. Donald, a British Columbia resident, observed that Canadians "are not under the same pressure as Americans are to become a member of the church, because that's sort of a social thing down there. If you're going to be a politician, and you're not a member of a church, you're probably dead in the water. In Canada, I don't think it would make much difference, in most cases."[14] While they identified America as the more religious country, many interviewees questioned the authenticity of this religiosity. As Anne observed, American piety is "not real. I think they are very religious, oh I pledge my allegiance to my God and my country. I think Americans are very much more so than Canadians. I don't know if it's true deep down, but on the outside looking in it certainly is that way."[15] People on both sides of the border echoed Anne's suspicions. Thomas, a Port Angeles resident, remarked that while the United States was highly religious "in form," Canada was the "truly religious" nation in practice: "I don't see the United States as being a Christian nation or even a religious one, in a broader sense, in terms of character as a nation … In terms of more truly conducting themselves in a Christian way, and respecting religion, I would say Canadians are way ahead of Americans."[16] Several interviewees commented on the "showy," "phony," and "surface" nature of American religiosity.[17] Such comments hint at the extent to which ingrained ideas about the religious differences between Canada and the United States were shared across the border.

According to Edward Ayers and Peter Onuf, people "carry in their heads quite powerful and uniform mental maps of the United States."[18] The oral interviews suggest that people carried powerful mental maps of religion in North America. When asked to consider the religious cultures of Canada and the United States, people commonly responded in regional terms. For instance, Sharon replied: "Well, when you talk about the South, you hear so much about religion there."[19] Others similarly commented on the widely known religious character of certain regions:

"All I knew was that Quebec was very religious."

"Canada is a little bit ahead of the United States. There's no deep South in Canada."

"I saw the South-East as heavily religious, and Utah as religious, California as not religious. There are pockets. The Midwest is more religious, but not so religious as the South-East."

"Well, I could see Quebec being quite religious because there are so many Catholics there and they are so religious."

"Oh, of course, we were well aware of the situation in the South, the bible belt."

"I think I've long had the sense of the South, the deep south, as more fundamentalist, Baptist, you know, the hoot and holler religion."[20]

As these remarks indicate, Quebec and the American South figured centrally in the widely held, mental maps of North American religion. When
asked whether her husband's parents were religious, Donna replied: "I
presume so, because they were in Quebec."[21] Like Donna, people carried with them presumptions about the religious character of particular
regions. In addition to Quebec and the South, Alberta, Utah, and the
Midwest were considered especially religious, and the Pacific Northwest and the entire West Coast non-religious. Northwesterners who had
lived in or visited other places found their own region to be relatively
non-religious. Even those who had rarely moved or travelled knew the
Northwest to be a comparatively secular place. Seattle resident Frank distinguished his own region from "back East where religion is taken a bit
more seriously."[22] In 1968, a humanist magazine matter-of-factly referred
to Atlantic Canada as a region "where religion still holds the field."[23]
Unlike many other regions, the Pacific Northwest assumed a relatively
secular place on the "mental map" of North American religion. This
imaginative map was not irrelevant but rather helped to further normalize and entrench indifference to organized religion in the region.

Church–State Relations

Celia Applegate notes that the study of regional cultures "does not so
much undermine national histories as complicate them and, especially
in the case of border regions, emphasize the ambiguities and instabili-
ties of the nationalizing project."[24] From a Pacific Northwest perspective, my work complicates certain national religious narratives, such as
those of secularization and Puritanism. In a 1975 speech, Episcopalian
minister Thomas Jessett remarked upon the unique character of Washington State: "The Biblical idea of being a people chosen of God that
permated [sic] the thinking of our New England ancestors has played an
important part in our national history. With it has gone both a sense of
privilege and a sense of responsibility. Neither of these appears to have
found lodgment [sic] in the thinking of the citizens of Washington."[25]
As Jessett's comment suggests, Washington never quite fit the dominant
story of American religion. The Puritan myth belies American diversity
generally, but it lacks particular resonance in the comparatively secular Northwest. Overarching national narratives such as Puritanism and
secularization look different from the view of this cross-border region.
This view also disrupts entrenched ideas about the nature of church–
state relations in Canada and the United States. Scholars often identify

church–state relations as the chief arena of religious difference between these two countries. It is something of a settled truth that a strict adherence to the separation of church and state has fundamentally distinguished America's religious culture from that of its neighbour to the north.[26] Few studies, however, have compared state interventions in religion in these two countries, particularly at the regional and local levels. Despite constitutional differences, British Columbia and Washington shared certain similarities in the realm of church–state relations, particularly when it came to the contested issues of Sabbath legislation and religion in the schools.

During the 1950s, Linda moved from Winnipeg to British Columbia and settled in Nanaimo. She recalled being struck by how different Sundays seemed in her new city: "It was different, it was freer, absolutely freer on Sundays. Difference of day and night actually. People boated a lot on Sundays in Nanaimo."[27] To Linda's surprise, Sundays seemed to be more about leisure than religion in Nanaimo. Christian leaders often glossed over such regional variations and constructed an idealized "Canadian Sunday," a nationally observed day of rest and worship that distinguished this country from its neighbour to the south. In 1957, a writer for the *Presbyterian Record* worried that the "Canadian Sunday" was at risk of becoming Americanized: "We need the Sunday for worship and, as Canadians, we ought to maintain our wholesome reverence for the Lord's Day. Let us see that opportunity to worship and create a nobler world is not further desecrated."[28] A writer for *Maclean's* magazine likewise imagined a distinctive "Canadian Sunday," describing this country as "the chief upholder of the closed Sunday in the English-speaking world."[29] The notion of a uniformly reverent, national Sunday was, of course, a fiction that excluded many Canadians, including those who observed different days of worship. References to *the* Canadian Sunday also obscured regional differences, such as those observed by Linda. Despite both legislative and imaginative efforts to define a national Sunday, there has never been a singular Canadian or American Sunday. Such efforts were regularly destabilized and challenged by ordinary people in local and regional contexts.

In Canada, the Lord's Day Act of 1906, which prohibited businesses from opening on Sundays, remained in effect until 1985. The Lord's Day Act should not be taken as a window on the Canadian Sunday, as over the years the act was variously enforced, contested, and amended across the country.[30] In the United States, Sunday closing laws were initiated by each state, including Washington, in 1909. In the postwar era, the "blue laws" in this cross-border region were widely viewed as outdated and unenforceable.[31] As early as 1937, a Washington newspaper observed: "One of the deadest of Washington's many dead laws is the Sunday closing law ... The statute has never been repealed, has been violated generally through the state every Sunday for the past quarter of a century."[32] In 1966, the *Seattle Magazine* reported that the majority of Washingtonians were "blithely unconcerned about legal limitations on their Sunday activities."[33] North of the border, religious leaders bemoaned the contemptuous disregard for the Sunday laws among legal officials themselves. As one Lord's Day Alliance spokesperson reported in 1957: "A police commissioner lent himself to attack the Sunday Observance Act of B.C. in some of its lapsed aspects, claiming that he had broken the law by failing to attend church on Sunday. His excuse was a 'sick wife.'"[34]

Stories told by some interviewees suggest that the blue laws prescribed, but did not determine, Sunday activities in the region. Through the postwar years, laws prohibiting the sale of alcohol on Sundays were subject to frequent contest in both British Columbia and Washington.[35] William recalled that during the 1950s in Tumwater, a city adjacent to Olympia, his parents and others easily evaded the Sunday liquor laws:

> My parents ... managed to get [liquor] from people who would bootleg for them on Sunday. In fact, you could call up and order it, and they'd bring it out. There was a man in town here, he had an ambulance, and he'd come out in his ambulance and deliver liquor out the back of his ambulance on Sunday, to people who needed alcohol on Sunday.[36]

Ordinary people navigated their way around the blue laws and found access to liquor on the "Lord's Day." Sunday liquor legislation was also challenged and ignored north of the border. Patrick recalled that on Sundays during the postwar years he regularly helped his friend "clean" a Nanaimo pub:

> he had a trap-door behind the bar, and it went down to his cellar, his basement. And we'd go down in there, and we'd drink the [inaudible] first to get rid of the beer in it so we could clean it. And the local constable would come by and knock on the side door, and he'd come in, and he'd party with us too, you know. So we used to have the police down there and everything. That was a – and I'll use the word "religious" – happening every Sunday.[37]

As these stories suggest, an understanding of Sunday legislation offers only a partial view of the lived experience of Sundays. Much to the chagrin of certain religious and government officials, ordinary people continued to reject and evade the blue laws and to go about their usual business on Sundays. In doing so, they were supported by, and helped to perpetuate, the wider, unchurched culture of the postwar Northwest.

Sunday closing legislation was challenged across both nations, not solely in British Columbia and Washington State. However, debates about Sunday laws served to maintain and disseminate the Northwest's distinct secularity. As the historian Katherine Morrissey observes, shared regional identities are made and entrenched, in part, during instances of conflict.[38] Through the 1950s and 1960s, British Columbia's secular identity was made visible in an ongoing contest around Sunday work in Canada's pulp and paper industry. Claiming that they needed to operate on Sundays in order to meet American competition, British Columbia mills defied the Lord's Day Act through these years. LDA officials complained that mill workers sought out Sunday work for the "financial advantage," and that mill owners were generally indifferent to the churches and actually encouraged "organized sport and other secular activities" on Sundays.[39] In disrespecting the Lord's Day, mill owners were seen as contributing to the widespread secularity of British Columbia's resource towns. As one LDA officer commented: "There appears to be a negative attitude on the part of most of the local company executives about Sunday in general and church attendance in particular – and this attitude seems to reflect inself [sic] in the attitude as a whole of the townspeople regarding the observance of the Sunday."[40] The persistence of Sunday work was blamed on the irreverence of, alternately, British Columbia's workers, its employers, and even its attorney general. Although national in scope, the Lord's Day Act was enforced by attorneys general at the provincial level. British Columbia's attorney general was especially resistant towards the Act, causing one LDA officer to remark: "Sunday difficulties in B.C. are in part a creation of the Attorney General's Department."[41] In a letter to the attorney general, the LDA executive urged the cessation of Sunday work in British Columbia's pulp and paper industry:

The variation in this industry which we experience in B.C. cannot help but exercise a harmful influence on the moral, social and spiritual climate of our people, for such policy permits the setting aside of the Lord's Day with its emphasis on spiritual values, as a day of special observance, in favour of the unchecked operation of the material factors of life.[42]

British Columbia's defiance of the Sunday laws was regularly called upon to pressure "the Governments of Eastern Provinces to permit continuous operation of pulp and paper mills in Ontario, Quebec and the Eastern Maritime Provinces."[43] This conflict over Sunday work brought regional variations to light, and is just one example of how secularity came to be taken for granted as part of Northwest culture.

We should not presume, of course, that everyone who opposed or ignored the Sunday laws was non-religious, or that all who supported such laws were religious. However, through public debates about such laws, the secular Northwest came to be known by those within and outside the region. In 1963, one journalist decried the "paradox" of Washington's blue laws:

> Washington State has one of the lowest church memberships in ratio to the population of any state of the fifty in our Union. It is a truth that at least one denomination has considered designating its Rosellini-land outposts as foreign missions. When we are this sinful I do not think it meet [sic] that pastors seek legislation to save either Sunday or Monday, Tuesday, Wednesday, Thursday, Friday or Saturday, for the family or anybody else.[44]

British Columbia's reputation for being "directly opposite the other nine provinces" on Sunday observance continued through 1980, when it became the first province to allow municipalities to enforce or abandon Sunday shopping legislation.[45] Public discourse on the Sunday laws set Washington and British Columbia apart, religiously, from other regions. On both sides of the border, contests over Sunday not only revealed but further entrenched the Northwest's secular identity.

In the postwar era, debates about the state's role in religion centred not only on Sundays but on schools. The First Amendment of the United States constitution explicitly supports the principle of church–state separation, whereas the Canadian constitution contains no such clause. Although regularly taken as proof of the rigid "wall" between church and state in the United States, the First Amendment was prescriptive rather than descriptive. In 1967, the Greater Seattle Council of Churches complained that the "strict separation of church and state in Washington [provides] one of the most difficult situations in the nation for maintaining working relations between religious bodies and governmental institutions."[46] American church leaders regularly complained that Washington's constitution was the most "strongly-worded" in the country with respect to the separation of church and state. When it came to the issue of religion and education, Washington joined most other states in prohibiting public aid to sectarian schools. However, it was one of the few states to forbid Bible reading in the schools and to disallow public support for the transportation of children to parochial schools.[47] The western states appeared to be uniquely committed to keeping religion out of the public schools. In 1962, an author for the secularist *Progressive World* noted that religious exercises were less prevalent in the western states: "The farther west you go, things get worse and worse, and when you come to California you find so many godless schools you begin to believe that the Constitution is really taken seriously by the inhabitants."[48] In the 1960s, a series of national surveys on religion in the schools revealed clear regional variances. Such surveys indicated that religion was far less prevalent in school systems of the West. For instance, when asked whether their schools aimed to teach "spiritual values," 21.3 percent of Americans replied in the negative, compared to 31.1 percent of the population of the western states. Also, 91.4 percent of westerners noted that their schools did not hold homeroom devotional services, compared to only 49.8 percent of the population nation-wide.[49] Despite generalized statements about church–state relations in the United States, regional discrepancies emerged in the arena of religious education. The states of the American West were comparatively strict in keeping religion out of the public schools, a fact that was lamented by religious leaders and celebrated by secularists.

Unlike its American counterpart, the Canadian constitution allowed for state-supported religious education. Provincial approaches to religious education varied across Canada. Like Washington, British Columbia was considered a "stronghold" of church–state separation. In postwar Canada, all provinces except British Columbia and Manitoba supported separate Catholic school systems. British Columbia was considered especially "extreme" in withholding state support for parochial schools.[50] In 1969, a British Columbia magazine urged Catholics in the province to "go east for a fair deal": "What a contrast! West of the Rockies Catholic schools get next to nothing in government support. Just east of the mountains, in Alberta and Saskatchewan, they've got it made."[51] Another writer pointed to the "grave injustices that Catholics in B.C. are enduring through its educational system, when all other provinces have much more favorable conditions."[52] In the 1950s, British Columbians debated about whether Catholic schoolchildren should be allowed to ride public school buses. A radio host contributed to the debate: "in British Columbia, it looks as if we haven't the same respect for the other fellow's viewpoint that they have in Quebec and Ontario. That sort of thing isn't normal in B.C. On most matters we're more than broad-minded."[53] Catholic and cultural observers described British Columbia's education system as uniquely "pagan," "un-Canadian," and "extremely secular."[54] In the postwar era, British Columbia's public school system made no provisions for religious instruction, and excluded the clergy from teaching positions.[55] In 1968, the editor of the *Canadian Register*, a Catholic periodical, remarked that British Columbia schools were "American-type public schools, basically non-religious."[56] Such evidence suggests the need to reconsider any easy truisms about the nature of church–state relations in these two countries. Despite their different constitutional traditions, British Columbia and Washington seemed to share more with each other than their counterparts to the east when it came to schools and Sundays.

The Habits of Region

The Pacific Northwest was, religiously and otherwise, a cross-border place. The "habits of region," writes historian Gerald Friesen, "are sunk deep in the Canadian soil and psyche."[57] The Northwest's secular "habits" did not suddenly appear in the 1950s but, rather, were "sunk deep" in the region's past. In 1860, a Protestant minister described his impressions of Olympia, Washington:

> Infidelity and skepticism are not nourished in secret; intemperance does not fix the same blot upon the escutcheon of individual reputation as in the older settled portions of our country. Many of the population ... seem to have forgotten the religious and moral restraints of early education and habit, and deem themselves emancipated from restraint and responsibility ... Many, also, are there who think less of God and the future than the excitements of money-making, the delirium of politics, or the delicious frenzy of intoxication.[58]

While partial and subjective, this minister's views hint at the historical roots of Northwest secularity. Scholars have traced the region's distinct irreligion back to the nineteenth century. In 1890, only 16.4 percent of people in Washington State adhered to organized religion, compared to 34.4 percent in the United States as a whole.[59] The Canadian historian Lynne Marks has shown that in 1901, British Columbians were far less involved in churches, and far more likely to be atheists, than their counterparts in other provinces. Northwest secularity must, then, be considered as part of a much longer history. Regional cultures are not stable essences but, rather, human constructions that shift across time. Contingent on time as well as place, Northwest secularity was not the same in 1950 as it was in 1900. In the earlier period, for example, the region's unique irreligion partially stemmed from a demographic preponderance of young, single males.[60] While this gender imbalance had levelled out by the postwar era, depictions of the Northwest as a "manly frontier" persisted through the 1970s and continued to influence the region's secularity.

Northwest irreligion was deeply rooted within families. As Rhys Williams writes, "people perform religious rituals precisely *because* they have been done repeatedly by their forebears – rituals connect people over time."[61] Although they are understood and practised in different ways across the generations, religious traditions are often passed on within families. To take secularity seriously as an element of regional culture is to acknowledge that it, too, is entangled in family histories. Karen, a retired nurse in Port Angeles, reflected on her mother's influence:

> as far as religion was concerned, apparently she hadn't had any particular influence in her family, from her mother and father, and she didn't pass any on to us. And I'm grateful for that, because it gave me a chance to do my own thinking. I think this is one of the biggest fallacies of religion, is the brainwashing in childhood. Because, you know, people will say 'I was born a Catholic' or 'I was born a Jew.' You're not, you're not born anything at all.

Karen continued this secular tradition when she became a parent: "Religion was just never that big a deal, I guess, to us because we didn't really talk about it the way some people do, and we didn't say grace at dinner, and we didn't bless everybody."[62] Like Karen, several interviewees attributed their secular inclinations at least partly to one or both of their parents. Of the forty-four individuals interviewed, more than half came from non-churchgoing families or families where one or both parents were non-religious; approximately sixteen of these were from families with longstanding histories in the Northwest.

Several scholars have demonstrated that how, or whether, one encounters religion in his or her childhood home is an important predictor of future religious involvement.[63] Donald recalled that in opting for atheism he had not consciously set out to "follow his dad," but had been deeply influenced by his father's religious scepticism.[64] Likewise, William attributed his avoidance of the churches in part to his family upbringing in Tumwater, near Olympia:

> I don't recall anybody in my family ever going to church. I don't recall my grandparents ever going to church, I don't recall my mother or father, or even my stepfather going to church. So, as far as I know, nobody in my family ever went to church. As far as I can recall. I mean, I know that I never went to church with my parents. I went to church one time with my uncle, and that was to a Catholic Church, one time, just because we were staying with him. But, none of my family went to church.[65]

In my conversations with people who lived in the region, I learned that irreligion was at least partly reproduced within Northwest households. According to historian Karen Wigen, it is in the "local spaces of everyday life" that regional identities were produced and disseminated. The household, Wigen maintains, is an "essential 'capillary' of regional reproduction, the level at which distinctive patterns of speech, labour, and sociability have been both forged and lost."[66] Secular traditions were reproduced, historically, within ordinary households, in actions taken and not taken in those "local spaces of everyday life," including the dinner table. They are more elusive than religious rituals, but distinctive, regional patterns of secularity were forged, and perpetuated across time, in Northwest families.

Northwest secularity was reproduced and disseminated not only in private but in public histories. Religion rarely appears in the dominant tellings of the Pacific Northwest's past. Popular and academic histories of the region that emerged in the postwar era typically ignored religion, or addressed it only in relation to Christian mission work in the nineteenth century.[67] For example, in 1957 the *Nanaimo Free Press* included an extensive supplement on the history of that city that included references to industry, leisure, and transportation, but not religion; likewise, Washington State's centennial celebrations in 1989 contained no mention of religion.[68] Cultural media not only circulated but also established the region's secular past. Popular histories disseminated the idea of Northwest secularity, helping to ingrain it in the public, historical memory. As one regional writer affirmed, in the Northwest "there are not even strong ties with the tradition of religion."[69] Social commentators in earlier years and today have reinforced the Northwest's secularity by depicting it as a place with a "pioneer, honky-tonk history" that was "free of religious constraints."[70] Historian Laurie Maffly-Kipp rightly notes that "religion as a social presence is either absent or at best, serves as a minor and ineffectual player" in popular and academic histories of the American West.[71] A number of scholars have countered this absence by highlighting evidence of informal, non-institutional religious practices in the region. Intent on showing religion's presence, scholars rarely acknowledge that secularity was itself an important aspect of Northwest regionalism. The Pacific Northwest's regional and secular identity became entwined, in part, through popular, and also academic, historical representations. In overlooking religion, such representations described, but also helped to make and affirm, this distinctive regional culture.

Reproduced and disseminated in both private and public histories, the secular "habits" of the Northwest were further reinforced by certain demographic patterns. As the existing scholarship confirms, Northwest irreligion was not demographically determined.[72] Demography is not, however, irrelevant to this story. Certain demographic elements, interwoven with the region's history and culture, helped to foster religious non-involvement and indifference. The region's highly mobile population was especially significant. Many scholars identify transiency as a defining characteristic of the Pacific Northwest. Mobility is not invariably secularizing, but in the specific context of the postwar Northwest, mobility facilitated disengagements from religion. As we saw in Chapter 5, moving often separated people from one of the chief motivations for religious practice: the family. Mobility also reproduced secularity in another way, which is hinted at in the following description of the American Northwest in *The Lutheran:*

> by cold and indisputable statistics a family moving to this region runs greater risk of losing its connection with the church, and of having its faith in God sicken and die, than it would anywhere else in the United States. (It should be pointed out that for Canada somewhat the same conditions prevail in British Columbia, which is also a part of the Pacific Synod). For the Christian Church this is an emergency area.[73]

Sociologists have shown that migrants often conform to the dominant religious culture of their new region. As Roger Stump argues, "changes in religious commitment among migrants reflect regional norms of religious behaviour."[74] When it came to religious behaviour, *where* a person moved was more important than *that* they moved; in other words, place was more significant to religious identity than moving itself. A distinct irreligion has been part of Northwest life since the nineteenth century. People who moved to the region in the postwar decades, as in earlier times, encountered a culture that ascribed comparatively little value to religious involvement. They may not have become godless, but migrants to the Pacific Northwest were likely to experience a decline in religious participation and commitment. Population mobility, then, helped to reproduce Northwest secularity over time. Mobility worked not only in historical but also imaginative ways to entrench norms of irreligion in the Northwest. Moving was constructed as a Northwest tradition, a central part of the region's independent, adventurous, and masculine identity. As my interviewees matter-of-factly affirmed, the impulse to "go west, young man" was about escaping tradition, including religion.[75]

Several interviewees hinted at another demographic factor that, along with mobility, may have contributed to the Northwest's distinct secularity: the relative absence of a stark Protestant–Catholic cultural divide in the region. British Columbia has always had a comparatively small Catholic population: in 1971, 46.2 percent of Canada's population identified as Catholic, compared to only 18.7 percent of British Columbia's population.[76] Certainly, British Columbia was not entirely free of anti-Catholicism. In 1951, the *BC Catholic* encouraged the distribution of Catholic reading material to "cut down prejudice in B.C. where only one in ten persons is of the Faith."[77] However, religion seems to have been a less prominent marker of difference in that province than in others. Sharon discovered that her identity as a nominal Catholic meant something quite different in Victoria than it had in her hometown of Edmonton. Sharon, who had confronted anti-Catholicism and had herself chanted: "Catholics, Catholics, ring the bell, Protestants, Protestants, go to hell!" in Edmonton, found that religious identities were unacknowledged or irrelevant in British Columbia.[78] Edward similarly discovered that being Catholic or Protestant mattered little in British Columbia, even in the realm of politics. He remarked: "there was more of a religious bias in Halifax. You were recognized as either Catholic or Protestant. The NDP were running a chap for city council in Halifax, and the consensus was that he wouldn't get in – not because he was NDP, but because he was Catholic."[79] Like Sharon and Edward, many Canadian interviewees were struck by the lack of Catholic–Protestant tensions in British Columbia. Linda, a nurse who was raised Protestant, moved from Winnipeg to Nanaimo in 1957. Having worked only with Protestant nurses in Winnipeg, Linda was "shocked" to discover that many of her Nanaimo colleagues were Catholic: "It was kind of jolting. The Nanaimo nurses just mixed together." According to Linda, anti-Catholicism was embedded in Winnipeg culture. When her Catholic friend dated a Protestant, "the family found out that she was Catholic, and they were just horrified."[80] The oral narratives suggest that British Columbia was neither as firmly nor as visibly divided along Catholic–Protestant lines as provinces to the east. Of course, as several scholars have shown, Catholic–Protestant conflicts have often been as much, or more, about ethnicity and race as about religion. The presence of a deep Catholic–Protestant divide is not reliable evidence of religiosity. However, the absence of such a divide in British Columbia likely reinforced the comparative irrelevance of public religious identities in Canada's westernmost province.

Scholars have identified a strand of anti-Catholic sentiment in American Northwest history, but this sentiment had waned by the postwar era.[81] Roman Catholics have long been the largest religious body in Washington and Oregon, consistently outnumbered only by those claiming no religion.[82] The American interviewees did not recall the existence of Catholic–Protestant tensions in postwar Washington. Brian remembered that as a child of atheist parents in Olympia, he counted Catholics as among some of his best friends: "It was never a big thing ... If you lived out here your whole life, you wouldn't have known the difference, because out here nobody really cared that much."[83] Historian Patricia Killen contends that Catholic religious identities have been more muted in the American Northwest than in other regions. She argues that Catholics who came to the Northwest did not link their ethnic identity "to religious identity in the way that greater numbers of Catholic immigrants to the eastern and Midwestern United States did."[84] The oral interviews suggest that there was a relative absence of anti-Catholicism in postwar Washington. The American interviewees, however, were less apt than their British Columbian counterparts to describe this absence as a striking regional phenomenon. Helen, who grew up Catholic in Olympia, encountered little religious prejudice:

I think there was more discrimination against blacks ... I can remember when
the first black people came to town, and I can remember there was this nice
black family – they happened to be Catholic, they went to church, they were
good people, they lived out by where my dad ... a couple of houses from
where my father lived – somebody burned a cross on their lawn, and then
they decided to move.[85]

As Helen's comments suggest, race outweighed religion as the dominant
terrain for defining and articulating difference in the Northwest. The
oral narratives, secondary sources, and printed materials point to deep
divisions of race in postwar British Columbia and Washington. Religious
divisions were less evident, distinguishing the Northwest from certain
other regions of North America. In the postwar era, the Northwest was
a place with neither extensive nor deeply ingrained Catholic–Protestant
antipathies. The relative lack of such antipathies did not cause irreligion. However, this did mean that religion was less a part of public discourse and identity in the Northwest than in places with more apparent
Catholic–Protestant divides.

"I just knew we were a hardier people":
Imagining the Secular Northwest

Growing up in Washington and northern Idaho, Susan was aware of the
limited appeal of organized religion in the region. When asked to reflect
on why this was so, she replied: "I just knew we were a hardier people."
What, I queried, did being "hardy" have to do with attitudes towards religion? She responded: "Well, you know, we were taught to be self-reliant,
and not depend on anybody. Like, you know, praying, that's fine – anybody can do that, and you can do it anywhere. But, you don't really need
a conductor up there leading the orchestra telling you how to do it."[86]
Like Donald, who we met at the outset of this chapter, Susan saw religious non-involvement as typical of a people who were especially independent, self-reliant, and "hardy." Scholars have identified such qualities
as particularly important to the distinctiveness of religion in the American West. As sociologist Mark Shibley writes: "Folks on the Pacific Coast
believe in God but are also less committed to traditional religious institutions. This privatization of religion in the West is not, however, an aber-
ration in American culture; rather, it is a product of our fundamental
national values of pluralism, voluntarism, and individualism."[87] Shibley
is not alone in his depiction of West Coast irreligion as quintessentially

American. Scholarly and popular observers regularly attribute the secularity of this region to the unique individualism of the American frontier. As we have seen, British Columbia and Washington shared strikingly low levels of commitment to formal religion. Northwest secularity should be understood, not as the product of uniquely American values, but as a cross-border, regional phenomenon.

A number of scholars attribute the dechristianizing currents of the 1960s to the ethos of individualism and anti-authoritarianism that emerged in that decade.[88] That ethos did not suddenly emerge on the Northwest scene during the sixties but, rather, had long characterized the region's identity and culture and was central to its deep-rooted secularity. Those within and outside the region helped to construct and disseminate dominant images of Northwesterners as independent, individualistic, anti-authoritarian, and frontier-minded. Cultural leaders and ordinary people shared in essentializing "the Northwesterner [as] sort of a solo, individual person."[89] Although it drew on wider western myths, the discourse on Northwest individualism and independence was regionally specific. Postwar cultural observers within the region often insisted on differentiating the Pacific Northwest from other Wests. As historian Stewart Holbrook wrote in 1952: "*This* Northwest is the one where men have their faces to the sea, and can go no farther. It's time Minnesotans gave up calling their state the Northwest." Holbrook went on: "one of the Northwest's charms is this feeling of being tucked away in a forgotten far corner of the United States ... The sense of isolation also contributes to the restless pioneering spirit, the opening-up-of-the-country idea."[90] In 1963, Roderick Haig-Brown remarked that British Columbia "is Canadian, but it is also West Coast Canadian, never quite forgetful of the mountains that divide."[91] Postwar religious leaders similarly imagined the Pacific Northwest as a sort of "West beyond the West."[92] In 1967, an Anglican minister identified "exclusiveness" as the chief characteristic of British Columbia. South of the border, a Washington minister observed that most "folks on the East Coast don't know Seattle is even out there. They are unconscious of the Northwest, and that gives Seattleites a kind of freedom."[93]

Secularity was very much entwined with regional myths of Northwest freedom and independence. Many of my interviewees described their own secularity as part of a shared regional sensibility. Irreligion, like independence, was understood to be intrinsic to the "true" Northwesterner. Richard reflected on the secularity of Washington State: "I think

it comes out of our pioneering experience. We were very lightly populated ... We were widely separated – we had time to think. We had to be
self-reliant. We didn't have anybody bailing us out."[94] Like Richard, several respondents called upon history to explain theirs and the region's
secularity.[95] As Joanne declared: "the people that founded Washington
State were generally more independent ... you know, the ones that
headed west when this was really the frontier, you know. That independence lives on ... people rebelling in terms of the union, and rebelling
in terms of the status quo of religion. They were the explorers."[96] Many
interviewees pointed matter-of-factly to the dependence and conformity
of those in more churchgoing regions; as Edna remarked: "they followed
the leader. Whereas here, everybody does their own thing."[97] Similarly,
Susan distinguished the "hardy" people of the Northwest from those on
the east coast who "don't know how to plant a seed or mow a lawn. They
don't know how to start a fire. They're really helpless."[98] Organized religion, my interviewees assured me, was a "crutch" that was not needed
in the Northwest. Geographer Rob Shields argues that regional myths
"motivate," have "social impacts," and are "articulated with a set of active
practices which are both institutional and personal."[99] The myth of the
"true" Northwesterner was a fiction with empirical consequences, particularly in the religious realm. In telling their stories, my interviewees
constructed this "far corner" – and themselves – as uniquely independent, anti-authoritarian, and secular. They reproduced regional myths
that, while partial and contested, helped to normalize the unimportance
of organized religion in the postwar Northwest.

Regional myths were constructed and disseminated by cultural and
religious leaders as well as ordinary people. Unlike religious leaders,
however, residents of the region often cast secularity as a positive element
of Northwest culture. For instance, in 1952 Northwest author Stewart
Holbrook described Oregon's secularity as a source of pride rather than
shame: "Any place where Billy Sunday could not draw a full house," he
wrote, "must be more civilized than most."[100] "In conversations with the
self," note sociologists Lee Cuba and David Humman, "cultural images
of places may ... be appropriated by individuals to elaborate self concep-
tion."[101] In "conversations with the self," Northwesterners called upon
irreligion to signal their own tolerance and broad-mindedness. Edward,
a socialist and retired public servant in Nanaimo, affirmed that to label
British Columbia non-religious was an "accolade" that showed the region
to be "a bit more laid back."[102] For David, who worked as a physician in

postwar Olympia, the relative lack of organized religion in this region reflected that "the farther west you went, the seemingly more under-standing, or less critical they would be."[103] Robert speculated about the causes of Northwest irreligion: "the further west you come in Canada, and the further north you come from the States, the less racial intoler-ance there is. We tend to be more tolerant in this area ... Maybe it's because we all believe in equality of life."[104] The ideal of Northwest toler-ance was and is belied by the region's history of racism and prejudice, but this ideal predominated in the regional imaginary. Frank echoed others in depicting the region's secularity as evidence of its openness: "Seattle," he remarked, "is probably one of the most liberal places in the country."[105] Others spoke with pride of the "unchurchy" and non-judgmental character of Northwesterners; as one interviewee noted, "there was never any anti-anything out here."[106]

Historian Callum Brown urges scholars to see people of "no religion" as more than lapsed Christians, and the rise of "no-religionism" as more than just the absence or decline of religion. As he convincingly argues, turning or staying away from religion was, for many, "a positive journey that affirms principles and meanings of life."[107] For most of the inter-viewees, rejecting organized religion was, indeed, a positive journey that affirmed their commitment to the Northwestern values of tolerance, resourcefulness, and autonomy. In many cases, such journeys involved seeking "meanings of life" in nature rather than religious institutions. For Nancy, the Northwest environment offered spiritual fulfillment:

> I feel connected to God through our environment. I guess that was part of why I was unhappy in Winnipeg. I guess we need prairies, we need farmers out there, we need this wheat, but you know what? I think they can do it without me [laughs]. The topography, the environment is very important to me. And it reflects, to me, what I perceive as the miracles of life. To others, it might be very different, they might not be miracles of life, but to me they are miracles of life. And I hold them as something very special, and I can ... [pause] ... feel spiritually fulfilled when I have gone for a walk in the woods.[108]

Susan similarly commented: "the area that we live in, we can go miles in any direction, and we have a cathedral anywhere we want to turn."[109] While some saw the Northwest's woods, waters, and mountains as inher-ently spiritual, many more emphasized the secular rather than sacred pleasures of the regional landscape. As Jean bluntly remarked: "Would you go to church today when you could be waterskiing right here?"[110] Several respondents looked to the landscape to explain their own secular behaviour, and that of others. Vancouver resident James stayed away from churches through much of his life because "B.C. is an outdoor type of place. On a Sunday I would just get in my car and drive down to Seattle or drive down to Whistler, and enjoy nature. More preferable than sitting for an hour in church. That didn't turn me on at all. I think people in B.C. have literally been drawn away from the church because we have other activities."[111] Another woman claimed that the church was irrelevant in Nanaimo because of "the absorbance of ... [pause] ... I'd call it nature, I don't know what else to call it."[112] Many interviewees attributed their absence from church to the Northwest's favourable climate. One British Columbia man, discussing his decision to stay away from the churches, simply affirmed: "We're living in Eden!"[113]

The Northwest's distinct secularity was not intrinsic to its natural environment, but it was partly a product of how that environment was defined. To recognize that regional identity is constructed is not to deny its relevance to human behaviour. As American historian Patricia Limerick argues, because "of an idea of the South and of Southernness, people have submitted to federal authority and resisted federal authority; they have stayed home and moved away; they have stood in solidarity and stood in one another's way; they have killed and been killed. Region is a mental act and region is real, at one and the same time."[114] Because of an idea of the Pacific Northwest, people approached and interpreted religion in particular ways. Because Northwesterners imagined themselves, and were perceived by others, as an "outdoorsy" people who opted for nature over churches, many did so. Although there was nothing inherent in the region's landscape that made people less "churchy," the people themselves suggest otherwise. Northwest regionalism was popularly viewed as "a quality of life thrust upon man by the mountains and the sea."[115] As the historian Carlos Schwantes notes: "Rugged mountains and gargantuan trees called forth strong-willed, self-reliant individuals to match them, or so Northwesterners have often claimed."[116] In the regional vernacular, the mountains, trees, and the sea were understood to be at least partially responsible for secularizing the quintessential Northwest lifestyle. As one American Episcopalian minister affirmed, the Northwest's "natural world dominates its reality," which makes "the work of a priest more difficult because the church's traditional forms are not as readily accessible as, say, a mountain landscape."[117] In an article titled

"So much sin in B.C. amid so much beauty," a Toronto United Church official described Canada's westernmost province as a place where "beneath the beauty there is something barren."[118] Canadian religious leaders regularly blamed the mountains for drawing British Columbians away from the church, and for acting as not only a geographical but spiritual barrier. One Protestant official anticipated that British Columbians would become more religious when the mountains became more passable: "the new highways through the mountains will make a difference, and B.C. people will be more in touch with Alberta."[119]

Church leaders often suggested that the Pacific Northwest's landscape dictated its secularity. Place shapes religious practice, but it must be understood in both material and symbolic terms. Contrary to the opinions of church officials, mountain ranges, forests, and other material geographic features did not, on their own, determine religious behaviour. As regional comparisons make clear, attention to cultural context is crucial. In Canada, an Anglican official matter-of-factly pointed out that the "Church's hold is always precarious" in northern British Columbia, because this "rough country" entails "dangerous journeys along a treacherous coast and arduous trips into a forbidding interior."[120] By contrast, on the opposite coast, a rugged geography was deemed responsible for inspiring deep attachments to religion and the churches:

> The Church occupies an important place in the life of the people of Newfoundland. It might be that because the people have been so closely related to the sea with its constant reminder of the power of God and with its heavy toll in human life, they seem to be more God conscious than people in inland areas. One of the results has been that Newfoundland has produced more ministers for the Christian Church in proportion to its population than any other area in Canada.[121]

As this example reveals, seemingly objective geographical characteristics could be considered inherently secularizing in one context, and sacralizing in another. Geography, then, does not determine culture but rather is mediated by it. In the postwar imaginary, the Northwest's topographical features were most often cast as secularizing. Interviewees helped to assign secular meanings to the Northwest's mountains, forests, and waters, geographical elements considered religiously inspiring in certain other contexts. In the wider regional imaginary, such elements rendered religious institutions irrelevant, and occasionally supplanted the sacred altogether.

When asked why she had never attended church, Donna explained: "Oh, I think a lot of the main reason is the circumstances of where we were – physically, we were out of town. We always seemed to live somewhere out of town. It was mostly, I think, probably the physical."[122] Several interviewees admitted to selecting religious institutions for weddings, baptisms, and Sunday school based on proximity. Muriel reflected upon how she chose the setting for her wedding: "I happened to live in Kerrisdale at the time, and I walked by this church every day, and I thought it looked like a real pretty English type church."[123] As these comments suggest, decisions about religion were often influenced, in very basic ways, by where one lived. While this often escapes the notice of scholars, ordinary people readily offer geographical explanations for their religious and non-religious behaviour. Northwesterners stayed away from the churches more than others, in part, because of the secular culture in which they lived. The religious associations of place are typically more apparent than the secular: few would contest the existence of a shared Mormon culture in Utah, a Baptist culture in the South, or a Catholic culture in Quebec, but the secular culture of the Pacific Northwest has gone largely unnoticed. This secular culture was partial, contested, and characterized mainly by a widespread detachment from organized religion. Secularity came to be part of Northwest culture through public contests over Sunday work and private decisions about family prayer, through popular histories of the region and in everyday constructions of religious and racial difference, through actions taken and not taken in governments and ordinary households. Like religion in other contexts, then, secularity became part of Northwest culture in multiple, overlapping, and sometimes conflicting ways. There was nothing inevitable about this secularity, but by the postwar era being "unchurchy" had come to seem typical of the "hardy," independent Northwesterner. Ordinary people were central to ongoing imaginings of the "true" Northwest, and to making non-involvement in religious institutions a normal, accepted, and even celebrated part of life in the region.

Conclusion

IN 1995, BRITISH COLUMBIA author Jim Christy wrote: "British Columbians are different from anybody else. The province is its own distinct
universe cut off from the rest of Canada ... The notion that every British
Columbian carries around in his or her head, whether acted upon or
not, is that this is the best of all possible places to do whatever the hell
you want to do."[1] In 1993, *Seattle Times* writer Curt Hopkins described the
American Northwest as "more than just a little off-center": "Northwesterners simply don't belong. They don't belong to the rest of the nation."
According to Hopkins, the Northwest is "The Last Weird Place," a region
that not only accepts but honours "the absurd, the deviant, [and] the pro-
foundly odd."[2] As these comments suggest, the Pacific Northwest is often
regarded as a unique and even strange place, inhabited by people with a
penchant for radical politics and alternative lifestyles. Home to a wider
array of religious groups than most other regions, the Northwest has also
long been considered a "distinct universe" with respect to religion. Spiritual traditions considered eccentric or peculiar in many other contexts,
such as the "Jesus Freak" movement of the 1970s, found acceptance and
flourished in the communities of Washington and British Columbia.[3]
The Northwest has been seen as a haven not only for those in search of
alternative spiritualities but also for those who wish to escape religion
altogether. The distinctly secular or unchurched nature of the Pacific
Northwest is often held up as further evidence of the region's peculiarity.

References to the unusual character of the Pacific Northwest typically
draw on ingrained regional stereotypes rather than actual research. In
this book, I have endeavoured to move beyond the stereotypes to examine one element of the Northwest's apparent distinctiveness: its secularity. The region was not wholly or exclusively secular, but irreligion
was a significant element of Northwest culture. Northwesterners were
more likely to reject, ignore, or otherwise "live against" religion, particularly in its organized forms, than their national counterparts. This

finding marked the starting point for my analysis, rather than its final conclusion. I was interested in exploring not only if and why but also how Northwesterners were secular, and what this meant in their day-to-day lives. What did it mean to reject religion, in any or all of its forms, in the postwar world? Did social and family identities influence decisions to avoid or engage religion? Guided by these sorts of questions, my work reaches into the relatively uncharted social history of secularity.

Scholars of popular and lived religion have done much to redirect our focus away from religious leaders and institutions and towards the spiritual lives of ordinary people. Although it focuses on the secular, my work contributes to this analytic redirection. Studies of secularization in North America have focused on elites and institutions, and have told us little about the secular in everyday life. Drawing on insights in the social history of religion, my work reveals the significance of race, class, and gender to secular identity and practice in the Northwest. Separated in this study for the purposes of analysis, these categories were commingled in human experience. Northwest secularity crossed lines of race and ethnicity, but was presumed to be made and perpetuated primarily by whites in the region. It was imagined as an element of the Northwest's frontier identity, an identity premised in part on unquestioned assumptions of whiteness. Men and women of all social classes in the Northwest shared a common awareness of the possibilities and parameters of secularity. All knew that public professions of atheism contravened social convention in the postwar years. At the same time, decisions about atheism were gendered and classed. Ingrained expectations of feminine piety partly explain why women were more hesitant than men to call themselves atheists. Middle-class ideals of religiosity also worked to constrain middle-class expressions of unbelief in the region. Masculine and working-class norms of impiety made it at least somewhat easier for working-class men in the region to cross the boundary of atheism. The churches were correct in identifying a strong working-class element to this regional secularism. However, they often overlooked the extent to which a distinct irreligion reached into the more "respectable" communities and homes of the Northwest. Staying away from religious institutions defied national middle-class ideals, but many middle-class Northwesterners did just that. Middle- and working-class residents also shared in criticizing the churches, although their critiques were occasionally class-specific. Inspired by studies in lived and popular religion, I identify a diffusive, everyday irreligion that embodied both cross-class and class-based elements.

Northwest secularity was found in unexpected places, including among women and within families. In suggesting that women and families had anything to do with secularity, my work contradicts conventional wisdom and also the wider literature on the subject. Gender historians have challenged popular images of postwar domestic bliss, and revealed family lives that were far more complicated than the "Leave it to Beaver" ideal implies.[4] My work contributes to this project, unveiling the tensions and contradictions of religion that simmered behind the domestic ideal in actual families. For many Northwesterners, religion was something tied to the family. Family and spiritual motivations were entwined, and some who participated in family religious rituals and celebrations did so reluctantly, in spite of their own secular inclinations. This book demonstrates that normative gender assumptions resonated powerfully in the realm of religion. Expectations of feminine piety made it difficult for women to disengage entirely from religion, especially as mothers. In efforts to reconcile their personal secularity with the religious obligations of motherhood, many unchurched women decided to at least briefly send their children to Sunday school. My work sheds light on the tensions and anxieties felt especially by women when it came to the religious education of children. I argue that many Northwest women sent their children to Sunday school for reasons that were neither superficial nor uncomplicatedly religious. Rather, many did so in an effort to fulfill democratic family and motherly ideals, and to nurture a sense of belonging for their children. Women and families played a central, albeit complex, role in Northwest irreligion.

Class, race, gender, and family influenced how people engaged, and disengaged from, religion in the postwar world. However, no single category alone explains the unusual secularity of the Pacific Northwest. Why was the Northwest distinctly secular? The three levels of sources consulted for this study offer somewhat competing answers to this question. The writings of religious and cultural observers suggest that Northwest secularity was mainly a product of white, working-class men and a lingering frontier mentality in the region. Quantitative materials indicate that this secularity was perpetuated not only by male loggers and miners in the region, but also by women, families, and the middle classes. The oral narratives reveal that the boundaries between sacred and secular were neither fixed nor stable, but rather fluid and contested within the realm of the everyday. My interviewees worked against religion in various ways, but they also sporadically engaged the sacred, often as family practice or in response to crises. In this study, the oral narratives, quantitative materials, and printed sources talk back to each other, revealing a more textured, nuanced view of the secular Northwest than may have been provided by any single source.

There is no single, settled truth of Northwest secularity, but place nurtured and sustained wider possibilities for the secular in the region. What did the schoolteacher in Bellingham, the pulp mill worker in Nanaimo, the businessperson in Vancouver, and the homemaker in Olympia have in common? Although subject to pressures and expectations based on class, gender, race, and various other factors, these people were loosely connected by place. In other words, they shared an organized world of meaning that was "the Pacific Northwest." There was nothing intrinsic or essential to the Pacific Northwest that made it comparatively less religious. Like all places, the region has changed and will continue to shift across time. However, in demographic, material, historical, and imaginative ways, irreligion was entwined with the regional identity of the Northwest. More than just a setting for wider secular processes, the region itself helped to create, and was partially defined by, irreligion.

In this study, I affirm the continued relevance of regions in twentieth-century North America. Regional cultures in Canada and the United States have been sustained, in part, by place-specific approaches to and understandings of religion.[5] Although this study focuses on one particular regional culture, my findings are not merely parochial. I demonstrate that practices occurring within the family did not simply reflect the wider world, but helped to shape and create it. I show that secularity was deeply gendered, and that women were central to its making. I indicate that, contrary to common assumption, working-class people were sometimes more than just "unconscious secularists." I reveal the cultural permeability of the Canada–United States border, and challenge many of the national meta-narratives that have dominated the study of religion in both countries. They were linked to each other by a sense of place, but Northwesterners encountered many of the same kinds of religious, gender, class, and family expectations as their national counterparts. For instance, people in the Northwest and beyond negotiated the religious ideals of motherhood, material barriers to churchgoing, masculine norms of impiety, and the spiritual obligations of family. In this work, I trace the existence of a regionally specific secularity, but my findings have broader implications for our understanding of religion, class, race, gender, family, and place in the postwar world.

The postwar Pacific Northwest was at the forefront of secularizing currents that, to this point, have shown little sign of reversing. Of course, the future of religion in the Northwest, as elsewhere, is unpredictable, a fact that becomes evident when we look at the growth of Christian evangelicalism in the region. Although still very much a minority tradition in British Columbia and Washington, evangelicalism has become increasingly popular among Northwesterners in recent years. At the same time, the proportion of the population claiming no religion has continued to grow steadily not only in the Pacific Northwest, but across both Canada and the United States. Data from the 2011 National Household Survey (NHS) in Canada and the 2008 American Religious Identification Survey (ARIS) indicate that approximately 24 percent of Canadians and 15 percent of Americans claim no religion. With 44.1 percent of its population claiming no religion, British Columbia has retained its distinction as the most secular of Canadian provinces. According to ARIS data, religious "nones" make up approximately 25 percent of Washington State's population; while Washington continues to be among the least religious of states, three other states have proportionately larger no religion populations.[6] The Pacific Northwest is more secular today than it was in the immediate postwar decades. However, the rise of the religiously unaffiliated in both countries has narrowed the gap between region and nation, making Northwest secularity somewhat less distinctive than it was in the earlier era.

A cursory internet search turns up countless articles about the growing population of religious "nones" in Canada and the United States. As many such articles point out, this growth is not straightforward evidence of religious decline, as most "nones" claim some form of religious belief. "Belief without belonging" is indeed becoming ever more common, and has long been a widely accepted way of approaching religion in the Pacific Northwest.[7] As we have seen, religious institutions held comparatively little appeal in the Northwest, but few people in the region called themselves atheists. Even in this relatively secular place, atheism marked a substantial departure from social convention. This book locates the majority of Northwesterners in the shifting, muddy ground between atheism and active religious involvement. It departs from most studies, however, in focusing on the secular impulses and practices that were part of this contested ground. We need to be careful not to overstate the religiosity of those Northwesterners who "believed without belonging." Relatively few people in the region identified as atheists or nonbelievers, but many were indifferent to or dismissive of religion. The interviewees urged me to take their irreligion seriously, and to see the freedom to be religiously uninvolved as a positive, valued element of Northwest culture. Many took special pride in being "unchurchy," and linked their own and the region's secularity to an anti-authoritarian, independent, and tolerant outlook. The rise of the religious "nones" reflects, in part, the growing popularity of non-institutional forms of religion. It also, however, reflects the fact that growing numbers of people are, like many in the postwar Northwest before them, turning away from religion and towards more secular ways of understanding and experiencing the world.

We still have much to learn about the sacred and secular in Northwest history and culture. Three subjects, in particular, beg for further research. First, we need to know much more about the religious and secular experiences of non-European, non-Christian populations in the region, especially in the latter half of the twentieth century. We have seen that race and ethnicity were central to constructions of religion and region in the postwar world. However, we need to learn much more about how those outside of the white, Christian mainstream negotiated the secularism of Northwest culture. Did they help to produce and perpetuate, ignore, or reject this secularism? By pursuing these sorts of questions, researchers will add further texture to our understanding of Northwest culture, and provide insights into the influence or relevance of this region's secularism outside of the dominant society. Second, the intersections between religion, irreligion, and leisure in the Pacific Northwest demand further research. My study indicates that the Northwest's natural world was invested with several competing meanings. In the postwar decades, religious leaders struggled to reaffirm the importance of churchgoing, but they also endeavoured to bring church to the people by establishing worship services on ski hills and in campgrounds. We need to know more about how the Northwest's emphasis on leisure, particularly in its nature-based forms, affected religious practice and identity in the region. Finally, more research is needed on the connections between the religious, political, and moral perspectives of Northwesterners. Opinion polls show that people in the region have held distinct views not only of religion but of such things as abortion, assisted suicide, and the environment.[8] Future studies should seek to make explicit the connections, if any, between the Northwest's irreligion and its seemingly unique moral and political culture. Research on these and other subjects will help to shed further light on the intersections between religion, irreligion, and place in the Pacific Northwest and beyond.

Notes

Introduction

1 Joe, personal interview, September 5, 2003.

2 Frank, personal interview, March 28, 2004.

3 Susan Lazaruk and Norma Greenaway, "Churches' role wanes in Canada," *Times Colonist,* May 14, 2003, A1; Knute Berger, "The God wars," *Weekly* (Seattle), March 24–30, 2004, 9; and Julia Duin, "Gallup poll finds Washington State least churchgoing," *Washington Times,* January 6, 1999, A2.

4 Lynne Marks, "'Leaving God Behind When They Crossed the Rocky Mountains': Exploring Unbelief in Turn-of-the-Century British Columbia," in *Household Counts: Canadian Households and Families in 1901,* ed. Peter Baskerville and Eric Sager (Toronto: University of Toronto Press, 2007), 371.

5 *Lutheran,* May 14, 1952, 12.

6 For studies that do address irreligion in the Pacific Northwest, see Patricia O'Connell Killen and Mark Silk, eds., *Religion and Public Life in the Pacific Northwest: The None Zone* (Walnut Creek: Altamira Press, 2004); Bob Stewart, "'That's the B.C. Spirit!' Religion and Secularity in Lotus Land," *Canadian Society of Church History Papers* (1983): 22–35; Lynne Marks, "Exploring Regional Diversity in Patterns of Religious Participation: Canada in 1901," *Historical Methods* 33: 4 (2000): 247–54; Marks, "'Leaving God Behind,'" 371–404; J.E. Veevers and D.F. Cousineau, "The Heathen Canadians: Demographic Correlates of Nonbelief," *Pacific Sociological Review* 23: 2 (April 1980): 199–216; Mark Silk and Andrew Walsh, *One Nation, Divisible: How Regional Religious Differences Shape American Politics* (Lanham, MD: Rowman and Littlefield, 2008); Tina Block, "Everyday Infidels: A Social History of Secularism in the Postwar Pacific Northwest," PhD diss., University of Victoria, 2006; and Frank Pasquale, "The 'Nonreligious' in the American Northwest," in *Secularism and Secularity: Contemporary International Perspectives,* ed. Barry Kosmin and Ariela Keysar (Hartford: Institute for the Study of Secularism and Society, 2007), 41–58.

7 W.F. Hart, "What Is Religion?," *Canadian Churchman,* February 20, 1958, 79.

8 Sandra, personal interview, March 27, 2004.

9 Barry Kosmin, "Contemporary Secularity and Secularism," in *Secularism and Secularity: Contemporary International Perspectives,* ed. Barry Kosmin and Ariela Keysar (Hartford, CT: Institute for the Study of Secularism and Society, 2007), 11.

10 See, for example, Lynne Marks, *Revivals and Roller Rinks: Religion, Leisure, and Identity in Late-Nineteenth-Century Small-Town Ontario* (Toronto: University of Toronto Press, 1996).

11 Callum Brown, *Religion and the Demographic Revolution: Women and Secularisation in Canada, Ireland, UK and USA since the 1960s* (Woodbridge: Boydell Press, 2012), 14, 61.

12 Claudio Lomnitz-Adler, *Exits from the Labyrinth: Culture and Ideology in the Mexican National Space* (Berkeley: University of California Press, 1992), 312.

13 Paul Groth and Chris Wilson, "The Polyphony of Cultural Landscape Study: An Introduction," in *Everyday America: Cultural Landscape Studies after J.B. Jackson,* ed. Chris Wilson and Paul Groth (Berkeley: University of California Press, 2003), 15; and Callum Brown, *Religion and Society in Twentieth-Century Britain* (Edinburgh Gate: Pearson, 2006), 14.

14 See, for example, Sarah Williams, *Religious Belief and Popular Culture in Southwark, 1880–1939* (Oxford: Oxford University Press, 1999); and David Hall, *Worlds of Wonder, Days of Judgment: Popular Religious Belief in Early New England* (New York: Knopf, 1989).

15 Williams, *Religious Belief and Popular Culture,* 13, 14.

16 David Hackett et al., "Forum: American Religion and Class," *Religion and American Culture* 15: 1 (2005): 1–29; William Sutton, "Tied to the Whipping Post: New Labor History and Evangelical Artisans in the Early Republic," *Labor History* 36: 2 (1995): 251–81; Bryan Palmer, "Historiographic Hassles: Class and Gender, Evidence and Interpretation," *Histoire Sociale* 33: 65 (2000): 105–44; and Lynne Marks, "Heroes and Hallelujahs – Labour History and the Social History of Religion in Canada: A Response to Bryan Palmer," *Histoire Sociale* 34: 67 (2001): 169–86.

17 The British historian Callum Brown notes that the concept of working-class absence from religion is often taken for granted; see his *Religion and Society,* 214.

18 Robert Orsi, "Everyday Miracles: The Study of Lived Religion," in *Lived Religion in America: Toward a History of Practice,* ed. David Hall (Princeton: Princeton University Press, 1997), 7.

19 Orsi, "Everyday Miracles," 9.

20 For two fine works on secularization in Canada, see Ramsay Cook, *The Regenerators: Social Criticism in Late Victorian English Canada* (Toronto: University of Toronto Press, 1985); and David Marshall, *Secularizing the Faith: Canadian Protestant Clergy and the Crisis of Belief, 1850–1940* (Toronto: University of Toronto Press, 1992).

21 See Brown, *Religion and the Demographic Revolution* and *the Death of Christian Britain: Understanding Secularisation, 1800–2000* (London: Routledge, 2001); and Hugh McLeod, *The Religious Crisis of the 1960s* (Oxford: Oxford University Press, 2007).

22 Hugh McLeod, "Reflections and New Perspectives," in *The Sixties and Beyond: Dechristianization in North America and Western Europe: 1945–2000,* ed. Nancy Christie and Michael Gauvreau (Toronto: University of Toronto Press, 2013), 453.

23 On secularization in the 1960s, see John Webster Grant, *The Church in the Canadian Era: The First Century of Confederation* (Toronto: McGraw-Hill Ryerson, 1972); Gary Miedema, *For Canada's Sake: Public Religion, Centennial Celebrations, and the Re-Making of Canada in the 1960s* (Montreal and Kingston: McGill-Queen's University Press, 2005); Catherine Gidney, *A Long Eclipse: The Liberal Protestant Establishment and the Canadian University, 1920–1970* (Montreal and Kingston: McGill-Queen's University Press, 2004); McLeod, *The Religious Crisis of the 1960s*; and Brown, *The Death of Christian Britain.*

24 *Time,* April 8, 1966; and Pierre Berton, *The Comfortable Pew: A Critical Look at Christianity and the Religious Establishment in the New Age* (Philadelphia: Lippincott, 1965). Also see John Robinson, *Honest to God* (Philadelphia: Westminster Press, 1963).

25 McLeod, *The Religious Crisis of the 1960s,* 261.

26 Sylvia, personal interview, June 24, 2003.

27 Grace Davie, *Religion in Britain since 1945: Believing Without Belonging* (Oxford: Blackwell, 1994); Mark Shibley, "Secular but Spiritual in the Pacific Northwest," in *Religion and Public Life in the Pacific Northwest: The None Zone,* ed. Patricia O'Connell Killen

and Mark Silk (Walnut Creek: AltaMira Press, 2004), 139–68; Mark Chaves, *American Religion: Contemporary Trends* (Princeton: Princeton University Press, 2011); Robert Putnam and David Campbell, *American Grace: How Religion Divides and Unites Us* (New York: Simon and Schuster, 2010); and Robert Fuller, *Spiritual but Not Religious: Understanding Unchurched America* (New York: Oxford University Press, 2001).

28 Brown, *Religion and the Demographic Revolution*, 62.

29 Mark Silk, "Religion and Region in American Public Life," *Journal for the Scientific Study of Religion* 44: 3 (2005): 266.

30 See David Livingstone, "Science and Religion: Foreword to the Historical Geography of an Encounter," *Journal of Historical Geography* 20: 4 (1994): 368; and John Agnew, *Place and Politics: The Geographical Mediation of State and Society* (Boston: Allen and Unwin, 1987), 2.

31 Samuel Hill, "Religion and Region in America," *Annals of the American Academy of Political and Social Science* 480 (1985): 140.

32 Orsi, "Everyday Miracles," 6. Also see Belden Lane, "Giving Voice to Place: Three Models for Understanding American Sacred Space," *Religion and American Culture* 11: 1 (Winter 2001): 58.

33 Rhys Williams, "Religion, Community, and Place: Locating the Transcendent," *Religion and American Culture* 12: 2 (June 2002): 260–61.

34 Rob Shields, *Places on the Margin: Alternative Geographies of Modernity* (London: Routledge, 1991), 10.

35 Hall, *Worlds of Wonder*, 4.

36 Bruce Curtis, *The Politics of Population: State Formation, Statistics, and the Census of Canada, 1840–1875* (Toronto: University of Toronto Press, 2001), 33. Also see Benedict Anderson, *Imagined Communities: Reflections on the Origin and Spread of Nationalism*, rev. ed. (London: Verso, 1991), 166.

37 Marshall, *Secularizing the Faith*, 132.

38 Curtis, *The Politics of Population*, 5.

39 Waldo Beach, "Faith and Morals on the College Campus," *Christianity and Crisis*, September 21, 1959, 125. Also see *New Religious Frontier*, September 28, 1955, 1; United Church of Canada (hereafter UCC), Board of Evangelism and Social Service (hereafter BESS), *Annual Report* (1960), 69–73; and Marjorie Oliver and Ron Kenyon, eds., *Signals for the Sixties* (Toronto: UCC Board of Information and Stewardship, 1961), 2–3.

40 Peter Viereck, "Drive-In Churches: The So-Called Return to Values," *Christianity and Society*, Summer 1956, 8.

41 UCC, BESS, *Annual Report* (1956), 32–36.

42 Ken Peters, "How Does One Evaluate U.S. Religious Boom?" *Register*, May 24, 1959, 7.

43 For discussions on the difficulties involved in quantifying religion, see Thomas Davenport, *Virtuous Pagans: Unreligious People in America* (New York: Garland Publishers, 1991), 34–73; and C. Kirk Haddaway, Penny Long Marler, and Mark Chaves, "What the Polls Don't Show: A Closer Look at US Church Attendance," *American Sociological Review* 58 (December 1993): 741–52.

44 Orsi, "Everyday Miracles," 8.

45 Callum Brown, "The Secularisation Decade: What the 1960s Have Done to the Study of Religious History," in *The Decline of Christendom in Western Europe, 1750–2000*, ed. Hugh McLeod and Werner Ustorf (Cambridge: Cambridge University Press, 2003), 42. For an eloquent discussion of the wide range of religious practices and beliefs that are missed by statistical measurements, see the introductory chapter to Williams, *Religious Belief and Popular Culture*.

46   H. Russell Bernard, *Research Methods in Anthropology: Qualitative and Quantitative Methods,* 3rd ed. (Walnut Creek: AltaMira Press, 2002); Paul Thompson, *The Voice of the Past: Oral History,* 3rd ed. (Oxford: Oxford University Press, 2000); Valerie Raleigh Yow, *Recording Oral History: A Practical Guide for Social Scientists* (Thousand Oaks: Sage, 1994); and Williams, *Religious Belief and Popular Culture,* 18–23.

47   Nancy Janovicek, "'If you'd told me you wanted to talk about the '60s, I wouldn't have called you back': Reflections on Collective Memory and the Practice of Oral History," in *Oral History Off the Record: Toward an Ethnography of Practice,* ed. Anna Sheftel and Stacey Zembrzycki (New York: Palgrave Macmillan, 2013), 192.

48   Yow, *Recording Oral History,* 2; and Maurice Punch, "Politics and Ethics in Qualitative Research," in *Handbook of Qualitative Research,* ed. Norman Denzin and Yvonna Lincoln (Thousand Oaks: Sage, 1994), 83–97.

49   See, for example, Thompson, *The Voice of the Past;* Daphne Patai, "Ethical Problems of Personal Narratives, or, Who Should Eat the Last Piece of Cake?" *International Journal of Oral History* 8: 1 (1987): 5–27; and Julie Cruikshank, "Oral Tradition and Oral History: Reviewing Some Issues," *Canadian Historical Review* 75: 3 (1994): 403–18.

50   Yow, *Recording Oral History,* 17.

51   I use the term "approximately" because these categories were fluid rather than fixed. There were those, for instance, who defined themselves as both atheistic and spiritual.

52   Williams, *Religious Belief and Popular Culture,* 19.

53   See, for example, Robert Orsi, *Thank You, St. Jude: Women's Devotion to the Patron Saint of Hopeless Causes* (New Haven: Yale University Press, 1996); R. Marie Griffith, *God's Daughters: Evangelical Women and the Power of Submission* (Berkeley: University of California Press, 1997); Williams, *Religious Belief and Popular Culture;* Brown, *Religion and Society;* and Brown, *The Death of Christian Britain.*

54   David Hall, "Introduction," in *Lived Religion in America: Toward a History of Practice,* ed. David Hall (Princeton: Princeton University Press, 1997), x.

55   Sheila McManus et al., "Challenging the Boundaries of Geography: A Roundtable on Comparative History," *Canadian Review of American Studies* 33: 2 (2003): 139–60; and William Westfall, "Voices from the Attic: Crossing the Canadian Border and the Writing of American Religious History," in *Retelling U.S. Religious History,* ed. Thomas Tweed (Berkeley: University of California Press, 1997), 181–99.

56   See, in particular, Seymour Lipset, *Continental Divide: The Values and Institutions of the United States and Canada* (New York: Routledge, 1990). The thesis is discussed and countered in Edward Grabb and James Curtis, *Regions Apart: The Four Societies of Canada and the United States* (Oxford: Oxford University Press, 2005).

57   See, for example, Ian McKay, "A Note on 'Region' in Writing the History of Atlantic Canada," *Acadiensis* 29: 2 (2000): 89–101; and Gerald Friesen, "The Evolving Meanings of Region in Canada," *Canadian Historical Review* 82: 3 (September 2001): 529–45.

58   Richard Maxwell Brown, "The Other Northwest: The Regional Identity of a Canadian Province," in *Many Wests: Place, Culture, and Regional Identity,* ed. David Wrobel and Michael Steiner (Lawrence: University Press of Kansas, 1997), 293.

59   Although I focus on Washington and British Columbia, Oregon has also maintained distinct patterns of secularism; see Mark Shibley, "Religion in Oregon: Recent Demographic Currents in the Mainstream," *Pacific Northwest Quarterly* 83: 3 (July 1992): 82–87.

60   See Don Alper, "The Idea of Cascadia: Emergent Transborder Regionalism in the Pacific Northwest-Western Canada," *Journal of Borderland Studies* 11: 2 (1996): 1–22; Matthew Sparke, "Excavating the Future in Cascadia: Geoeconomies and the Imagined Geographies of a Cross-Border Region," *BC Studies* 127 (2000): 5–44; Patrick Smith, "Cascading Concepts in Cascadia: A Territory or a Notion?," *International Journal of*

Canadian Studies 25 (2002): 113–48; Joel Garreau, *The Nine Nations of North America* (Boston: Houghton Mifflin, 1981); and Carlos Schwantes, *Radical Heritage: Labor, Socialism, and Reform in Washington and British Columbia, 1885–1917* (Seattle: University of Washington Press, 1979).

61 For discussions on the socio-economic development of the Pacific Northwest following the Second World War, see Carlos Schwantes, *The Pacific Northwest: An Interpretive History*, rev. ed. (Lincoln: University of Nebraska Press, 1996), 429–522; Jean Barman, *The West beyond the West: A History of British Columbia*, rev. ed. (Toronto: University of Toronto Press, 1996), 270–321; and Brown, "The Other Northwest," 300.

62 For an exception, see Rodney Stark and William Bainbridge, *The Future of Religion: Secularization, Revival, and Cult Formation* (Berkeley: University of California Press, 1985).

63 The historiography on the relationship between class and religion is rich and growing; see, for example, Marks, *Revivals and Roller Rinks;* Brown, *The Death of Christian Britain;* Williams, *Religious Belief and Popular Culture;* Nancy Christie, "On the Threshold of Manhood: Working-Class Religion and Domesticity in Victorian Britain and Canada," *Histoire Sociale* 36: 71 (2003): 145–74; and Norman Knowles, "Christ in the Crowsnest: Religion and the Anglo-Protestant Working Class in the Crowsnest Pass, 1898–1918," in *Nations, Ideas, Identities: Essays in Honour of Ramsay Cook,* ed. Michael Behiels and Marcel Martel (New York: Oxford University Press, 2000), 57–72.

64 For exceptions, see Maureen Fitzgerald, "Losing Their Religion: Women, the State, and the Ascension of Secular Discourse," in *Women and Twentieth Century Protestantism,* ed. Margaret Bendroth and Virginia Brereton (Urbana: University of Illinois Press, 2002), 280–303; Evelyn Kirkley, *Rational Mothers and Infidel Gentlemen: Gender and American Atheism, 1865–1915* (Syracuse: Syracuse University Press, 2000); Lori Ginzberg, "'The Hearts of Your Readers Will Shudder': Fanny Wright, Infidelity, and American Freethought," *American Quarterly* 46: 2 (June 1994): 195–226; Tina Block, "'Going to church just never even occurred to me': Women and Secularism in the Postwar Pacific Northwest," *Pacific Northwest Quarterly* 96 (Spring 2005): 61–68; and Tina Block, "Ungodly Grandmother: Marian Sherman and the Social Dimensions of Atheism in Postwar Canada," *Journal of Women's History* 26: 4 (Winter 2014): 132–54.

65 Ann Braude, "Women's History *Is* American Religious History," in *Retelling U.S. Religious History,* ed. Thomas Tweed (Berkeley: University of California Press, 1997), 87.

66 For studies that seek to "place" religion see, for example, Wilbur Zelinsky, "An Approach to the Religious Geography of the United States: Patterns of Church Membership in 1952," *Annals of the Association of American Geographers* 51 (1961): 139–93; James Shortridge, "A New Regionalization of American Religion," *Journal for the Scientific Study of Religion* 16: 2 (1977): 143–53; Hill, "Religion and Region in America"; Lane, "Giving Voice to Place"; and Williams, "Religion, Community, and Place."

67 On western exceptionalism, see David Bercuson, "Labour Radicalism and the Western Industrial Frontier, 1897–1919," *Canadian Historical Review* 58: 2 (1977): 154–75. For further discussions on the thesis, see Schwantes, *Radical Heritage;* Mark Leier, "W[h]ither Labour History: Regionalism, Class, and the Writing of BC History," *BC Studies* 111 (1996): 61–75; and John Belshaw, "The West We Have Lost: British Columbia's Demographic Past and an Agenda for Population History," *Western Historical Quarterly* 29 (Spring 1998): 25–47.

68 See, in particular, Agnew, *Place and Politics;* John Agnew and Jonathan Smith, eds., *American Space/American Place: Geographies of the Contemporary United States* (New York: Routledge, 2002); and Shields, *Places on the Margin.*

69 See *Western Regular Baptist,* March 1954, 11; and Marks, "Leaving God Behind When They Crossed the Rocky Mountains."

Chapter 1: Constructing the Secular Northwest

1 Joanne, personal interview, March 30, 2004; Linda, personal interview, October 14, 2003; Richard, personal interview, March 22, 2004; and Margaret, personal interview, September 10, 2003.

2 University of Washington Manuscripts and Special Collections (hereafter UWM), Greater Seattle Council of Churches (hereafter GSCC), Acc. 1358-7, Box 3, File 6: Notebooks, "Suggestions for Implementation" by Gertrude Apel, 1958; and Edwin Bracher and Marjory Bracher, "The Northwest is Growing," *Lutheran,* March 26, 1952, 15.

3 UCC, Board of Information, *Outreach* (1966), 78–79.

4 *United Church Observer,* October 1971, 11; R.E. Milam, "Impressions of the British Columbia Bible Conference," *Western Regular Baptist,* February 1952, 12; and UCC, British Columbia Conference (hereafter BCC), *Minutes* (1954), 1318.

5 Elizabeth Furniss demonstrates the continuing significance of the frontier myth to the regional identity of British Columbia in her fascinating study, *The Burden of History: Colonialism and the Frontier Myth in a Rural Canadian Community* (Vancouver: UBC Press, 1999). Also see Carlos Schwantes, "The Case of the Missing Century, or Where Did the American West Go After 1900?" *Pacific Historical Review* 70: 1 (2001): 1–20.

6 Gerald Friesen, "The Evolving Meanings of Region in Canada," *Canadian Historical Review* 82: 3 (September 2001): 542.

7 Randy Widdis, "Borders, Borderlands, and Canadian Identity: A Canadian Perspective," *International Journal of Canadian Studies* 15 (1997): 56; Donald Worster, "Wild, Tame, and Free: Comparing Canadian and U.S. Views of Nature," in *Parallel Destinies: Canadian-American Relations West of the Rockies,* ed. John Findlay and Kenneth Coates (Seattle: University of Washington Press, 2002), 260–61; and Brown, "The Other Northwest," 302.

8 Edward Ayers and Peter Onuf, "Introduction," in *All Over the Map: Rethinking American Regions,* ed. Edward Ayers et al. (Baltimore: Johns Hopkins University Press, 1996), 3.

9 Presbyterian Church in the United States (hereafter PCU), Board of National Missions, *Annual Report* 33 (1956), 98.

10 Furniss, *The Burden of History,* 207.

11 UWM, Washington and Northern Idaho Council of Churches and Christian Education (hereafter WNICC), Acc. 1567-2, Box 3, File: Writings, "The State of the Church in the Northwest," n.d.

12 UWM, GSCC, Acc. 1358-7, Box 4, File 2: Notebooks, "Denominational Executives Advisory Committee," June 15–16, 1964.

13 Harvey Shepherd, "BC's Swinging Seminary," *United Church Observer,* February 1, 1967, 27.

14 Rillmond Schear, "The Stone Cold Spirit That Stalks Seattle's Churches," *Seattle Magazine,* December 1965, 21.

15 UWM, WNICC, Acc. 1567-2, Box 2, File: Writings, "The State of the Church in the Northwest," n.d.; and UWM, WNICC, 1920–66, Acc. 1567-1, Box 1, File 19: Incoming Letters, M-N, Letter from Gertrude Apel to Dr. Norman Vincent Peale, October 11, 1949.

16 Kay Cronin, *Cross in the Wilderness* (Vancouver: Mitchell Press, 1960), 240.

17 UCC, British Columbia Conference Archives (hereafter UCBCA), Home Missions Committee Papers, *Minutes,* "Prince Rupert-General Recommendations," March 1–2, 1966, 3. Also see Presbyterian Church in Canada (hereafter PCC), *Acts and Proceedings of the General Assembly* (1952), 16, 17; and Roy Manwaring, "Cariboo is Calling," *Canadian Churchman,* December 15, 1955, 584.

18 *Catholic Northwest Progress,* March 3, 1961, 3; "Full Text of Archbishop Duke's Sermon at Nuns' Investiture," *BC Catholic,* March 29, 1951, 4.

19 "Wanted: Clergymen!," *Fort Nelson News,* May 11, 1960, 2. Also see Anglican Church of Canada (hereafter ACC), Diocese of British Columbia, *Journal of Synod* (1959), 17; (1960), 16; and United Methodist Church in the United States (hereafter UMC), Pacific Northwest Conference, *Annual Journal* (1970), 84–89.

20 UWM, WNICC, Acc. 1567-2, Box 9, File: Faith and Order, "The State of the Church in the Pacific Northwest," n.d.

21 Lutheran Church in America (hereafter LCA), Western Canada Synod, *Minutes of Annual Convention* (May 1964), 27.

22 Len Thorpe, "The Call of the North," *Western Regular Baptist,* March 1953, 4; F.A. Schole, "This is Kitimat," *Canadian Lutheran,* November 15, 1955, 4; PCU, General Assembly, *Minutes* (1955), 73–79; and UWM, WNICC, Acc. 1567-1, Box 1, File 19: Incoming Letters, M-N, Letter from Gertrude Apel to Norman Vincent Peale, October 11, 1949.

23 See Furniss, *The Burden of History,* 53; Belshaw, "The West We Have Lost," 35–36; and Cole Harris, *The Resettlement of British Columbia: Essays on Colonialism and Geographical Change* (Vancouver: UBC Press, 1997), xi.

24 PCC, *Acts and Proceedings of the General Assembly* (1952), 16, 17; and "The Diocese of Cariboo," *Canadian Churchman,* January 3, 1952, 6.

25 ACC, General Synod, *Journal of Proceedings* (1959), 381.

26 "Geography, A Problem in the West," *Western Lutheran,* February 9, 1953, 4.

27 See, for example, Hugh McCullum, "Diocese tries ecumenical parishes," *Canadian Churchman,* May 1971, 19; Robert Smith, "Canada's 'Zoom Town,'" *United Church Observer,* February 15, 1961, 25; and Episcopal Church, Diocese of Olympia, *Annual Journal* (1953), 45.

28 Thomas Tweed, "Introduction: Narrating U.S. Religious History," in *Retelling U.S. Religious History,* ed. Thomas Tweed (Berkeley: University of California Press, 1997), 12.

29 Schole, "This is Kitimat," 5.

30 Methodist Church in the United States (hereafter MCU), Pacific Northwest Conference, *Annual Journal* (1965), 92.

31 Ron Strickland, ed., *Whistlepunks and Geoducks: Oral Histories from the Pacific Northwest* (Corvallis: Oregon State University Press, 2001), 292; and UWM, WNICC, Acc. 1567-2, Box 3, File: Writings, "The State of the Church in the Northwest," n.d.

32 UCBCA, Lord's Day Alliance (hereafter LDA), BC-Alta Branch Papers, Box 3, File 9: "Sunday" by Walter Cavert, n.d.

33 *Vancouver Sun,* September 28, 1966, 4.

34 "Archbishop's Annual Report: Notes Growing Lawlessness, Material Progress on BC Coast," *BC Catholic,* February 3, 1955, 1.

35 Shepherd, "BC's Swinging Seminary," 28.

36 "The Farmer and Sunday," *United Church Observer,* April 1, 1952, 4. Also see W.S. Sutherland, "The Rural Church," *Presbyterian Record,* February 1951, 62; UCC, BESS, *Annual Report* (1957), 54–59, 81–82; (1962), 260–61; UCC, *Outreach* (1962), 5; Church of England in Canada (hereafter CEC), Council for Social Service (hereafter CSS), *Bulletin,* February 1, 1952, 1–22.

37 CEC, CSS, *Bulletin,* February 1, 1952, 16, 19.

38 Robert Ficken and Charles LeWarne, *Washington: A Centennial History* (Seattle: University of Washington Press, 1988), 130–31.

39 UWM, Thomas Jessett, "The Influence of the Church in Washington State – Is This God's Country?" Typescript of speech given at a meeting of the clergy, concerned laity, and visiting ministers of the Diocese of Spokane, November 20, 1975, 5.

40   Clifford Merrill Drury, *Presbyterian Panorama: 150 Years of National Missions History* (Philadelphia: Board of Christian Education, Presbyterian Church in the United States, 1952), 282; and UWM, WNICC, Acc. 1567-1, Box 7, File 41: Division of Christian Missionaries, Minutes, 1958–66.

41   UWM, WNICC, Acc. 1567-2, Box 8, File: Conference on Church and Minority Peoples, Minutes, Seattle, 1944; Box 14, File: Migrant: General Correspondence, "Memo to Members of the Okanogan County Council of Churches," 1961; Box 15, File: Yakima, "Migrant Ministry," 1964; and Box 17, File: Lower Yakima Valley, "Witness to the Laboring Migrant," n.d. UWM, WNICC, Acc. 1567-1, Box 9, File 4: Incoming Letters, C-W, 1941–65, Letter from Velma Shotwell to Soren Kring, September 3, 1953.

42   CEC, CSS, *Bulletin,* February 1, 1952, 2; and Norman Clark, *Washington: A Bicentennial History* (New York: W.W. Norton, 1976), 189.

43   "Spotlight on Kimberley," *Western Regular Baptist,* May 1965, 2.

44   UCBCA, LDA Papers, Box 1, File 3: Letter from Rev. J.N. Allan to Rev. R.A. Redman, November 17, 1954; Box 1, File 5: Letter from Rev. R.A. Redman to Mr. McGrath; Box 1, File 3: Letter from A.S. McGrath to Rev. R.A. Redman, April 28, 1955.

45   UWM, WNICC, Acc. 1567-2, Box 9, File: Faith and Order, "The State of the Church in the Pacific Northwest," n.d.

46   Bracher and Bracher, "The Northwest Is Growing," 12.

47   UCC, BCC, *Minutes* (1971), 7.

48   "'Interfaith Chapel' Would Meet Needs of Transient Population," *Canadian Register,* December 9, 1967, 9.

49   John McNab, "Church Extension Beckons in the West!" *Presbyterian Record,* September 1955, 18–20; and E.L. Homewood, "Lay Preacher of the Queen Charlottes," *United Church Observer,* January 15, 1960, 14, 18.

50   "Priest Serves West Coast 'Instant' Towns," *Catholic Northwest Progress,* 8 July 1966, 2.

51   UWM, WNICC, Acc. 1567-2, Box 3, File: Writings, "The State of the Church in the Northwest," n.d.

52   Bracher and Bracher, "The Northwest is Growing," 12–15; and UWM, WNICC, Acc. 1567-2, Box 9, File: Long-Range Planning Conference, "Cooperative Planning Consultation," 1963.

53   UWM, WNICC, Acc. 1567-2, Box 17, File: Lower Yakima Valley, "Witness to the Laboring Migrant," n.d.

54   Thorpe, "The Call of the North," 4–5.

55   UCC, BCC, *Minutes* (1964), 81.

56   Joel Connelly, "God vs. outdoors: State's church rolls dwindling," *Seattle Post-Intelligencer,* January 2, 1977, A1, A16.

57   Ian McKay, *The Quest of the Folk: Antimodernism and Cultural Selection in Twentieth-Century Nova Scotia* (Montreal and Kingston: McGill-Queen's University Press, 1994), 270; and Friesen, "The Evolving Meanings of Region," 534–35.

58   Ayers and Onuf, "Preface," in *All Over the Map,* 3; and Edward Ayers, "What We Talk About When We Talk About the South," in *All Over the Map,* 64.

59   UCC, BESS, *Annual Report* (1955), 28; and (1957), 45.

60   E. Harold Toye, "The Church and the People," *United Church Observer,* October 15, 1952, 18; UCC, BESS, *Annual Report* (1955), 28; and D. Glenn Campbell, "The Un-Automated Man," *Presbyterian Record,* September 1966, 3.

61   Edgar Stride, "The Gospel and Industry," *Christianity Today,* August 27, 1965, 14; and Norman Birnbaum, "The Secularization of Society," *Christianity and Crisis,* March 2, 1959, 21.

62 UCC, BESS, *Annual Report* (1962), 67.

63 See *Western Regular Baptist,* March 1954, 11; and Marks, "Leaving God Behind When They Crossed the Rocky Mountains."

64 Schear, "The Stone Cold Spirit," 20; PCU, Board of National Missions, *Annual Report* (1957), 560; and UWM, GSCC, Acc. 1358-7, Box 13, File 27: Meetings – Annual, 1962–66, House of Delegates, January 31, 1965, 21.

65 UCBCA, LDA Papers, Box 1, File 5: Letter from Rev. R.A. Redman to Mr. McGrath, December 1, 1954.

66 UCBCA, LDA Papers, Box 2, File 11:Memo to P. Mallon, January 13, 1961; and Box 3, File 11: Report of the Sunday Labour Questions Committee, June 20, 1961, 2.

67 *BC Catholic,* 20 September 1951, 4.

68 Harvey Shepherd, "When clergy join the working man," *United Church Observer,* February 1, 1968, 21.

69 Donald Smith, "Let's bridge the gulf between the church and industrial workers," *Presbyterian Record,* September 1966, 12–14.

70 "The Layman's Corner," *Canadian Churchman,* June 3, 1955, 255.

71 "C.C.D. Notes: Interesting Men in the Confraternity," *BC Catholic,* February 15, 1951, 1.

72 UWM, WNICC, Acc. 1567-2, Box 18, File: Newspaper Clippings, UCW, *Seattle Times,* October 17, 1964, 2; MCU, Pacific Northwest Conference, *Annual Journal* (1951), 551.

73 Elaine Bulmer, "Women in the Church," *Canadian Churchman,* May 1960, 4; Roy Hamilton, "Is Christianity a Man's Religion?," *Presbyterian Record,* May 1957, 8–9; Amy Haufschild, "What Do Children Do on Sunday Afternoon?," *United Church Observer,* April 15, 1957, 19–20; Cynthia Clark Wedel, "Opportunities for Women in the Life of the Church," *Forth,* October 1952, 11; and UWM, GSCC, Acc. 1358-7, Box 7, File 14: Newsletters-Others, "The Congregational Way," May 1959, 15.

74 "The Episcopal Address," *Daily Christian Advocate,* April 26, 1956, 16.

75 James Taylor, "The Worker and His Boss: Is One Church Big Enough for Both?," *United Church Observer,* December 1, 1968, 13.

76 "Too Many Women?," *Canadian Churchman,* November 18, 1954, 394. Also see UWM, WNICC, 1567-1, Box 8, File 15: General Correspondence, Letter from Mrs. Ralph Jones to Rev. Stanley, January 12, 1955; and UWM, WNICC, 1567-2, Box 17, File: United Church Men, National Council, "Speaker's Manual: 22nd Annual Observance of Men and Missions Day," October 12, 1952, 11.

77 *Presbyterian Record,* September 1967, 6.

78 UWM, WNICC, Acc. 1567-1, Box 3, File 20: Reports, 1954–60, "Report of the Laymen's Group at Seabeck," n.d.; and *United Church Observer,* October 15, 1962, 19.

79 E.L. Homewood, "The 160-Point Parish," *United Church Observer,* September 1, 1960, 10.

80 UWM, WNICC, Acc. 1567-2, Box 15, File: Tonasket, Letter from R.H. Litherland to Mrs. Beryl McIvor, July 7, 1961; and Box 14, File: Migrant-General Correspondence, "Migrant Ministry Report," 1967.

81 Tom York, "Tasu – end of the line for the Prodigal Son," *United Church Observer,* October 1, 1968, 18–19.

82 On the feminization of religion in the nineteenth century, see Lynne Marks, *Revivals and Roller Rinks: Religion, Leisure, and Identity in Late-Nineteenth-Century Small Town Ontario* (Toronto: University of Toronto Press, 1996), 14; and Barbara Welter, "The Feminization of American Religion: 1800–1860," in *Clio's Consciousness Raised: New Perspectives on the History of American Women,* ed. Mary Hartman and Lois Banner (New York: Harper Torchbooks, 1974): 137–57.

83 Bulmer, "Women in the Church," 4; and "Does the church present a female image?," *Presbyterian Record,* April 1966, 20.

84 *BC Catholic,* November 18, 1965, 8.

85 "Men and the Church," *Living Church,* January 29, 1950, 14–15.

86 F.H. Wooding, "A Frontier Church: The Columbia Coast Mission," *Canadian Churchman,* January 1961, 16.

87 UCC, *Outreach* (1966), 86.

88 Furniss, *The Burden of History,* 84.

89 James Taylor, "A Man's Man in a Man's Town," *United Church Observer,* November 15, 1968, 16–18.

90 UWM, GSCC, Acc. 1358-7, Box 3, File 12: Notebooks, "So That You May Know," December 11, 1962.

91 Drury, *Presbyterian Panorama,* 248.

92 "Random Thoughts by Rex," *Canadian Churchman,* June 17, 1954, 184.

93 Furniss, *The Burden of History,* 78; and Laurie Maffly-Kipp, "Historicizing Religion in the American West," in *Perspectives on American Religion and Culture,* ed. Peter Williams (Malden: Blackwell, 1995), 11.

94 UWM, WNICC, Acc. 1567-1, Box 3, File 16, Reports c.a. 1945–57, "Report of Department of Minority Relations," July 5, 1945, 1.

95 *Census of Canada,* Vol. 1, Part 4, Bulletin 7, Table 19 (1971); United States, Bureau of the Census, *1970 Census of Population, Characteristics of the Population, U.S. Summary,* Vol. 1, Part 1, Section 1, Table 59 (1970); and United States, Bureau of the Census, *Historical Statistics of the United States, Colonial Times to 1970* (Washington: United States Department of Commerce, 1975), Series A 23–28. In 1970, 95.4 percent of Washington's population identified as white. The *Census of Canada* documents ethnic origins, but not racial identities; in 1971, 93 percent of British Columbia residents claimed to be of British or European heritage.

96 See Jean Barman, *The West Beyond the West: A History of British Columbia,* rev. ed. (Toronto: University of Toronto Press, 1996), 305–16; and Carlos Schwantes, *The Pacific Northwest: An Interpretive History,* rev. ed. (Lincoln: University of Nebraska Press, 1996) 450–51.

97 *Presbyterian Record,* September 1964, 4.

98 MCU, Pacific Northwest Conference, *Annual Journal* (1958), 610; and PCU, Board of National Missions, *Annual Report* (1954), 18.

99 "Project Equality, The Workingman's Crusade," *Catholic Northwest Progress,* July 15, 1966, 4.

100 *United Church Observer,* June 1, 1962, 2.

101 Mariana Valverde, "Building Anti-Delinquent Communities: Morality, Gender, and Generation in the City," in *A Diversity of Women: Ontario, 1945–1980,* ed. Joy Parr (Toronto: University of Toronto Press, 1995), 20–21; Myra Rutherdale, *Women and the White Man's God: Gender and Race in the Canadian Mission Field* (Vancouver: UBC Press, 2002), xxx; and Kay Anderson, *Vancouver's Chinatown: Racial Discourse in Canada, 1875–1980* (Montreal and Kingston: McGill-Queen's University Press, 1991), 211.

102 "Multi-racial Worshippers," *United Church Observer,* March 1, 1969, 3.

103 Episcopal Church, Diocese of Olympia, *Annual Journal* (1956), 40.

104 UWM, GSCC, Acc. 1358-07, Box 3, File 14: Notebooks, 1960–64, "Seattle Clergy Speak on Racial Integration," June 30, 1963.

105 "The Theory of Relativity," *Catholic Northwest Progress,* March 11, 1966, 4.

106 Quintard Taylor, "'There was no better place to go': The Transformation Thesis Revisited: African American Migration to the Pacific Northwest, 1940–1950" in *Terra Pacifica: People and Place in the Northwest States and Western Canada,* ed. Paul Hirt (Pullman:

Washington State University Press, 1998), 206–7; and Quintard Taylor, *In Search of the Racial Frontier: African-Americans in the American West, 1528–1990* (New York: Norton, 1998).

107 Taylor, "There was no better place to go," 210–11.

108 UWM, Christian Friends for Racial Equality Records (hereafter CFRE), Acc. 4040-3, Box 1, File 2: Historical Features: "Twenty Years History of the Christian Friends for Racial Equality," Seattle, 1942–62, 27.

109 Hilda Bryant, "Churches meeting race issue?," *Seattle Post-Intelligencer,* September 13, 1967, 5.

110 Barman, *The West Beyond the West,* 379; and *1970 Census of Population, Characteristics of the Population, U.S. Summary,* Vol. 1, Part 1, Section 1, Table 60 (1970).

111 Norman Knowles, "Religious Affiliation, Demographic Change, and Family Formation among British Columbia's Chinese and Japanese Communities: A Case Study of Church of England Missions, 1861–1942," *Canadian Ethnic Studies* 27: 2 (1995): 67–68; and UWM, CFRE, Acc. 4040-3, Box 1, File 1: Historical Features: "Twenty Years History of the Christian Friends for Racial Equality," 1962, 2.

112 Anderson, *Vancouver's Chinatown,* 239.

113 E.L. Homewood, "Lillian Lee's Church in Chinatown," *United Church Observer,* February 1, 1958, 13.

114 Anglican Provincial Synod of British Columbia and Yukon Archives (hereafter APSA), Provincial Board of Missions to Orientals, Box 1, Series 4, PSA 4/6, File: Board Minutes, 1956–65, "Minutes of a Meeting of the Provincial Board of Missions to Orientals," Vancouver, September 25, 1963, 3.

115 F.H. Wooding, "Hong Kong and Japan: Human Needs – Christian Opportunities," *Canadian Churchman,* February 1963, 8–9.

116 Rutherdale, *Women and the White Man's God,* 40.

117 "The Pickerings write from Japan," *Western Regular Baptist,* November 1952, 7–8; Marian Pickering, "Mrs. Pickering Writes ...," May 1956, 13. Also see APSA, Provincial Board of Missions to Orientals, Box 1, Series 4, PSA 4/6, Minutes 1956–65, "Minutes," September 25, 1963; and John Harbron, "Christianity in Japan," *Canadian Churchman,* March 1964, 8, 12.

118 Drury, *Presbyterian Panorama,* 298.

119 Peter Duffy, "Prince George's Chinese community observes ancient traditions while fully integrated," *Prince George Progress,* November 16, 1966, 1.

120 John Findlay, "A Fishy Proposition: Regional Identity in the Pacific Northwest," in *Many Wests: Place, Culture, and Regional Identity,* ed. David Wrobel and Michael Steiner (Lawrence: University Press of Kansas, 1997), 46; and Laurie Mercier, "Reworking Race, Class, and Gender into Pacific Northwest History," *Frontiers* 22: 3 (2001): 61.

121 Barman, *The West Beyond the West,* 132–48; Pat Roy, *A White Man's Province: British Columbia Politicians and Chinese and Japanese Immigrants, 1858–1914* (Vancouver: UBC Press, 1989); and Adele Perry, *On the Edge of Empire: Gender, Race, and the Making of British Columbia* (Toronto: University of Toronto Press, 2001).

122 Catherine Hall, *White, Male, and Middle Class: Explorations in Feminism and History* (New York: Routledge, 1992), 205–54.

123 Episcopal Church, Diocese of Olympia, *Annual Journal* (1961), 48.

124 Judith Weisenfeld, "On Jordan's Stormy Banks: Margins, Centers, and Bridges in African-American Religious History," in *New Directions in American Religious History,* ed. Harry Stout and D.G. Hart (New York: Oxford University Press, 1997), 419.

125 PCC, *Acts and Proceedings of the General Assembly* (1952), 16, 17.

126 Margaret, personal interview, September 10, 2003.

Chapter 2: A "mounting tide of criticism"

1 Larry, personal interview, March 28, 2004.

2 See Nancy Christie and Michael Gauvreau, eds., *The Sixties and Beyond: Dechristianization in North America and Western Europe: 1945–2000* (Toronto: University of Toronto Press, 2013); Callum Brown, *The Death of Christian Britain: Understanding Secularisation, 1800–2000* (London: Routledge, 2001); and Hugh McLeod, *The Religious Crisis of the 1960s* (Oxford: Oxford University Press, 2007).

3 Patricia O'Connell Killen and Mark A. Shibley, "Surveying the Religious Landscape: Historical Trends and Current Patterns in Oregon, Washington, and Alaska," in *Religion and Public Life in the Pacific Northwest,* ed. Patricia O'Connell Killen and Mark Silk, 25–50; George Gallup Jr. and Jim Castelli, *The People's Religion: American Faith in the 90s* (New York: MacMillan, 1989), 118–20; Barry Kosmin and Seymour Lachman, *One Nation Under God: Religion in Contemporary American Society* (New York: Crown Trade Paperbacks, 1993), 82–87; and Gallup Organization, *Religion in America: 50 years, 1935–1985* (Princeton: Gallup Organization, 1985), 27.

4 These surveys are reprinted in Martin Marty, Stuart Rosenberg, and Andrew Greeley, *What Do We Believe? The Stance of Religion in America* (New York: Meredith Press, 1968), 177–346.

5 *Gallup Opinion Index* 70 (April 1971), 57, 70–81.

6 *Gallup Opinion Index* 70 (April 1971), 70; *Census of Canada,* Series 5, Special Bulletin, Table 1, 1971.

7 Killen and Shibley, "Surveying the Religious Landscape," 25–50; Gallup and Castelli, *The People's Religion,* 28–29; and Susan Lazaruk and Norma Greenaway, "Churches' role wanes in Canada," *Times Colonist,* May 14, 2003, A1.

8 UWM, WNICC, Acc. 1567-2, Box 13, File: Kent Fellowship Evangelism Mission, Letter from Bob Ortmeyer to Gertrude Apel, c. 1956.

9 "The Problem of Missing and 'Lost Anglicans,'" *BC Diocesan Post,* May 1968, 2–3; Ben Metcalfe, "Rare churchgoers ticked off," *Vancouver Province,* July 14, 1958, 1–2; Jurgen Hesse, "Religious faith faces test in materialistic Canada," *Colonist,* December 16, 1962, 1–2; W.F. Hart, "What Is Religion?" *Canadian Churchman,* February 20, 1958, 79–80; and "The World's Most Important Religions," *Christianity and Crisis,* July 25, 1955, 103–4.

10 Robert Burkinshaw, *Pilgrims in Lotus Land: Conservative Protestantism in British Columbia, 1917–1981* (Montreal and Kingston: McGill-Queen's University Press, 1995), 5; and Reginald Bibby, *Fragmented Gods: The Poverty and Potential of Religion in Canada* (Toronto: Irwin Publishers, 1987), 89.

11 Data Laboratories Research Consultants (hereafter DLRC), *Report of a Survey of Canadians' Participation in Organized Religion* (Montreal, 1977), 9, 13. Also see Bibby, *Fragmented Gods,* 89.

12 UCC, BESS, *Annual Report* (1953), 81; (1963), 148; and *Yearbook of American and Canadian Churches,* 1973.

13 "Random Thoughts by Rex," *Canadian Churchman,* November 6, 1952, 336; "The Parliament of the Church," *Canadian Churchman,* October 2, 1952, 299; *Canadian Churchman,* October 1962, 9; "Church Pulse Livened by Campaign for British Columbia College," *Canadian Churchman,* June 1963, 8; and "Two Million Different Adherents," *United Church Observer,* September 1, 1962, 8. There is evidence of similar regional discrepancies among Canadian Lutherans. See J.M. Zimmerman, "President's Column," *Western Canada Lutheran,* June 1967, 2; and Victor Meyer, *Canadian Lutheran,* August 1967, 6.

14 National Council of Churches of Christ in the United States of America (hereafter NCCC), *Churches and Church Membership in the United States: An Enumeration and Analysis by Counties, States, and Regions,* Series A-E (New York: Bureau of Research and Survey, 1956); and Douglas Johnson, Paul Picard, and Bernard Quinn, eds., *Churches and Church Membership in the United States: An Enumeration by Region, State, and County, 1971* (Washington: Glenmary Research Center, 1974). These studies, which consist of membership statistics collected from the denominations themselves, are not without problems: they must be approached with caution due to the omission of certain key groups, and the persistence of inconsistent, multiple definitions of membership across and even within religious groups. For discussions and critiques of these membership studies, see William Newman and Peter Halvorson, "The Church Membership Studies: An Assessment of Four Decades of Institutional Research," *Review of Religious Research* 35: 1 (1993): 55–61; William Newman, Peter Halvorson, and Jennifer Brown, "Problems and Potential Uses of the 1952 and 1971 National Council of Churches' 'Churches and Church Membership in the United States' Studies," *Review of Religious Research* 18 (1977): 167–73; William Newman and Peter Halvorson, "Updating an Archive: 'Churches and Church Membership in the US, 1952–1980,'" *Review of Religious Research* 24 (September 1982): 54–60; Rodney Stark and William Bainbridge, *The Future of Religion: Secularization, Revival, and Cult Formation* (Berkeley: University of California Press, 1985) , 69–70; Wilbur Zelinsky, "An Approach to the Religious Geography of the United States: Patterns of Church Membership in 1952," *Annals of the Association of American Geographers* 51 (1961): 139–93; and Mark Shibley, "Religion in Oregon: Recent Demographic Currents in the Mainstream," *Pacific Northwest Quarterly* 83: 3 (July 1992): 83.

15 While the figures for Protestant groups in this study represent approximately 75 percent of the total membership reported in the 1953 edition of the *Yearbook of American Churches,* Roman Catholic membership numbers in this study approximate the totals in the 1953 *Official Catholic Directory.* Although it does not include county-level figures from Jewish synagogue rolls, this study draws "cultural membership" counts of the wider American Jewish population from the 1955 *American Jewish Yearbook.* To mitigate the absence of data from African-American denominations, the African-American population was removed from the total population figures in this study. The published reports of this study include statistics that were adjusted to at least partially account for the several omissions and for the inconsistencies in the meanings of membership across denominations. For an in-depth discussion of the procedures used and the religious bodies involved in this study, consult NCCC, *Churches and Church Membership,* Series A, No. 1 and No. 2.

16 NCCC, Churches and Church Membership in the United States, Series A, No. 3, Table 6.

17 NCCC, Churches and Church Membership, Series A, No. 3, Table 6; Series C, No. 57, Table 127, Part II; and Series A, No. 3, Table 6.

18 Like its earlier counterpart, the 1971 membership study provides only a partial picture of religious involvement in America. For an assessment of this study, see Stark and Bainbridge, *The Future of Religion,* 69–75, in which the authors find that adjusting the figures to account for omissions does not disrupt the strikingly unchurched character of the West Coast.

19 Johnson, Picard, and Quinn, *Churches and Church Membership in the United States, 1971,* Tables 1, 2, and 3; and United States Bureau of Census, *1970 Census of Population: Number of Inhabitants, United States Summary,* Table 8, 1971. The 1971 study is based

on membership data gathered from 53 Christian denominations (approximately 80.8 percent of the total Christian membership in the United States). In an effort to account for different definitions of church membership, the assemblers of this study created a "total adherents" category; in cases where denominations reported only communicant, confirmed, or full members, total adherents were estimated using a formula based on 1970 census returns.

20 Kevin William Welch, "Church Membership in American Metropolitan Areas, 1952–1971" (PhD diss., University of Washington, 1985), 31; Stark and Bainbridge, *The Future of Religion,* 69–77; and James Shortridge, "Patterns of Religion in the United States," *Geographical Review* 66: 4 (1976): 420–21.

21 UWM, WNICC, Acc. 1567-1, Box 3, File 17: "Percentage of Church Members by States," 1945.

22 UWM, WNICC, Acc. 1567-1, Box 3, File 17: "Percentage of Church Members by States," 1945; Box 3, File 7: "Area Meeting, First Methodist Church, Yakima, Washington," March 31–April 1, 1952; Box 7, File 26: "Report presented by Professor Arthur Frederick to a joint meeting of The Home Missions Council and the Department of Church Planning and Strategy of the Washington Council of Churches," December 1946; Box 12, File 6: An Address "To All Ministers in Tacoma, and Guests of the College of Puget Sound," November 2, 1954; Box 3, File 17: "Annual Report of the Council of Churches and Christian Education for Washington and Northern Idaho," n.d.; and Box 11, File 3: "Study of the Sizes of Churches in State of Washington, and Negro Population in Washington State," December 1952. UWM, WNICC, Acc. 1567-2, Box 4, "Annual Report, Council of Churches and Christian Education for Washington and Northern Idaho," 1951; Arthur Frederick and Ross Sanderson, *The Columbia Basin Project Area and Its Churches* (Seattle: Washington State Council of Churches, 1950); and Rillmond Schear, "The Stone Cold Spirit That Stalks Seattle's Churches," *Seattle Magazine,* December 1965, 20.

23 UWM, WNICC, Acc. 1567-1, Box 3, File 13: "Church Membership, Bible School Enrolment, Compared with Total Population in Spokane County, Washington," April 1956.

24 Marty, Rosenberg, and Greeley, *What Do We Believe?,* 277; and George H. Gallup, *The Gallup Poll: Public Opinion 1935–1971* (New York: Random House, 1972), 1253.

25 Killen and Shibley, "Surveying the Religious Landscape," 30. Also see Kosmin and Lachman, *One Nation under God,* 82–83.

26 UWM, GSCC, Acc. 1358-7, Box 13, File 26: "Report of Division Assembly, House of Delegates Meeting," January 31, 1965.

27 Marty, Rosenberg, and Greeley, *What Do We Believe?,* 214. For secondary analyses that further illustrate strikingly low church attendance rates in the postwar American West, and particularly the Northwest, see Stark and Bainbridge, *The Future of Religion,* 75–78; Shibley, "Religion in Oregon," 82; and Dean Hoge and David Roozen, "Research on Factors Influencing Church Commitment," in *Understanding Church Growth and Decline, 1950–1978,* ed. Dean Hoge and David Roozen (New York: Pilgrim Press, 1979), 47–48.

28 E.L. Homewood, "B.C.'s Building Boom," *United Church Observer,* March 1, 1960, 12.

29 Hans Mol, "Major Correlates of Churchgoing in Canada," in *Religion in Canadian Society,* ed. Stewart Crysdale and Les Wheatcroft (Toronto: MacMillan of Canada, 1976), 241–42.

30 DLRC, *Report of a Survey,* 9, 13.

31 "How many of us go to church regularly?" *Vancouver Province,* May 11, 1956, 21; "Who is My Neighbour?," *Presbyterian Record,* July–August 1956, 14; Jurgen Hesse, "'Fringe'

Forgets Worship of God," *Daily Colonist,* December 29, 1962, 2; "What a Truly Religious Person Should Be Most Concerned With," *BC Diocesan Post,* September 1969, 2; and "Church's public image needs to be improved," *Nanaimo Free Press,* October 16, 1963, 9.

32 Robert Putnam and David Campbell, *American Grace: How Religion Divides and Unites Us* (New York: Simon and Schuster, 2010), 97; Kurt Bowen, *Christians in a Secular World: The Canadian Experience* (Montreal and Kingston: McGill-Queen's University Press, 2005), 273; and Mark Noll, "What Happened to Christian Canada?," *Church History* 75: 2 (2006): 245–73.

33 Canadian Institute of Public Opinion (CIPO), *Gallup Report,* April 16, 1960; August 18, 1965; April 25, 1970; and Gallup, *The Gallup Poll: Public Opinion,* 1222, 1389, 1479, 1746, 1856, 1978, 2095, 2173, 2276.

34 Callum Brown, *Religion and the Demographic Revolution: Women and Secularisation in Canada, Ireland, UK and USA since the 1960s* (Woodbridge: Boydell Press, 2012), 29. Also see John Webster Grant, *The Church in the Canadian Era: The First Century of Confederation* (Toronto: McGraw-Hill Ryerson, 1972); Gary Miedema, *For Canada's Sake: Public Religion, Centennial Celebrations, and the Re-Making of Canada in the 1960s* (Montreal and Kingston: McGill-Queen's University Press, 2005); Catherine Gidney, *A Long Eclipse: The Liberal Protestant Establishment and the Canadian University, 1920–1970* (Montreal and Kingston: McGill-Queen's University Press, 2004); McLeod, *The Religious Crisis of the 1960s*; and Brown, *The Death of Christian Britain.*

35 "The Hidden Failure of Our Churches," *Maclean's,* February 25, 1961, 50. Also John Robinson, *Honest to God* (Philadelphia: Westminster Press, 1963); Pierre Berton, *The Comfortable Pew: A Critical Look at Christianity and the Religious Establishment in the New Age* (Philadelphia: Lippincott, 1965); and *Time,* April 8, 1966.

36 UMC, Pacific Northwest Conference, *Annual Journal* (1968), 89.

37 UCC, BESS, *Annual Report* (1966), 18.

38 William Portman, "Priest Quits Parish: Seeks Christ of the Streets," *Canadian Churchman,* April 1968, 24; and Schear, "The Stone Cold Spirit," 20.

39 *Seattle Post-Intelligencer,* February 6, 1971, 4.

40 See, for example, Brown, *Religion and the Demographic Revolution,* 63–64.

41 *Census of Canada,* Vol. 1, Part 4, Tables 7 and 8, 1971; Vol. 1, Part 4, Bulletin 7, Tables 18 and 19.

42 Nancy Christie and Michael Gauvreau, "'Even the hippies were only very slowly going secular': Dechristianization and the Culture of Individualism in North America and Western Europe," in *The Sixties and Beyond,* ed. Christie and Gauvreau, 25. On the link between dechristianization and the challenge to moral and sexual codes in the 1960s, see Brown, *Religion and Society,* 230; Putnam and Campbell, *American Grace,* 99; and Grace Davie, *Religion in Britain since 1945: Believing Without Belonging* (Oxford: Blackwell, 1994), 33.

43 Nancy, personal interview, September 19, 2003.

44 Thomas, personal interview, 11 November 2003.

45 Sandra, personal interview, 27 March 2004.

46 Larry, personal interview, 28 March 2004.

47 Christie and Gauvreau, "Even the hippies," 26. Also see Brown, *The Death of Christian Britain,* Chapter 8; Gidney, *A Long Eclipse,* xv; McLeod, *The Religious Crisis,* 246; Miedema, *For Canada's Sake,* 35; Noll, "What Happened to Christian Canada?" 251; and Alan Petigny, "The Spread of Permissive Religion," *Canadian Review of American Studies* 39: 4 (2009): 415.

48 Larry, personal interview, March 28, 2004.

49 Christie and Gauvreau, "Even the hippies," 25.

50 George, personal interview, October 21, 2003.

51 Helen, personal interview, March 25, 2004.

52 Margaret, personal interview, September 10, 2003; Patricia, personal interview, August 18, 2003.

53 Larry, personal interview, March 28, 2004.

54 Mary, personal interview, March 24, 2004.

55 Sarah Williams, *Religious Belief and Popular Culture in Southwark, 1880–1939* (Oxford: Oxford University Press, 1999), 12.

56 Robert Rutherdale, "Fatherhood and the Social Construction of Memory: Breadwinning and Male Parenting on a Job Frontier, 1945–1966," in *Gender and History in Canada,* ed. Joy Parr and Mark Rosenfeld (Toronto: Copp Clark, 1996), 372.

57 *Seattle Post-Intelligencer,* May 15, 1971, 12.

58 *Canadian Churchman,* May 1967, 18.

59 Meg Grant, "Who's New in the Pew: The post-war generation rediscovers religion," *Weekly* (Seattle), September 17, 1986, 33.

60 Nancy, personal interview, September 19, 2003.

61 Susan, personal interview, October 30, 2003.

62 Anne, personal interview, September 16, 2003.

63 Donna, personal interview, August 29, 2003 and November 19, 2003; and Thomas, personal interview, November 11, 2003.

64 Patrick, personal interview, September 3, 2003.

65 Margaret, personal interview, September 10, 2003.

66 Deborah, personal interview, March 29, 2004.

67 Jean and Donald, personal interview, June 23, 2003; Thomas, personal interview, November 11, 2003; and George, personal interview, October 21, 2003.

68 Williams, *Religious Belief and Popular Culture,* 113–15.

69 Hesse, "'Fringe' Forgets Worship of God," 1.

70 "What a Truly Religious Person Should Be Most Concerned With," 2. Also see Metcalfe, "Rare churchgoers ticked off," 1–2; Hesse, "Religious faith faces test in materialistic Canada," 1, 2; and Hart, "What Is Religion?," 79–80.

71 See Brown, *Religion and Society,* 316.

72 Ray Rupert, "State least churched in U.S., study shows," *Seattle Times,* May 8, 1974, B9; Joel Connelly, "Seeking God – Seattle-style," *Seattle Post-Intelligencer,* January 3, 1977, A1, A20; *Vancouver Province,* May 11, 1956, 21; Jurgen Hesse, "Canada's history deeply marked by two faiths," *Colonist,* December 20, 1962, 6.

73 Schear, "The Stone Cold Spirit," 21.

74 Richard, personal interview, March 22, 2004.

75 William, personal interview, March 23, 2004.

76 Charles, personal interview, October 30, 2003.

77 Rhys Williams, "Religion, Community, and Place: Locating the Transcendent," *Religion and American Culture* 12: 2 (June 2002): 250–51.

78 Sandra, personal interview, March 27, 2004.

79 John, personal interview, September 8, 2003.

80 Sharon, personal interview, September 22, 2003.

81 Deborah and Steven, personal interview, March 29, 2004.

82 Frank, personal interview, March 28, 2004.

83 Joanne, personal interview, March 30, 2004.

84 *Argus,* May 9, 1980, 6.

85 Joanne, personal interview, March 30, 2004.

86 Edna, personal interview, March 25, 2004.

87 Charles, personal interview, October 30, 2003; Edward, personal interview, August 26, 2003.

88 Rutherdale, "Fatherhood and the Social Construction of Memory," 358.

89 Ruth, personal interview, October 21, 2003; Helen, personal interview, March 25, 2004; Muriel, personal interview, October 21, 2003; Joanne, personal interview, March 30, 2004; Mary, personal interview, March 24, 2004; Robert, personal interview, October 17, 2003; and George, personal interview, October 21, 2003.

90 Muriel, personal interview, October 21, 2003.

Chapter 3: Class, Gender, and Religious Involvement

1 Sylvia, personal interview, 24 June 2003.

2 Patricia, personal interview, August 18, 2003.

3 Patricia O'Connell Killen and Mark Shibley, "Surveying the Religious Landscape: Historical Trends and Current Patterns in Oregon, Washington, and Alaska," in *Religion and Public Life in the Pacific Northwest: The None Zone,* ed. Patricia O'Connell Killen and Mark Silk (Walnut Creek: AltaMira Press, 2004), 41–42. Also see Dean Hoge and David Roozen, "Research on Factors Influencing Church Commitment," in *Understanding Church Growth and Decline, 1950–1978,* ed. Dean Hoge and David Roozen (New York: Pilgrim Press, 1979), 47; Bob Stewart, "That's the B.C. Spirit! Religion and Secularity in Lotus Land," *Canadian Society of Church History Papers* (1983): 22–35; J.E. Veevers and D.F. Cousineau, "The Heathen Canadians: Demographic Correlates of Nonbelief," *Pacific Sociological Review* 23: 2 (1980): 210; and Kevin William Welch, "Church Membership in American Metropolitan Areas, 1952–1971" (PhD diss., University of Washington, 1985), 31.

4 Veevers and Cousineau, "The Heathen Canadians," 207.

5 United States, Bureau of the Census, *1970 Census of Population, Characteristics of the Population, U.S. Summary,* Vol. 1, Part 1, Sections 1 and 2; and United States, Bureau of the Census, *Historical Statistics of the United States, Colonial Times to 1970* (Washington: United States Department of Commerce, 1975).

6 Welch, "Church Membership," 26. Also see Thomas Davenport, *Virtuous Pagans: Unreligious People in America* (New York: Garland Publishers, 1991), 79; and Wade Clark Roof and William McKinney, *American Mainline Religion: Its Changing Shape and Future* (New Brunswick: Rutgers University Press, 1987), 124.

7 *Gallup Opinion Index* 70 (April 1971), 57–68. These figures are based on interviews with a representative sample of Americans rather than on the United States Census. As such, the population figures differ slightly from those in the census.

8 *Gallup Opinion Index* 70 (April 1971), 70–81.

9 For two different views on the effects of migration on religiosity, see Timothy Smith, "Religion and Ethnicity in America," *American Historical Review* 83: 5 (December 1978): 1155–85; and John Bukowczyk, "The Transforming Power of the Machine: Popular Religion, Ideology, and Secularization among Polish Immigrant Workers in the United States, 1880–1940," *International Labor and Working Class History* 34 (1989): 22–38.

10 See, for example, Robert Orsi, *The Madonna of 115th Street: Faith and Community in Italian Harlem, 1880–1950* (New Haven: Yale University Press, 1985); and Mark McGowan, *The Waning of the Green: Catholics, the Irish, and Identity in Toronto, 1887–1922* (Montreal and Kingston: McGill-Queen's University Press, 1999).

11 Brian, personal interview, 22 March 2004.

12 See, for example, Jace Weaver, ed., *Native American Religious Identity: Unforgotten Gods* (Maryknoll: Orbis Books, 1998); Lee Irwin, "Native Voices in the Study of Native American Religions," *European Review of Native American Studies* 12: 2 (1998): 25–40; Lance Laird, "Religions of the Pacific Rim in the Pacific Northwest," in *Religion and Public Life in the Pacific Northwest*, 110–11; and John Wunder, "Pacific Northwest Indians and the Bill of Rights," in *Terra Pacifica: People and Place in the Northwest States and Western Canada*, ed. Paul Hirt (Pullman: Washington State University Press, 1998), 179.

13 Kazuo Ito, *Issei: A History of Japanese Immigrants in North America*, trans. Shinichiro Nakamura and Jean Gerard (Seattle: Japanese Community Service, 1973), 231; and Laurie Maffly-Kipp, "Historicizing Religion in the American West," in *Perspectives on American Religion and Culture*, ed. Peter Williams (Malden: Blackwell, 1999), 15.

14 *Asian Family Affair*, May 1976, 9.

15 Judith Weisenfeld, "On Jordan's Stormy Banks: Margins, Center, and Bridges in African American Religious History," in *New Directions in American Religious History*, ed. Harry Stout and D.G. Hart (New York: Oxford University Press, 1997), 418.

16 *Census of Canada*, Vol. 5, Part 1, Table 14, 1971.

17 *Census of Canada*, Vol. 3, Table 7, 1971, 94–736.

18 *Census of Canada*, Vol. 5, Part 1, Table 16, 1971, 49–50.

19 Class is not, of course, defined solely by income but also by occupation, education, and a range of cultural factors.

20 United States, Bureau of the Census, *1970 Census of Population, Characteristics of the Population, U.S. Summary*, Vol. 1, Part 1, Sections 1 and 2; and United States, Bureau of the Census, *Historical Statistics of the United States, Colonial Times to 1970* (Washington: United States Department of Commerce, 1975).

21 *Gallup Opinion Index* 70 (April 1971), 57–68. National surveys conducted by the *Catholic Digest* in the postwar decades revealed that occupation was not a significant predictor of church involvement. See Martin Marty, Stuart Rosenberg, and Andrew Greeley, *What Do We Believe? The Stance of Religion in America* (New York: Meredith Press, 1968), 276–77.

22 *Gallup Opinion Index* 44 (February 1969), 33; and 70 (April 1971), 59, 70–81.

23 *Gallup Opinion Index* 70 (April 1971), 57–68, 70–81.

24 See Welch, "Church Membership," 60–61; and Hoge and Roozen, "Research on Factors," 47–48.

25 *Census of Canada*, Vol. 5, Part 1, Table 8, 1971, 26.

26 *Census of Canada*, Vol. 1, Part 3, Bulletin 3, Table 11, 1971.

27 *Census of Canada*, Vol. 1, Part 3, Bulletin 3, Table 13, 1971.

28 *Gallup Opinion Index* 70 (April 1971), 57–68.

29 *Gallup Opinion Index* 70 (April 1971), 70–81.

30 Rodney Stark and William Bainbridge, *The Future of Religion: Secularization, Revival, and Cult Formation* (Berkeley: University of California Press, 1985), 69–75. Using data from the 1952 and 1971 church membership studies, Stark and Bainbridge analyze church involvement in census metropolitan areas and reveal an "unchurched belt" along the Pacific Coast of Canada and the United States.

31 NCCC, *Churches and Church Membership in the United States, 1952*, Series C, No. 57, Table 127; Series A, No. 3, Table 6; and Douglas Johnson, Paul Picard, and Bernard Quinn, eds. *Churches and Church Membership in the United States: An Enumeration by Region, State, and County, 1971* (Washington: Glenmary Research Center, 1974), Table 3.

32 Alice, personal interview, March 23, 2004.

33 Robert Wuthnow, *The Restructuring of American Religion: Society and Faith since World War II* (Princeton: Princeton University Press, 1988), 226; and Ellen Gee, "Gender Differences in Church Attendance in Canada: The Role of Labor Force Participation," *Review of Religious Research* 32: 3 (1991): 267–73.

34 *Census of Canada*, Vol.1, Part 3, Bulletin 3, Table 10 (1971); and United States, Bureau of Census, *1970 Census of Population, Characteristics of the Population, U.S. Summary*, Vol. 1, Part 1, Section 1, Table 59 (1970).

35 See Norval Glenn, "The Trend in 'No Religion' Respondents to US National Surveys, Late 1950s to Early 1980s," *Public Opinion Quarterly* 51: 3 (1987): 304; George Gallup Jr. and Jim Castelli, *The People's Religion: American Faith in the 90s* (New York: MacMillan, 1989), 50–51; and Jackson Carroll, Douglas Johnson, and Martin Marty, *Religion in America, 1950 to Present* (New York: Harper and Row, 1979), 21.

36 United States Bureau of Census, *1970 Census of Population*, Vol. 1, Part 49, Table 35 (1970); Johnson, Picard, and Quinn, *Churches and Church Membership in the United States, 1971*, Table 3.

37 UWM, WNICC, Acc. 1567-02, Box 4, File: Statistics, Reports, "Survey of the Protestant Churches of Metropolitan Seattle," 1945.

38 *Gallup Opinion Index* 70 (April 1971), 57, 62, 70–81.

39 DLRC, *Report of a Survey*, 14, 15; CIPO, *Gallup Report*, 15 January 1969, 1; and Mol, "Major Correlates of Churchgoing," 244–45.

40 *Census of Canada*, Vol. 1, Table 38, 1951; *Census of Canada*, Vol. 1, Bulletin 3, Table 10, 1971.

41 Callum Brown, *The Death of Christian Britain: Understanding Secularisation, 1800–2000* (London: Routledge, 2001), especially Chapter 8.

42 Susan, personal interview, October 30, 2003.

43 Ralph Allen, "The Hidden Failure of Our Churches," *Maclean's*, February 25, 1961, 48.

44 UWM, WNICC, Acc. 1567-2, Box 17, File: Untitled, Annual Meeting, Washington Council of Churches and Christian Education, Seattle, January 6, 1941.

45 See, for example, Doug Owram, *Born at the Right Time: A History of the Baby Boom Generation* (Toronto: University of Toronto Press, 1996), 103–9; Margaret Bendroth, *Growing Up Protestant: Parents, Children, and Mainline Churches* (New Brunswick: Rutgers University Press, 2002), 99–103; and Mary Louise Adams, *The Trouble with Normal: Postwar Youth and the Making of Heterosexuality* (Toronto: University of Toronto Press, 1997), 21.

46 Rillmond Schear, "The Stone Cold Spirit That Stalks Seattle's Churches," *Seattle Magazine*, December 1965, 20, 24.

47 Joel Connelly, "God vs. outdoors: State's church rolls dwindling," *Seattle Post-Intelligencer*, January 2, 1977, A1, A16.

48 Jurgen Hesse, "Canada's history deeply marked by two faiths," *Colonist*, December 20, 1962, 6.

49 As cited in Hugh McLeod, *Piety and Poverty: Working-Class Religion in Berlin, London, and New York, 1870–1914* (New York: Holmes and Meier, 1996), 131.

50 UCBCA, LDA Papers, Box 1, File 5: Letter from Rev. R.A. Redman to Mr. McGrath, December 1, 1954.

51 See, for example, Nancy Christie, "'On the Threshold of Manhood': Working-Class Religion and Domesticity in Victorian Britain and Canada," *Histoire Sociale* 36: 71 (2003): 145–74; Norman Knowles, "Christ in the Crowsnest: Religion and the Anglo-Protestant Working Class in the Crowsnest Pass, 1898–1918," in *Nations, Ideas,*

Identities: Essays in Honour of Ramsay Cook, ed. Michael Behiels and Marcel Martel (New York: Oxford University Press, 2000), 57–72; and Sarah Williams, *Religious Belief and Popular Culture in Southwark, 1880–1939* (Oxford: Oxford University Press, 1999).

52 Sylvia, personal interview, June 24, 2003.

53 Anne, personal interview, September 16, 2003.

54 Larry, personal interview, March 28, 2004.

55 Bill, personal interview, 4 September 2003.

56 UCBCA, LDA Papers, Box 2, File 7: "Special Meeting of the Lord's Day Alliance of Canada," May 18, 1955; Box 2, File 11: "Memo to P. Mallon," January 13, 1961.

57 Frank, personal interview, March 28, 2004.

58 Margaret, personal interview, September 10, 2003.

59 Sylvia, personal interview, June 24, 2003.

60 David, personal interview, March 24, 2004.

61 John, personal interview, September 8, 2003.

62 Muriel, personal interview, October 21, 2003.

63 Anne, personal interview, September 16, 2003.

64 Robert Orsi, "Everyday Miracles: The Study of Lived Religion," in *Lived Religion in America: Toward a History of Practice,* ed. David Hall (Princeton: Princeton University Press, 1997), 6.

65 Patrick, personal interview, September 3, 2003.

66 Richard, personal interview, March 22, 2004.

67 Gary, personal interview, November 19, 2003.

68 Edward, personal interview, August 26, 2003.

69 Alice, personal interview, March 23, 2004.

70 Anne, personal interview, September 16, 2003.

71 Charles, personal interview, October 30, 2003.

72 Carlos Schwantes, *Radical Heritage: Labor, Socialism, and Reform in Washington and British Columbia, 1885–1917* (Seattle: University of Washington Press, 1979), 220–23; Tom Langford and Chris Frazer, "The Cold War and Working Class Politics in the Coal Mining Communities of the Crowsnest Pass, 1945–1958," *Labour/Le Travail* 49 (Spring 2002): 19; George Taft, "Socialism in North America: The Case of BC and Washington State, 1900–1960" (PhD diss., Simon Fraser University, 1983), 107; and Dorothy Johansen and Charles Gates, *Empire of the Columbia: A History of the Pacific Northwest,* 2nd ed. (Seattle: Diocese of Olympia Press, 1967), 473.

73 Taft, "Socialism in North America," 305–6; Schwantes, *A Radical Heritage,* x; Jean Barman, *The West Beyond the West: A History of British Columbia,* rev. ed. (Toronto: University of Toronto Press, 1996), 364; and UCC, BESS, *Annual Report* (1968), 166.

74 Laurie Mercier, "Reworking Race, Class, and Gender into Pacific Northwest History," *Frontiers* 22: 3 (2001): 61. Also see Barman, *The West Beyond the West,* 364; Stewart Holbrook, *Far Corner: A Personal View of the Pacific Northwest* (New York: MacMillan, 1952), 233; and Ruth Sandwell, "Peasants on the Coast? A Problematique of Rural British Columbia," *Canadian Papers in Rural History* 10 (1996): 275.

75 One of the Nanaimo interviewees admitted that because working-class lifestyles were so valorized and normative in the region, he had always felt uncomfortable admitting that he had attended university.

76 Margaret, personal interview, September 10, 2003.

77 Brian, personal interview, March 22, 2004; and James, personal interview, October 22, 2003.

78 Sharon, personal interview, September 22, 2003.

79 Beverly, personal interview, September 4, 2003.

80 UWM, WNICC, Box 17, File: United Church Men, "Speakers Manual: 22nd Annual Observance of Men and Missions Day," October 12, 1952; Roy Hamilton, "Is Christianity a Man's Religion?," *Presbyterian Record,* May 1957, 8–9; and "Does the church present a female image?," *Presbyterian Record,* April 1966, 20–22.

81 "Being a Real Christian Is Not a Sissy Thing," *Nanaimo Free Press,* September 24, 1960, 4.

82 MCU, Pacific Northwest Conference, *Annual Journal* (1951), 551.

83 UWM, WNICC, Acc. 1567-02, Box 17, File: Laymen's Committee, *Advance,* July 1950, 18.

84 Ann Braude notes this tendency in her article, "Women's History *Is* American Religious History," in *Retelling U.S. Religious History,* ed. Thomas Tweed (Berkeley: University of California Press, 1997), 104.

85 Elaine Bulmer, "Women in the Church," *Canadian Churchman,* May 1960, 4; Agnes Markle, "A Woman's Voice: Wanted: a Genuine Partnership," *Canadian Churchman,* February 1966, 16; and Katherine Rhodes, "The best – regardless of sex," *Canadian Churchman,* March 1966, 20; and UMC, Pacific Northwest Conference, *Annual Journal* (1969), 123.

86 Charles, personal interview, October 30, 2003.

87 Donald, personal interview, June 23, 2003.

88 Jean, personal interview, June 23, 2003.

89 James, personal interview, October 22, 2003.

90 Margaret, personal interview, September 10, 2003.

91 Brian, personal interview, March 22, 2004.

92 George, personal interview, October 21, 2003.

93 Ruth, personal interview, October 21, 2003.

94 Reginald Bibby also found that Canadians during the 1970s and 1980s typically identified their mothers as more religious than their fathers; see his *Fragmented Gods: The Poverty and Potential of Religion in Canada* (Toronto: Irwin Publishers, 1987), 100.

95 Larry, personal interview, March 28, 2004.

96 Donald, personal interview, June 23, 2003.

97 Thomas, personal interview, November 11, 2003; and James, personal interview, October 22, 2003.

98 Charles, personal interview, October 30, 2003.

99 David, personal interview, March 24, 2004; and Sylvia, personal interview, June 24, 2003.

100 Jean, personal interview, June 23, 2003.

101 *Canadian Churchman,* May 1964, 4.

102 Shirley, personal interview, March 22, 2004.

103 Bill, personal interview, September 4, 2003.

104 Edna, personal interview, March 25, 2004.

105 Williams, *Religious Belief and Popular Culture,* 21.

106 Lynne Marks, *Revivals and Roller Rinks: Religion, Leisure, and Identity in Late-Nineteenth-Century Small-Town Ontario* (Toronto: University of Toronto Press, 1996), 29–30.

107 Muriel, personal interview, October 21, 2003.

108 Linda, personal interview, October 14, 2003; Patricia, personal interview, August 18, 2003; Donna, personal interview, August 29, 2003, and November 19, 2003; Karen, personal interview, November 19, 2003; Alice, personal interview, March 23, 2004; Edna, personal interview, March 25, 2004; and Joanne, personal interview, March 30, 2004.

109 Joanne, personal interview, March 30, 2004; and Sandra, personal interview, March 27, 2004.
110 Edna, personal interview, March 25, 2004.
111 Susan, personal interview, October 30, 2003.
112 Sharon, personal interview, September 22, 2003.
113 Carolyn Purden, "Women and the Church," *Canadian Churchman,* March 1968, 1, 9; Isabel McLaren, "Let's Look at Women's Work," *Presbyterian Record,* September 1971, 7–8; Patricia Clarke, "Marilyn Huband: Church Work Can Be Beautiful," *United Church Observer,* February 1, 1970, 12–14; UWM, GSCC, Acc. 1358-7, Box 39, File 42: Women and Religion Task Force, Statements, 1972–78, "Church Council of Greater Seattle, Task Force on Women and Religion," January 17, 1977; "Role of Women in Church Discussed by Panelists," *Olympia Churchman,* April 1966, 7; and UMC, Pacific Northwest Conference, *Annual Journal* (1971), 84–87.
114 Patricia, personal interview, August 18, 2003.
115 Margaret, personal interview, September 10, 2003.
116 Beverly, personal interview, September 4, 2003.
117 Barbara Bagnell, "The Feminists," *United Church Observer,* May 1, 1970, 12–15.
118 Although a few studies point to the importance of religion to the North American women's movement, the relationship between religion and feminism demands far more research. See Ann Braude, "A Religious Feminist: Who Can Find Her? Historiographical Challenges from the National Organization for Women," *Journal of Religion* 84: 4 (October 2004), 555–56; and Susan Hartmann, "Expanding Feminism's Field and Focus: Activism in the National Council of Churches in the 1960s and 1970s," in *Women and Twentieth-Century Protestantism,* ed. Margaret Bendroth and Virginia Brereton (Urbana: University of Illinois Press, 2002), 50.
119 See Brown, *The Death of Christian Britain,* 176–80.
120 Charles, personal interview, October 30, 2003.
121 Richard, personal interview, March 22, 2004.
122 Bill, personal interview, September 4, 2003.
123 Patrick, personal interview, September 3, 2003.
124 See, for example, Marks, *Revivals and Roller Rinks,* 175–77.
125 Gary, personal interview, November 18, 2003.
126 James, personal interview, October 22, 2003.
127 Richard, personal interview, March 22, 2004.
128 Larry, personal interview, March 28, 2004; and Thomas, personal interview, November 11, 2003.

Chapter 4: Belief and Unbelief

1 Anne, personal interview, September 16, 2003.
2 Robert Orsi, "Everyday Miracles: The Study of Lived Religion," in *Lived Religion in America: Toward a History of Practice,* ed. David Hall (Princeton: Princeton University Press, 1997), 11.
3 Sarah Williams, *Religious Belief and Popular Culture in Southwark, 1880–1939* (Oxford: Oxford University Press, 1999), 2.
4 Patricia, personal interview, August 18, 2003; and James, personal interview, October 22, 2003.
5 Hugh McLeod, *The Religious Crisis of the 1960s* (Oxford: Oxford University Press, 2007), 241.
6 For discussions on the available data on religious belief, see Jackson Carroll, Douglas Johnson, and Martin Marty, *Religion in America: 1950 to the Present* (New York: Harper

and Row, 1979), 28–34; Hans Mol, *Faith and Fragility: Religion and Identity in Canada* (Burlington: Trinity Press, 1985); and Reginald Bibby, *Fragmented Gods: The Poverty and Potential of Religion in Canada* (Toronto: Irwin Publishers, 1987), 88.

7 *Angus Reid Poll,* April 21, 2000.

8 Bibby, *Fragmented Gods,* 88.

9 Data Laboratories Research Consultants [hereafter DLRC], *Report of a Survey of Canadians' Participation in Organized Religion* (Montreal, 1977), 9, 13.

10 George H. Gallup, *The Gallup Poll: Public Opinion 1935–1971* (New York: Random House, 1972), 473–74.

11 *Gallup Opinion Index* (February 1969), 14.

12 Martin Marty, Stuart Rosenberg, and Andrew Greeley. *What Do We Believe? The Stance of Religion in America* (New York: Meredith Press, 1968) 216–19.

13 Rodney Stark and William Bainbridge, *The Future of Religion: Secularization, Revival, and Cult Formation* (Berkeley: University of California Press, 1985), 79.

14 Gallup, *The Gallup Poll: Public Opinion,* 474–75; *Gallup Opinion Index* (February 1969), 18; and Marty, Rosenberg, and Greeley, *What Do We Believe?,* 236–39, 246–47. Drawing on social surveys from the 1970s, Thomas Davenport argues that residents of the Pacific region were the least certain about life after death, and the most unreligious people in America; see his *Virtuous Pagans: Unreligious People in America* (New York: Garland Publishers, 1991), 82 and 97.

15 Stark and Bainbridge, *The Future of Religion,* 79. A 2001 survey found that 15.2 percent of residents in the Pacific region claimed to be atheists or agnostics, compared to 10.5 percent of Americans more generally. For an analysis of this survey, and other current trends in atheism, see William Bainbridge, "Atheism," *Interdisciplinary Journal of Research on Religion* 1: 1 (2005), 22.

16 DLRC, *Report of a Survey,* 9, 13.

17 Gallup, *The Gallup Poll: Public Opinion,* 698; Gallup Organization, *Religion in America: 50 Years, 1935–1985* (Princeton: Gallup Organization, 1985), 10.

18 DLRC, *Report of a Survey,* 11.

19 Marty, Rosenberg, and Greeley, *What Do We Believe?,* 184–85.

20 David, personal interview, 24 March 2004.

21 Larry, personal interview, 28 March 2004.

22 Patricia, personal interview, 18 August 2003.

23 See, for example, Williams, *Religious Belief and Popular Culture;* Robert Orsi, *The Madonna of 115th Street: Faith and Community in Italian Harlem, 1880–1950* (New Haven: Yale University Press, 1985); and Norman Knowles, "Christ in the Crowsnest: Religion and the Anglo-Protestant Working Class in the Crowsnest Pass, 1898–1918," in *Nations, Ideas, Identities: Essays in Honour of Ramsay Cook,* ed. Michael Behiels and Marcel Martel (New York: Oxford University Press, 2000), 57–72.

24 *BC Catholic,* July 18, 1951, 3; and *Catholic Northwest Progress,* March 10, 1961, 7.

25 Robert, personal interview, October 17, 2003.

26 Thomas, personal interview, November 11, 2003.

27 Susan, personal interview, October 30, 2003.

28 Susan, personal interview, October 30, 2003; and Richard, personal interview, March 22, 2004.

29 Donald, personal interview, June 23, 2003.

30 Mark Shibley, "Secular but Spiritual in the Pacific Northwest," in *Religion and Public Life in the Pacific Northwest: The None Zone,* ed. Patricia O'Connell Killen and Mark Silk (Walnut Creek: AltaMira Press, 2004), 139–68.

31 Mary, personal interview, March 24, 2004.

32   Robert Putnam, and David Campbell, *American Grace: How Religion Divides and Unites Us* (New York: Simon and Schuster, 2010), 126; Grace Davie, *Religion in Britain since 1945: Believing Without Belonging* (Oxford: Blackwell, 1994); and Patricia O'Connell Killen and Mark Silk, eds., *Religion and Public Life in the Pacific Northwest: The None Zone* (Walnut Creek: AltaMira Press, 2004).

33   Edward, personal interview, August 26, 2003.

34   Robert, personal interview, October 17, 2003.

35   Sylvia, personal interview, June 24, 2003.

36   James, personal interview, October 22, 2003.

37   David, personal interview, March 24, 2004.

38   Beverly, personal interview, September 4, 2003.

39   Callum Brown, *Religion and the Demographic Revolution: Women and Secularisation in Canada, Ireland, UK and USA since the 1960s* (Woodbridge: Boydell Press, 2012), 62, 28.

40   Joanne, personal interview, March 30, 2004.

41   Donna, personal interview, August 29, 2003, and November 19, 2003.

42   Nancy Ammerman, "Golden Rule Christianity: Lived Religion in the American Mainstream," in *Lived Religion in America,* ed. David Hall (Princeton: Princeton University Press, 1997), 203.

43   Nancy, personal interview, September 19, 2003.

44   Patrick, personal interview, September 3, 2003.

45   Ammerman, "Golden Rule Christianity," 207.

46   Donald, personal interview, June 23, 2003.

47   Henry, personal interview, August 27, 2003.

48   Muriel, personal interview, October 21, 2003.

49   Charles, personal interview, October 30, 2003.

50   Margaret, personal interview, September 10, 2003.

51   Thomas, personal interview, November 11, 2003.

52   Frank, personal interview, March 28, 2004.

53   Karen, personal interview, November 19, 2003.

54   Lee Canipe, "Under God and Anti-Communist: How the Pledge of Allegiance Got Religion in Cold War America," *Journal of Church and State* 45: 2 (Spring 2003): 312; Carlos Schwantes, *The Pacific Northwest: An Interpretive History,* rev. ed. (Lincoln: University of Nebraska Press, 1996), 438; Putnam and Campbell, *American Grace,* 1; Hugh Robert Orr, "In God We Trust," *Progressive World,* October 1956, 3; and Norman Meese, "The 'Christian Amendment,'" *Progressive World,* November 1956, 19–21.

55   Putnam and Campbell, *American Grace,* 564.

56   Samuel Reimer, "A Look at Cultural Effects on Religiosity: A Comparison between the United States and Canada," *Journal for the Scientific Study of Religion* 34: 4 (1995): 445–46; and Penny Edgell, Joseph Gerteis, and Douglas Hartmann, "Atheists as 'Other': Moral Boundaries and Cultural Membership in American Society," *American Sociological Review* 71: 2 (April 2006): 212.

57   Nancy Ammerman observes that scholars tend to implicitly measure religiosity "against a norm defined by evangelicalism"; see her "Golden Rule Christianity," 196.

58   UWM, WNICC, Acc. 1567-2, Box 13, File: "Kent Fellowship Evangelism Mission," 24–28 February 1956, 7.

59   Sylvia Fraser, "What Makes an Atheist Tick?" *Star Weekly,* September 11, 1965, 7.

60   For references to the stigma against atheism in the United States vs. Canada, and in the west vs. the east, see Ralph Bois, "Atheist Broadcasts in Canada," *Progressive World,* March 1952, 177–78; and Corliss Lamont, "Speaking Tour for Humanism," *Progressive World,* August 1958, 7.

61 "Atheism Blocks Adoption," *Progressive World,* January 1964, 27; "Unbelievers Denied Citizenship," *Progressive World,* November 1964, 28; "Atheists are citizens, too," *BC Catholic,* March 25, 1965, 4; and "Perjury case thrown out by local court," *Nanaimo Free Press,* June 13, 1951, 1, 3.

62 Jurgen Hesse, "Argument futile on belief issue," *Daily Colonist,* January 6, 1963, 10.

63 Joanne, personal interview, March 30, 2004.

64 John, personal interview, September 8, 2003.

65 Karen, personal interview, November 19, 2003.

66 Gary, personal interview, November 19, 2003.

67 Thomas, personal interview, November 11, 2003.

68 Helen, personal interview, March 25, 2004.

69 On anti-communism in the postwar United States, see Elaine Tyler May, *Homeward Bound: American Families in the Cold War Era* (New York: Basic Books, 1988), 10; and Schwantes, *The Pacific Northwest,* 424–28.

70 Alice, personal interview, March 23, 2004.

71 Frank, personal interview, March 28, 2004.

72 In David Hackett et al., "Forum: American Religion and Class," *Religion and American Culture* 15: 1 (2005): 9, 15.

73 British Columbia Archives (hereafter BCA), Marian Noel Sherman Papers (hereafter MNS), MS-0409, Box 2, File: Correspondence re: 'What Makes an Atheist Tick,' Letter to Sherman, September 9, 1965.

74 BCA, MNS, MS-0409, Box 2, File: Correspondence re: 'What Makes an Atheist Tick,' Letter to Sherman, September 14, 1965. For further analysis on Sherman's class position and her atheist activism, see Tina Block, "Ungodly Grandmother: Marian Sherman and the Social Dimensions of Atheism in Postwar Canada," *Journal of Women's History* 26: 4 (Winter 2014): 140–41.

75 Deborah, personal interview, March 29, 2004.

76 Jurgen Hesse, "Religious issue disturbs city teachers," *Colonist,* December 28, 1962, 1.

77 Mona Gleason, *Normalizing the Ideal: Psychology, Schooling, and the Family in Postwar Canada* (Toronto: University of Toronto Press, 1999), 120.

78 Stark and Bainbridge, *The Future of Religion,* 92–93.

79 Leo Adolph, "No Jobs for Atheists," *Progressive World,* May 1964, 12–17.

80 Alice, personal interview, March 23, 2004.

81 Henry, personal interview, August 27, 2003; and Frank, personal interview, March 28, 2004.

82 BCA, MNS, Box 3, File: Humanism, Clippings, Unpublished Papers, Pamphlets etc., Herbert Rosenfeld, "American Humanism: Can It Grasp Its Opportunities," 12, n.d.

83 BCA, MNS, Box 4, File: Publications-C, *The Canadian Humanist,* January 1965, 1.

84 Roger Blanchard, "Church on Campus Driven by Imperative Command," *Forth,* September 1951, 13.

85 "Are Our Universities Irreligious?" *Canadian Churchman,* April 2, 1953, 112; and Donald Collier, "Is the Church Losing Out on Campus?," *Presbyterian Record,* February 1963, 4.

86 Roger Blanchard, "College Work Today," *Living Church,* June 25, 1950, 13.

87 Linda, personal interview, October 14, 2003.

88 Charles, personal interview, October 30, 2003.

89 Alice, personal interview, March 23, 2004.

90 UWM, Stuart Carter Dodd Papers (hereafter SCD), Acc. 1686-71-12, Box 3, File: Humanist Association Correspondence, 1963, "Who Are These Humanists," Edwin Wilson, Exec. Director, AHA.

91 BCA, MNS, Box 1, File: Victoria Humanist Fellowship: Notes, Minutes, Correspondence, ca.1957–1964, Executive Minutes Book, July 26, 1959; Box 3, File: Victoria Humanist Fellowship: Correspondence, Minutes, 1969, "VHF: List of Members in the Victoria Area."

92 Richard, personal interview, March 22, 2004.

93 Gallup Organization, *Religion in America*, 22, 45; *Gallup Opinion Index* 70 (April 1971), 49, 52; and Marty, Rosenberg, and Greeley, *What Do We Believe?*, 184, 230, 236, and 276.

94 *Gallup Opinion Index* 44 (February 1969), 15. Also see, Marty, Rosenberg, and Greeley, *What Do We Believe?*, 216.

95 Samuel Mueller and Angela Lane, "Tabulations from the 1957 Current Population Survey on Religion," *Journal for the Scientific Study of Religion* 11 (1972): 84; and *Gallup Opinion Index* 70 (April 1971), 63–65, 76, 79–81.

96 DLRC, *Report of a Survey*, 14, 15; CIPO, *Gallup Report*, January 15, 1969, 1; and Hans Mol, "Major Correlates of Churchgoing in Canada," in *Religion in Canadian Society*, ed. Stewart Crysdale and Les Wheatcroft (Toronto: MacMillan of Canada, 1976), 244–45.

97 David, personal interview, March 24, 2004.

98 Thomas, personal interview, November 11, 2003.

99 John, personal interview, September 8, 2003.

100 Frank, personal interview, March 28, 2004.

101 Brian, personal interview, March 22, 2004.

102 Edna, personal interview, March 25, 2004.

103 Beverly, personal interview, September 4, 2003.

104 Sharon, personal interview, September 22, 2003.

105 BCA, MSN, MS-0409, Box 2, File: Correspondence re: CBC Interview, Letter to Sherman, 1966.

106 Block, "Ungodly Grandmother," 144–46.

107 Alice, personal interview, March 23, 2004; BCA, MNS, MS-0409, Box 3, File: Victoria Humanist Fellowship, Correspondence, Minutes, 1969, "VHF: List of Members in Victoria Area"; and Box 3, File: Victoria Humanist Fellowship, Notes, Correspondence, 1967, 1968, "Humanist Mailing List," 1967.

108 Brown, *Religion and the Demographic Revolution*, 266.

Chapter 5: "The closest thing to me"

1 Muriel, personal interview, October 21, 2003.

2 Robert Orsi, "Everyday Miracles: The Study of Lived Religion," in *Lived Religion in America: Toward a History of Practice*, ed. David Hall (Princeton: Princeton University Press, 1997), 8.

3 Neil Smith, "Faith begins at home," *Presbyterian Record*, June 1961, 6–7.

4 See, for example, Nancy Christie, ed., *Households of Faith: Family, Gender, and Community in Canada, 1760–1969* (Montreal and Kingston: McGill-Queen's University Press, 2002); Tina Block, "'Families that pray together, stay together': Religion, Gender, and Family in Postwar Victoria, British Columbia," *BC Studies* 145 (Spring 2005): 31–54; and Robert Orsi, *The Madonna of 115th Street: Faith and Community in Italian Harlem, 1880–1950* (New Haven: Yale University Press, 1985).

5 See, for example, Joy Parr, ed., *A Diversity of Women: Ontario, 1945–1980* (Toronto: University of Toronto Press, 1995); and Joanne Meyerowitz, ed., *Not June Cleaver: Women and Gender in Postwar America, 1945–1960* (Philadelphia: Temple University Press, 1994).

6 Cynthia Comacchio, "'The History of Us': Social Science, History, and the Relations of Family in Canada," *Labour/Le Travail* 46 (Fall 2000): 217.

7 Nancy Christie, "Introduction," in Christie, ed., *Households of Faith: Family, Gender, and Community in Canada, 1760–1969* (Montreal: McGill-Queen's University Press, 2002), 6.

8 Nancy, personal interview, September 19, 2003.

9 The tendency of interviewees to situate their stories of religion within the context of family reflects the broader emphasis on familism in the postwar decades. For a discussion of the postwar ideology of familism, see Veronica Strong-Boag, "'Their Side of the Story': Women's Voices from the Ontario Suburbs, 1945–1960," in *A Diversity of Women: Ontario, 1945–1980,* ed. Joy Parr (Toronto: University of Toronto Press, 1995), 52–53.

10 Robert, personal interview, October 17, 2003.

11 Sarah Williams, *Religious Belief and Popular Culture in Southwark, 1880–1939* (Oxford: Oxford University Press, 1999), 19.

12 Jean, personal interview, June 23, 2003.

13 Joanne, personal interview, March 30, 2004.

14 Richard, personal interview, March 22, 2004.

15 Charles, personal interview, October 30, 2003.

16 Patrick, personal interview, September 3, 2003.

17 Frank, personal interview, March 28, 2004.

18 Comacchio, "'The History of Us,'" 193, 216; Karen Dubinsky, *Improper Advances: Rape and Heterosexual Conflict in Ontario, 1880–1929* (Chicago: University of Chicago Press, 1993); Linda McDowell, *Gender, Identity, and Place: Understanding Feminist Geographies* (Minneapolis: University of Minnesota Press, 1999); and Jeanne Kay, "Landscapes of Women and Men: Rethinking the Regional Historical Geography of the United States and Canada," *Journal of Historical Geography* 17: 4 (1991): 435–52.

19 Sidney Warren, *Farthest Frontier: The Pacific Northwest* (Port Washington: Kennikat Press, 1949), 326.

20 Divorce rates were unusually high in the Pacific Northwest. See BC Council for Families, *Diversity and Change: A Profile of British Columbia Families* (Vancouver: BC Council for Families, 1997), 21; UWM, GSCC, 1358-7, Box 4, File 14: Speeches and Writings, 1964–68, "Religion and Welfare: A New Look at an Old Partnership," Seattle, February 4, 1964, 4; UCC, BESS, *Annual Report* (1969), 182; Canada, *Vital Statistics* (1965), 37; and J.E. Veevers, and D.F. Cousineau, "The Heathen Canadians: Demographic Correlates of Nonbelief," *Pacific Sociological Review* 23: 2 (1980): 211.

21 UCC, BCC, *Minutes* (1957), 1443; and (1960), 1630.

22 "Home and the Family," *BC Catholic,* March 8, 1951, 4.

23 George, personal interview, October 21, 2003.

24 George, personal interview, October 21, 2003.

25 Jean Barman, *The West beyond the West: A History of British Columbia,* rev. ed. (Toronto: University of Toronto Press, 1996), 343; Rodney Stark and William Bainbridge, *The Future of Religion: Secularization, Revival, and Cult Formation* (Berkeley: University of California Press, 1985), 94; and Robert Burkinshaw, *Pilgrims in Lotus Land: Conservative Protestantism in British Columbia, 1917–1981* (Montreal and Kingston: McGill-Queen's University Press, 1995), 4.

26 See, for example, Bob Stewart, "That's the B.C. Spirit! Religion and Secularity in Lotus Land," *Canadian Society of Church History Papers* (1983), 32; Veevers and Cousineau, "The Heathen Canadians," 211; Burkinshaw, *Pilgrims in Lotus Land,* 4; and Stark and Bainbridge, *The Future of Religion,* 94.

27 Thomas, personal interview, November 11, 2003.

28 Robert, personal interview, October 17, 2003.

29 David, personal interview, March 24, 2004.

30 George, personal interview, October 21, 2003.

31 Gary, personal interview, November 19, 2003.

32 Rillmond Schear, "The Stone Cold Spirit That Stalks Seattle's Churches," *Seattle Magazine,* December 1965, 21.

33 James, personal interview, October 22, 2003.

34 Margaret, personal interview, September 10, 2003.

35 Joe, personal interview, September 5, 2003.

36 Susan, personal interview, October 30, 2003.

37 George, personal interview, October 21, 2003.

38 Suzanne Morton, "Gender, Place, and Region: Thoughts on the State of Women in Atlantic Canadian History," *Atlantis* 25: 1 (Fall/Winter 2000): 122.

39 "Hitchhiking to Heaven?," *Olympia Churchman,* October 1960, 2. Also see UWM, WNICC, Acc. 1567-1, Box 9, File 4: Incoming Letters, C-W, Letter from Velma Shotwell to Soren Kring, September 3, 1953.

40 "Lost, 400,000 Presbyterians!" *Presbyterian Record,* October 1962, 16.

41 "Country Club Religion No Remedy for These Times," *Canadian Churchman,* January 1961, 10.

42 See, for example, Orsi, *The Madonna of 115th Street,* xvi; Williams, *Religious Belief and Popular Culture,* 163; and Jeffrey Cox, *The English Churches in a Secular Society: Lambeth, 1870–1930* (Oxford: Oxford University Press, 1982).

43 Williams, *Religious Belief and Popular Culture,* 163.

44 Reginald Bibby, *Fragmented Gods: The Poverty and Potential of Religion in Canada* (Toronto: Irwin Publishers, 1987), 55, 76–77.

45 Reginald Bibby, *Restless Gods: The Renaissance of Religion in Canada* (Toronto: Novalis, 2004), 29.

46 United States Department of Health, Education, and Welfare, "Marriage and Divorce," *Vital Statistics of the United States, 1972,* Vol. 3 (Rockville: National Center for Health Statistics, 1976), 6.

47 *United Church Observer,* 15 October 1960, 12; and D. Crawford Smith, "Why Young Couples Need Preparation for Marriage," *Presbyterian Record,* November 1965, 2.

48 Bibby, *Fragmented Gods,* 89.

49 Smith, "Why Young Couples Need Preparation for Marriage," 2.

50 Muriel, personal interview, October 21, 2003.

51 Jean, personal interview, June 23, 2003.

52 Anne, personal interview, September 16, 2003.

53 Edward, personal interview, August 26, 2003.

54 James, personal interview, October 22, 2003.

55 David, personal interview, March 24, 2004.

56 Linda, personal interview, October 14, 2003.

57 Thomas, personal interview, November 11, 2003.

58 "Godparents Wanted," *Olympia Churchman,* April 1964, 7.

59 Bibby, *Fragmented Gods,* 89. Also see UCC, *Yearbook* (1972), Vol. 1, 1–2; and ACC, General Synod, *Journal of Proceedings* (1967), 399.

60 Anne, personal interview, September 16, 2003.

61 Patrick, personal interview, September 3, 2003.

62 Nancy, personal interview, September 19, 2003.

63 *Olympia Churchman,* April 1959, 6.

64 See, for example, Leigh Eric Schmidt, *Consumer Rites: The Buying and Selling of American Holidays* (Princeton: Princeton University Press, 1995).

65   Patrick, personal interview, September 3, 2003.

66   "Christianity's Lost Radiance," *Presbyterian Record,* April 1953, 10; E.A. Callanan, "Our Paganized Holidays," *Canadian Churchman,* December 20, 1951, 395–97; and Ruby Lornell, "Is Santa Claus Bigger Than Jesus?," *Lutheran,* December 5, 1951, 16–17.

67   According to an American survey conducted in 1962, schools in the western states were least likely to observe religious holidays. See Richard Dierenfield, *Religion in American Public Schools* (Washington: Public Affairs Press, 1962), 68.

68   Gary, personal interview, November 19, 2003.

69   Jean and Donald, personal interview, June 23, 2003; Helen, personal interview, March 25, 2004; and Patrick, personal interview, September 3, 2003.

70   Sharon, personal interview, September 22, 2003.

71   Edna, personal interview, March 25, 2004.

72   See, for example, Orsi, *The Madonna of 115th Street.*

73   Charles, personal interview, October 30, 2003; Edward, personal interview, August 26, 2003; John, personal interview, September 8, 2003; Joe, personal interview, September 5, 2003; Karen, personal interview, November 19, 2003; Linda, personal interview, October 14, 2003; Philip, personal interview, October 22, 2003; and Deborah and Steven, personal interview, March 29, 2004.

74   Parr, "Introduction," in *A Diversity of Women,* 7. Also see Elaine Tyler May, *Homeward Bound: American Families in the Cold War Era* (New York: Basic Books, 1988).

75   *Catholic Northwest Progress,* August 5, 1966, 3; Gordon Walker, "What Is the Church Doing to Save Family Life?" *BC Diocesan Post,* October 1971, 2; T.M. Bailey, "The Fate of Today's Family," *Presbyterian Record,* May 1970, 7; UCC, BESS, *Annual Report* (1963), 102–3; and ACC, Diocese of British Columbia, *Journal of Synod* (1958), 15.

76   "Atheism Blocks Adoption," *Progressive World,* January 1964, 27; and "Religion and Child Adoption," *Progressive World,* April 1964, 27.

77   *Port Angeles Evening News,* December 1, 1951, 1.

78   Amy Haufschild, "What Do Children Do on Sunday Afternoon," *United Church Observer,* April 15, 1957, 19–20; "Parents," *Canadian Churchman,* August 4, 1955, 359; "Up-Island visitors gather in city," *Nanaimo Free Press,* December 2, 1966, 6; and "Be It Ever So Humble There Is No Place Like Home," *Torch,* March 1950, 3–4.

79   Katherine Arnup, *Education for Motherhood: Advice for Mothers in Twentieth-Century Canada* (Toronto: University of Toronto Press, 1994), 150.

80   See Joan Sangster, "Doing Two Jobs: The Wage-Earning Mother, 1945–1970," in *A Diversity of Women,* 104.

81   Joanne, personal interview, March 30, 2004.

82   Thomas, personal interview, November 11, 2003.

83   Beverly, personal interview, September 4, 2003.

84   Sharon, personal interview, September 22, 2003.

85   George, personal interview, October 21, 2003.

86   Robert, personal interview, October 17, 2003; and James, personal interview, October 22, 2003.

87   Bibby, *Fragmented Gods,* 89. According to Bibby, in 1985 20 percent of British Columbians sought out church school for their children, as compared to 25 percent in Canada as a whole. Also see Burkinshaw, *Pilgrims in Lotus Land,* 5; MCU, Pacific Northwest Conference, *Annual Journal* (1962), 93; and UWM, WNICC, Acc. 1567-2, Box 4, File: Statistics, Reports, "Survey of the Protestant Churches of Metropolitan Seattle, Washington," 1945, 7.

88   *Canadian Churchman,* July-August 1966, 4; and June 1964, 4. Also see "Sunday School Orphans," *United Church Observer,* January 15, 1959, 18; UWM, WNICC, 1567-2, Box 4,

File: Statistics, Reports, "Survey of the Protestant Churches in Metropolitan Seattle, Washington," 1945, 9; and UWM, GSCC, Box 14, File 16: United Church Men of Seattle, 1946–57, "Minutes for Laymen's Committee Meeting," May 15, 1950, 1.

89 Margaret Bendroth, *Growing Up Protestant: Parents, Children, and Mainline Churches* (New Brunswick: Rutgers University Press, 2002), 101.

90 Doug Owram, *Born at the Right Time: A History of the Baby-Boom Generation* (Toronto: University of Toronto Press, 1996), 108.

91 Violet Berringer, "On Being a Humanist Mother," *Victoria Humanist,* Late Summer 1967, 13.

92 BCA, MNS, MS-0409, Box 2, File: Correspondence re: What Makes an Atheist Tick? Letter to Sherman, September 13, 1965.

93 BCA, MNS, MS-0409, Box 2, File: Correspondence re: CBC Interview, Letter to Sherman, 1966.

94 Jean, personal interview, June 23, 2003.

95 Joanne, personal interview, March 30, 2004.

96 Edna, personal interview, March 25, 2004.

97 Anne, personal interview, September 16, 2003.

98 Annalee Golz, "Family Matters: The Canadian Family and the State in the Postwar Period," *Left History* 1: 2 (1993): 27; and Mona Gleason, *Normalizing the Ideal: Psychology, Schooling, and the Family in Postwar Canada* (Toronto: University of Toronto Press, 1999), 140.

99 Karen, personal interview, November 19, 2003.

100 Ruth, personal interview, October 21, 2003.

101 Gleason, *Normalizing the Ideal,* 140.

102 BCA, MNS, MS-0409, Box 3, File: Humanism: Clippings, Unpublished Papers, Pamphlets, etc., "American Humanism: Can It Grasp Its Opportunities," by Herbert Rosenfeld, 22.

103 BCA, MNS, MS-0409, Box 4, File: Publications-A; *Humanist,* September 1962, "Forming a Humanist Group," by Ernest Poser, 272–74.

104 Alice, personal interview, March 23, 2004.

105 Joanne, personal interview, March 30, 2004. Also see Marian Sherman, "How I Came To Be a Humanist," *Humanist in Canada,* Winter Solstice, 1968, 7.

106 Patricia, personal interview, August 18, 2003.

107 Linda, personal interview, October 14, 2003.

108 Sharon, personal interview, September 22, 2003.

109 Donna, personal interview, August 29, 2003, and November 19, 2003.

110 Linda, personal interview, October 14, 2003.

111 Sharon, personal interview, September 22, 2003.

112 Muriel, personal interview, October 21, 2003.

113 Orsi, "Everyday Miracles," 8.

Chapter 6: "So much sin amid so much beauty"

1 Donald, personal interview, June 23, 2003.

2 Wilbur Zelinsky, "An Approach to the Religious Geography of the United States: Patterns of Church Membership in 1952," *Annals of the Association of American Geographers* 51 (1961): 164.

3 John Agnew, "Introduction," in *American Space/American Place: Geographies of the Contemporary United States,* ed. John Agnew and Jonathan Smith (New York: Routledge, 2002).

4 See Edward Ayers and Peter Onuf, "Introduction," in *All Over the Map: Rethinking American Regions*, ed. Ayers et al. (Baltimore: Johns Hopkins University Press, 1996), 3.

5 Susan, personal interview, October 30, 2003.

6 R.E. Milam, "Impressions of the British Columbia Bible Conference," *Western Regular Baptist*, February 15, 1952, 12.

7 Katherine Morrissey, *Mental Territories: Mapping the Inland Empire* (Ithaca: Cornell University Press, 1997), 16.

8 Don Alper, "The Idea of Cascadia: Emergent Transborder Regionalism in the Pacific Northwest-Western Canada" *Journal of Borderland Studies* 11: 2 (1996): 1–22; Matthew Sparke, "Excavating the Future in Cascadia: Geoeconomics and the Imagined Geographies of a Cross-Border Region," *BC Studies* 127 (2000): 5–44; and Joel Garreau, *The Nine Nations of North America* (Boston: Houghton Mifflin, 1981).

9 Stewart Holbrook, *Far Corner: A Personal View of the Pacific Northwest* (New York: MacMillan, 1952), 48; and Murray Morgan, *The Northwest Corner: The Pacific Northwest, Its Past and Present* (New York: The Viking Press, 1962), 7.

10 UCC, BESS, *Annual Report* (1954), 7.

11 *Victoria Humanist*, December 1964, 2.

12 William New, *Borderlands: How We Talk About Canada* (Vancouver: UBC Press, 1998), 40.

13 Ralph Bois, "Atheist Broadcasts in Canada," *Progressive World*, March 1952, 78.

14 Donald, personal interview, June 23, 2003.

15 Anne, personal interview, September 16, 2003.

16 Thomas, personal interview, November 11, 2003.

17 James, personal interview, October 22, 2003; Frank, personal interview, March 28, 2004; John, personal interview, September 8, 2003; Gary, personal interview, November 19, 2003; Philip, personal interview, October 22, 2003; and Ruth, personal interview, October 21, 2003.

18 Ayers and Onuf, "Introduction," in *All Over the Map*, 3.

19 Sharon, personal interview, September 22, 2003.

20 Brian and Shirley, personal interview, March 22, 2004; Sharon, personal interview, September 22, 2003; Frank, personal interview, March 28, 2004; Deborah and Steven, personal interview, March 29, 2004; Beverly and Bill, personal interview, September 4, 2003; Charles, personal interview, October 30, 2003; Gary, personal interview, November 19, 2003; Karen, personal interview, November 19, 2003; Ruth, personal interview, October 21, 2003; Thomas, personal interview, November 11, 2003; and William, personal interview, March 23, 2004.

21 Donna, personal interview, August 29, 2003.

22 Frank, personal interview, March 28, 2004.

23 *Humanist in Canada*, Fall 1968, 24.

24 Celia Applegate, "A Europe of Regions: Reflections on the Historiography of Sub-National Places in Modern Times," *American Historical Review* 104: 4 (1999): 1179.

25 UWM, Thomas Jessett, "The Influence of the Church in Washington State – Is This God's Country?" Typescript of speech given at a meeting of the clergy, concerned laity, and visiting ministers of the Diocese of Spokane, November 20, 1975, 20.

26 Kevin Christiano, "Church and State in Institutional Flux: Canada and the United States," in *Rethinking Church, State, and Modernity: Canada Between Europe and America*, ed. David Lyon and Marguerite Van Die (Toronto: University of Toronto Press, 2000), 69; Seymour Lipset, *Continental Divide: The Values and Institutions of the United States and Canada* (New York: Routledge, 1990); and Douglas Baer, Edward Grabb, and William Johnston, "The Values of Canadians and Americans: A Critical Analysis and Reassessment," *Social Forces* 68: 3 (March 1990): 693–713.

27 Linda, personal interview, October 14, 2003.

28 "Will a Man Rob God?" *Presbyterian Record,* April 1957, 3. For an expression of concern about the "Americanization" of the Canadian Sunday, see UCBCA, LDA, Box 2, File 23: Letter from Rev. Allen to Harvey Smith, October 11, 1961.

29 John Gray, "They're Fighting to Save What's Left of Sunday," *Maclean's,* February 15, 1955, 32.

30 See Paul Laverdure, *Sunday in Canada: The Rise and Fall of the Lord's Day* (Yorkton: Gravelbooks, 2004).

31 "Sunday laws not enforced, unlikely to be," *Seattle Times,* March 23, 1961, 6; *Seattle Magazine,* July 1966, 21; UWM, WNICC, Acc. 1567-1, Box 8, File 42: Reports, News Releases, Programs, C.A. 1956–64 (Legislative Committee), "Why Sunday Observance Legislation Is Desirable," n.d.

32 *Argus,* August 28, 1937, 3.

33 *Seattle Magazine,* July 1966, 22.

34 UCBCA, LDA, Box 1, File 9: Letter from Rev. Allen to Rev. A.S. McGrath, November 2, 1957.

35 United Presbyterian Church in the United States (hereafter UPC), Synod of Washington, Annual Session, *Minutes* (1952), 331; *Argus,* 8 December 1961, 1; Emmett Watson, "Our city," *Seattle Post-Intelligencer,* December 10, 1964, 21; and "Will a Man Rob God?" *Presbyterian Record,* April 1957, 3.

36 William, personal interview, March 23, 2004.

37 Patrick, personal interview, September 3, 2003.

38 Morrissey, *Mental Territories,* 17–18.

39 UCBCA, LDA, Box 1, File 9: Letter from Rev. Allen to Rev. McGrath, November 2, 1957; Box 2, File 7: Special Meeting of the LDA of Canada, BC Executive, May 18, 1955; and Box 2, File 9: Minutes of Policy Committee, April 1, 1959.

40 UCBCA, LDA, Box 2, File 11: Memo to P. Mallon, Archbishop's Representative, LDA Committee, January 13, 1961.

41 UCBCA, LDA, Box 3, File 9: Review and Observations for 1961, Field Secretary for Alberta and BC.

42 UCBCA, LDA, Box 2, File 24: Letter from LDA Executive to the Attorney General, May 14, 1960.

43 UCBCA, LDA, Box 1, File 12: Letter from Rev. Allen to Rev. MacGrath, June 23, 1960; Box 2, File 7: Special Meeting of the Lord's Day Alliance of Canada, BC Executive, May 18, 1955; Box 2, File 9: Minutes of Meeting, Policy Committee, BC Branch of LDA, March 23, 1961; Box 1, File 3: Letter from Rev. Redman to Hon. Robt. Bonner, Attorney General of BC, August 26, 1954; and "Sunday work ban in pulp industry sought," *Nanaimo Free Press,* June 3, 1959, 5.

44 Philip Westwood, "Save Me from a Saved Sunday," *Argus,* March 1, 1963, 4.

45 UCBCA, LDA, Box 4, File 3: Letter from Les Kingdon, General Secty, to the Honourable Allan Williams, Atty-General, Province of BC, July 9, 1980.

46 UWM, GSCC, Acc. 1358-7, Box 4, File 7: Notebooks, 1967, "An Ecumenical Metropolitan Ministry in the Puget Sound Region," April 22, 1967, 3. Also see MSN, WNICC, 1567-2, Box 8, File: Campus Ministry, 1966–68, "Proposal for a Christian Higher Educational Center and Research Institute," Bellingham, November 28, 1966, 1.

47 Paul Blanshard, *Religion and the Schools: The Great Controversy* (Boston: Beacon Press, 1963), 97; and Richard Dierenfield, *Religion in American Public Schools* (Washington: Public Affairs Press, 1962), 21, 23, and 37.

48 "Geography and Religion," *Progressive World,* July 1962, 29. Also see *Seattle Times,* June 17, 1963, 6; Thomas Pangle, "The Accommodation of Religion: A Tocquevillian

Perspective," in *The Canadian and American Constitutions in Comparative Perspective,* ed. Marian McKenna (Calgary: University of Calgary Press, 1993), 3–5; and Samuel Reimer, *Evangelicals and the Continental Divide: The Conservative Protestant Subculture in Canada and the United States* (Montreal and Kingston: McGill-Queen's University Press, 2003), 30.

49 These surveys did not include state-level data; see Dierenfield, *Religion in American Public Schools,* 47–94; and David Roozen and Jackson Carroll, "Recent Trends in Church Membership and Participation: An Introduction," in *Understanding Church Growth and Decline, 1950–1978,* ed. Dean Hoge and David Roozen (New York: Pilgrim Press, 1979), 34.

50 Vincent McNally, "Church–State Relations and American Influence in British Columbia before Confederation," *Journal of Church and State* 34: 1 (1992): 94, 108; Ronald Manzer, "Public Philosophy and Public Policy: The Case of Religion in Canadian State Education," *British Journal of Canadian Studies* 7: 2 (1992), 260; Hans Mol, *Faith and Fragility: Religion and Identity in Canada* (Burlington: Trinity Press, 1985), 202, 269; APSA, Provincial Council, Minutes of Executive Committee, PSA 00, File PSA 00/02, Minutes, May 28, 1964, 1; APSA, Douglas Percy Watney Papers, Box 481, File 1: Religion in Public Education, "Memorandum to the House of Bishops of the Province of British Columbia," April 8, 1952; and ACC, Diocese of British Columbia, *Journal of Synod* (1952), 11, 30–32.

51 Stephen Brown, "Go east, R.C.'s for fair deal!," *BC Catholic,* February 6, 1969, 9.

52 "Maillardville Makes a Stand," *Torch,* April 1951, 3–5, 7.

53 "News Commentator Supports School Campaign," *BC Catholic,* May 3, 1951, 1.

54 *Torch,* May 1952, 3–4; "The Catholic School Struggle Here," *BC Catholic,* October 11, 1951, 8; November 1, 1951, 4; March 3, 1955, 1; "BC Education Flayed as 'Pagan'; Discrimination Charged by Minister," *Colonist,* March 11, 1950, 6; *Catholic Northwest Progress,* April 13, 1951, 5; and ACC, Provincial Synod of British Columbia, *Journal of Proceedings* (1953), 42–43.

55 Doug Owram, *Born at the Right Time: A History of the Baby-Boom Generation* (Toronto: University of Toronto Press, 1996), 104; Vincent McNally, "Challenging the Status Quo: An Examination of the History of Catholic Education in British Columbia," *Historical Studies: Canadian Catholic Historical Association* 65 (1999): 8; and Manzer, "Public Philosophy and Public Policy," 259.

56 "Diversity in Education," *Canadian Register,* July 20, 1968, 5.

57 Gerald Friesen, "Homer's Odyssey and a Region of Rednecks: What Communication History Can Tell Us about Canada as a Country of Region," *British Journal of Canadian Studies* 15: 1/2 (2002): 37, 39.

58 UWM, Thomas Jessett Papers, Acc. 1832, Box. 9, File: Proposed Writing of History of Episcopal Church in Northwest, "The Episcopate of Thomas Fielding Scott," 13.

59 Patricia O'Connell Killen and Mark Shibley, "Surveying the Religious Landscape: Historical Trends and Current Patterns in Oregon, Washington, and Alaska," in *Religion and Public Life in the Pacific Northwest: The None Zone,* ed. Patricia O'Connell Killen and Mark Silk (Walnut Creek: AltaMira Press, 2004), 30–31; and Jessett, "The Influence of the Church," 6.

60 Lynne Marks, "'Leaving God Behind When They Crossed the Rocky Mountains': Exploring Unbelief in Turn-of-the-Century British Columbia," in *Household Counts: Canadian Households and Families in 1901,* ed. Peter Baskerville and Eric Sager (Toronto: University of Toronto Press, 2007), 371–404; and Lynne Marks, "Exploring Regional Diversity in Patterns of Religious Participation: Canada in 1901," *Historical Methods* 33: 4 (2000): 251, 252.

61 Rhys Williams, "Religion, Community, and Place: Locating the Transcendent," *Religion and American Culture* 12: 2 (June 2002): 250.

62 Karen, personal interview, November 19, 2003.

63 See, for example, Reginald Bibby, *Fragmented Gods: The Poverty and Potential of Religion in Canada* (Toronto: Irwin Publishers, 1987), 236–37; Mark Chaves, *American Religion: Contemporary Trends* (Princeton: Princeton University Press, 2011), 52; and Steve Bruce, *God Is Dead: Secularization in the West* (Oxford: Blackwell, 2002), 240.

64 Donald, personal interview, June 23, 2003.

65 William, personal interview, March 23, 2004.

66 Karen Wigen, "Culture, Power, and Place: The New Landscapes of East Asian Regionalism," *American Historical Review* 104: 4 (1999), 1200–1.

67 For early works that largely overlooked religion, see Dorothy Johansen and Charles Gates, *Empire of the Columbia: A History of the Pacific Northwest*, 2nd ed. (New York: Harper and Row, 1967); Holbrook, *Far Corner*; and Ken Liddell, *This Is British Columbia* (Toronto: Ryerson Press, 1958). For more recent discussions on the neglect of religion in studies of the Northwest's past, see Norman Knowles, "New Perspectives on the History of Religion in BC," *Journal of the Canadian Church Historical Society* 38: 1 (1996): 6; and Ferenc Szasz, "The Clergy and the Myth of the American West," *Church History* 59: 4 (1990): 497–500.

68 *Nanaimo Free Press*, October 31, 1957, 2; and "The spiritual side of state's history," *Seattle Times*, October 21, 1989, A15.

69 Charles Booth, *The Northwestern United States* (New York: Van Nostrand Reinhold, 1971), v.

70 Helen Grieve, "Seattle has no soul," *UW Daily*, October 19, 1979, 9; Gil Bailey, "State's churchgoers are fewer but more fervent, leader says," *Seattle Post-Intelligencer*, July 18, 1992, A6; and Carol Ostrom, "State has rich religious history," *Seattle Times*, August 20, 1988, A14.

71 Laurie Maffly-Kipp, "Historicizing Religion in the American West," in *Perspectives on American Religion and Culture*, ed. Peter Williams (Malden: Blackwell, 1999), 11. Also see Szasz, "The Clergy," 500; and Patricia O'Connell Killen, "Writing the Pacific Northwest into Canadian and U.S. Catholic History: Geography, Demographics, and Regional Religion," *Historical Studies: Canadian Catholic Historical Association* 66 (2000): 75–76.

72 See, for example, Stewart, "Religion and Secularity," 22–35; Killen and Shibley, "Surveying the Religious Landscape," 41–42; and Tina Block, "Religion, Irreligion, and the Difference Place Makes: The Case of the Pacific Northwest, 1950–1970," *Histoire sociale/Social History* 43: 85 (May 2010): 1–30.

73 Edwin Bracher and Marjory Bracher, "The Northwest Is Growing," *Lutheran*, March 26, 1952, 14.

74 Roger Stump, "Regional Migration and Religious Commitment in the U.S.," *Journal for the Scientific Study of Religion* 23: 3 (1984): 302. Also see Killen, "Writing the Pacific Northwest," 82.

75 George, personal interview, October 21, 2003; James, personal interview, October 22, 2003; and Beverly and Bill, personal interview, September 4, 2003.

76 *Census of Canada*, Special Series #5, Table 1, 1971.

77 J.J. Molley, "Around the Diocese with the C.W.L.," *BC Catholic*, January 25, 1951, 2. For an American example, see *Catholic Northwest Progress*, January 20, 1961, 5.

78 Sharon, personal interview, September 22, 2003.

79 Edward, personal interview, August 26, 2003.

80 Linda, personal interview, October 14, 2003.

81 Steven Avella, "Catholicism in the Twentieth-Century American West: The Next Frontier," *Catholic Historical Review* 97: 2 (April 2011): 234, 244; Dale Soden, "Contesting for the Soul of an Unlikely Land: Mainline Protestants, Catholics, and Jews in the Pacific Northwest," in *Religion and Public Life in the Pacific Northwest: The None Zone*, ed. Patricia O'Connell Killen and Mark Silk (Walnut Creek: AltaMira Press, 2004), 61; Kristofer Allerfeldt, *Race, Radicalism, Religion, and Restriction: Immigration in the Pacific Northwest, 1890–1924* (Westport: Praeger, 2003), 32, 41, 61; and Patricia O'Connell Killen, "The Geography of a Religious Minority: Roman Catholicism in the Pacific Northwest," *US Catholic Historian* 18: 3 (Summer 2000): 51–72.

82 Killen and Shibley, "Surveying the Religious Landscape," 33.

83 Brian, personal interview, March 22, 2004.

84 Killen, "Writing the Pacific Northwest," 82–83.

85 Helen, personal interview, March 25, 2004.

86 Susan, personal interview, October 30, 2003.

87 Mark Shibley, "Religion in Oregon: Recent Demographic Currents in the Mainstream," *Pacific Northwest Quarterly* 83: 3 (July 1992): 86.

88 Nancy Christie and Michael Gauvreau, "'Even the hippies were only very slowly going secular': Dechristianization and the Culture of Individualism in North America and Western Europe," in *The Sixties and Beyond: Dechristianization in North America and Western Europe: 1945–2000*, ed. Nancy Christie and Michael Gauvreau (Toronto: University of Toronto Press, 2013), 3–38; Callum Brown, *The Death of Christian Britain: Understanding Secularisation, 1800–2000* (London: Routledge, 2001), Chapter 8; Catherine Gidney, *A Long Eclipse: The Liberal Protestant Establishment and the Canadian University, 1920–1970* (Montreal and Kingston: McGill-Queen's University Press, 2004), xv; Hugh McLeod, *The Religious Crisis of the 1960s* (Oxford: Oxford University Press, 2007), 246; Gary Miedema, *For Canada's Sake: Public Religion, Centennial Celebrations, and the Re-Making of Canada in the 1960s* (Montreal and Kingston: McGill-Queen's University Press, 2005) 35; Mark Noll, "What Happened to Christian Canada?" *Church History* 75: 2 (2006): 251; and Alan Petigny, "The Spread of Permissive Religion," *Canadian Review of American Studies* 39: 4 (2009): 415.

89 Ron Strickland, ed., *Whistlepunks and Geoducks: Oral Histories from the Pacific Northwest* (Corvallis: Oregon State University Press, 2001), 295.

90 Holbrook, *Far Corner*, 4, 6.

91 Stewart Holbrook, Nard Jones, and Roderick Haig-Brown, *The Pacific Northwest*, ed. Anthony Netboy (Garden City: Doubleday, 1963), 176.

92 Jean Barman, *The West Beyond the West: A History of British Columbia*, rev. ed. (Toronto: University of Toronto Press, 1996).

93 ACC, General Synod, *Journal of Proceedings* (1967), 10; and Strickland, ed., *Whistlepunks and Geoducks*, 291.

94 Richard, personal interview, March 22, 2004.

95 Sandra, personal interview, March 27, 2004; Susan, personal interview, October 30, 2003; Thomas, personal interview, November 11, 2003; Donna, personal interview, August 29, 2003, and November 19, 2003; Jean and Donald, personal interview, June 23, 2003; and Brian and Shirley, personal interview, March 22, 2004.

96 Joanne, personal interview, March 30, 2004.

97 Edna, personal interview, March 25, 2004.

98 Susan, personal interview, October 30, 2003.

99 Rob Shields, *Places on the Margin: Alternative Geographies of Modernity* (London: Routledge, 1991) 6, 199.

100 Holbrook, *Far Corner,* 10.
101 Lee Cuba and David Hummon, "A Place to Call Home: Identification with Dwelling, Community, and Region," *Sociological Quarterly* 34: 1 (1993), 113.
102 Edward, personal interview, August 26, 2003.
103 David, personal interview, March 24, 2004.
104 Robert, personal interview, October 17, 2003.
105 Frank, personal interview, March 28, 2004.
106 William, personal interview, March 23, 2004; Mary, personal interview, March 24, 2004; Helen, personal interview, March 25, 2004; Robert, personal interview, October 17, 2003; Edward, personal interview, August 26, 2003; David, personal interview, March 24, 2004; and Larry, personal interview, March 28, 2004.
107 Callum Brown, *Religion and the Demographic Revolution: Women and Secularisation in Canada, Ireland, UK and USA since the 1960s* (Woodbridge: Boydell Press, 2012), 25–26.
108 Nancy, personal interview, September 19, 2003.
109 Susan, personal interview, October 30, 2003.
110 Jean, personal interview, June 23, 2003.
111 James, personal interview, October 22, 2003. In the postwar decades, church leaders also often constructed the Pacific Northwest as a place of leisure. In 1967, the Washington and Northern Idaho Council of Churches began studying the possibilities of bringing the church to people in parks and other leisure areas. See MCU, Pacific Northwest Conference, *Annual Journal* (1967), 164; and UMC, Pacific Northwest Conference, *Annual Journal* (1971), 122.
112 Donna, personal interview, November 19, 2003.
113 Robert, personal interview, October 17, 2003.
114 Patricia Limerick, "Region and Reason," in *All Over the Map: Rethinking American Regions,* ed. Edward Ayers et al. (Baltimore: Johns Hopkins University Press, 1996), 103.
115 Norman Clark et al., "The Pacific Northwest as Cultural Region: A Symposium," *Pacific Northwest Quarterly* 64 (1973): 156–57. Also see Carlos Schwantes, *The Pacific Northwest: An Interpretive History,* rev. ed. (Lincoln: University of Nebraska Press), 7.
116 Schwantes, *The Pacific Northwest,* 7.
117 Strickland, *Whistlepunks and Geoducks,* 295.
118 A.C. Forrest, "So much sin in B.C. amid so much beauty," *Vancouver Sun,* October 22, 1955, 15.
119 "Growing?," *United Church Observer,* October 15, 1963, 11, 46.
120 ACC, General Synod, *Journal of Proceedings* (1959), 381.
121 Geo. A. Williams, "First Impressions of Newfoundland," *United Church Observer,* October 1, 1951, 13.
122 Donna, personal interview, November 19, 2003.
123 Muriel, personal interview, October 21, 2003.

Conclusion

1 Jim Christy, "Visions of Columbia," *Raw Vision* (Spring 1995): 40–45.
2 Curt Hopkins, "The ends of the Earth: How the Northwest came to be more than just a little of-center," *Seattle Times,* June 6, 2003.
3 Bernard Weiner, "They call themselves the 'new Christians," *Seattle Post-Intelligencer,* August 23, 1970, 4–5; and Earl Hansen, "Jesus people army seeking a Seattle explosion of 'babes in the Lord," *Seattle Post-Intelligencer,* November 4, 1970, 19.
4 See, for example, Joanne Meyerowitz, ed., *Not June Cleaver: Women and Gender in Postwar America, 1945–1960* (Philadelphia: Temple University Press, 1994); and Joy Parr, ed., *A Diversity of Women: Ontario, 1945–1980* (Toronto: University of Toronto Press, 1995).

5 Mark Silk, "Religion and Region in American Public Life," *Journal for the Scientific Study of Religion* 44: 3 (2005): 265, 269.
6 Statistics Canada, *National Household Survey*, 2011, Statistics Canada Catalogue no. 99-010-X2011032, http://www12.statcan.gc.ca/nhs-enm/2011/dp-pd/dt-td/Rp-eng. cfm; and Barry Kosmin and Ariela Keysar, with Ryan Cragun and Juhem Navarro-Rivera, *American Nones: The Profile of the No Religion Population* (Hartford: Institute for the Study of Secularism in Society and Culture, 2009), i, 19. Washington tied with Maine for the fourth highest population of religious "nones," behind Vermont, New Hampshire, and Wyoming.
7 Grace Davie, *Religion in Britain since 1945: Believing without Belonging* (Oxford: Blackwell, 1994); Mark Shibley, "Secular but Spiritual in the Pacific Northwest," in *Religion and Public Life in the Pacific Northwest: The None Zone*, ed. Patricia O'Connell Killen and Mark Silk (Walnut Creek: AltaMira Press, 2004); and Robert Fuller, *Spiritual but Not Religious: Understanding Unchurched America* (New York: Oxford University Press, 2001).
8 Silk, "Religion and Region," 267–69; and J.E. Veevers and D.F. Cousineau, "The Heathen Canadians: Demographic Correlates of Nonbelief," *Pacific Sociological Review* 23: 2 (1980): 211.

Selected Bibliography

Archival Collections

Anglican Provincial Synod of British Columbia and Yukon Archives, Vancouver
Douglas Percy Watney Papers
Provincial Board of Missions to Orientals, Minutes, Series 4, PSA 4/6
Provincial Council, Minutes of Executive Committee, PSA 00

British Columbia Archives, Victoria
Marian Noel Sherman Papers, MS 0409

United Church of Canada, British Columbia Conference Archives, Vancouver
Home Missions Committee Papers
Lord's Day Alliance, BC–Alberta Branch Papers

University of Washington Manuscripts and Special Collections, Seattle
Christian Friends for Racial Equality Records, Acc. 4040-3
Greater Seattle Council of Churches Records, Acc. 1358-07
Stuart Carter Dodd Papers, Acc. 1686-71-12
Thomas Jessett. "The Influence of the Church in Washington State – Is This God's Country?" Typescript of speech given at a meeting of the clergy, concerned laity, and visiting ministers of the Diocese of Spokane, November 20, 1975
Thomas Jessett Papers, Acc. 1832
University of Washington Religious Directors' Association, Acc. 3454
Washington and Northern Idaho Council of Churches and Christian Education Records, Acc. 1567 and 1567-2

Newspapers and Periodicals
Argus (Northwest)
BC Catholic
BC Diocesan Post
Bulletin (Seattle Council of Churches)
Canadian Churchman
Canadian Lutheran
Canadian Register (Roman Catholic)
Catholic Northwest Progress
Christianity and Crisis
Christianity and Society
Christianity Today
Daily Christian Advocate (Methodist)

Fort Nelson News
Forth (Episcopalian)
Humanist (Ohio)
Humanist in Canada
Living Church (Episcopalian)
Lutheran
Maclean's
Nanaimo Free Press
New Religious Frontier (Seattle, Church of the People)
Olympia Churchman (Episcopalian)
Ottawa Citizen
Port Angeles Evening News
Presbyterian Record
Prince George Progress
Progressive World (United Secularists of America)
Register (Denver, Roman Catholic)
Seattle Magazine
Seattle Post-Intelligencer
Seattle Times
Star Weekly (Toronto)
Torch (Victoria, Roman Catholic)
Toronto Daily Star
United Church Observer
Vancouver Province
Vancouver Sun
Victoria Daily Colonist/Times Colonist/Colonist
Victoria Humanist
Washington Times
Weekly (Seattle)
Western Canada Lutheran
Western Lutheran
Western Regular Baptist

Proceedings and Annual Reports

Anglican Church of Canada, Diocese of British Columbia. *Journal of Synod.* 1952–71.
Anglican Church of Canada, General Synod. *Journal of Proceedings.* 1955–71.
Anglican Church of Canada, Provincial Synod of British Columbia. *Journal of Proceedings.* 1950–70.
Augustana Evangelical Lutheran Church, Columbia Conference. *Minutes of Annual Convention.* 1956.
Church of England in Canada, Council for Social Service. *Bulletin.* 1951–71.
Episcopal Church, Diocese of Olympia. *Annual Journal.* 1951–69.
Lutheran Church in America, Western Canada Synod. *Minutes of Annual Convention.* 1962–71.
Methodist Church in the United States, Pacific Northwest Conference. *Annual Journal.* 1951–60, 1962–67.
National Council of the Churches of Christ in the United States of America. *Yearbook of American Churches.* 1951–72.
National Council of the Churches of Christ in the United States of America. *Yearbook of American and Canadian Churches.* 1973–79.

Presbyterian Church in Canada. *Acts and Proceedings of the General Assembly*. 1952–61.
Presbyterian Church in the United States, Board of Christian Education. *Annual Report*. 1952–53, 1956.
Presbyterian Church in the United States, Board of National Missions. *Annual Report*. 1951–52, 1954–57.
Presbyterian Church in the United States, General Assembly. *Minutes*. 1951, 1954–55.
Presbytery of Victoria, Annual Meeting. *Minutes*. 1951–62.
United Church of Canada. *Yearbook*. 1965–72.
United Church of Canada, Board of Evangelism and Social Service. *Annual Report*. 1951–71.
United Church of Canada, Board of Information. *Outreach*. 1962–66.
United Church of Canada, British Columbia Conference. *Minutes*. 1951–71.
United Lutheran Church in America, Biennial Convention. *Minutes*. 1958–60.
United Methodist Church in the United States, Pacific Northwest Conference. *Annual Journal*. 1968–71.
United Presbyterian Church in the United States, Synod of Washington, Annual Session. *Minutes*. 1951–61.

Statistical Sources and Government Documents

American Institute of Public Opinion. *Gallup Opinion Index*. 1967–75.
Angus Reid Poll. April 21, 2000.
BC Council for Families. *Diversity and Change: A Profile of British Columbia Families*. Vancouver: BC Council for Families, 1997.
Canada. *Census of Canada*. 1951–01.
Canada. *Vital Statistics*. Ottawa: Dominion Bureau of Statistics, 1960–71.
Canadian Institute of Public Opinion. *Gallup Poll of Canada*. 1956–67.
Canadian Institute of Public Opinion. *Gallup Report*. 1967–75.
Data Laboratories Research Consultants. *Report of a Survey of Canadians' Participation in Organized Religion*. Montreal, 1977.
Gallup, George H. *The Gallup Poll: Public Opinion 1935–1971*. New York: Random House, 1972.
Gallup, George Jr., and Jim Castelli. *The People's Religion: American Faith in the 90s*. New York: MacMillan, 1989.
Gallup Organization. *Religion in America: 50 Years, 1935–1985*. Princeton: Gallup Organization, 1985.
Gallup Organization, et al. *The Unchurched American*. Princeton: Princeton Religion Research Center, 1978.
Johnson, Douglas, Paul Picard, and Bernard Quinn, eds. *Churches and Church Membership in the United States: An Enumeration by Region, State, and County, 1971*. Washington: Glenmary Research Center, 1974.
National Council of Churches of Christ in the United States of America. *Churches and Church Membership in the United States: An Enumeration and Analysis by Counties, States, and Regions*. Series A-E. New York: Bureau of Research and Survey, 1956.
Statistics Canada. *National Household Survey, 2011*. Statistics Canada Catalogue no. 99–010-X2011032. http://www12.statcan.gc.ca/nhs-enm/2011/dp-pd/dt-td/Rp-eng.cfm.
United States. Bureau of the Census. *Census of Population*. 1950–70.
United States. Bureau of the Census. *Historical Statistics of the United States, Colonial Times to 1970*. Washington: United States Department of Commerce, 1975.

United States. Bureau of the Census. "Religion reported by the civilian population of the United States: March 1957." *Current Population Reports.* Series P-20, Washington: United States Department of Commerce, 1958.

United States Department of Health, Education, and Welfare. "Marriage and Divorce." *Vital Statistics of the United States, 1972.* Vol. 3. Rockville: National Center for Health Statistics, 1976.

Washington State, Bureau of Vital Statistics. *Vital Statistics Summary, Washington State.* Olympia: Department of Social and Health Services, 1970–75.

Other Sources

Adams, Mary Louise. *The Trouble with Normal: Postwar Youth and the Making of Heterosexuality.* Toronto: University of Toronto Press, 1997.

Agnew, John. "Introduction." In Agnew and Smith, *American Space/American Place,* 1–20.

–. *Place and Politics: The Geographical Mediation of State and Society.* Boston: Allen and Unwin, 1987.

Agnew, John, and Jonathan Smith, eds. *American Space/American Place: Geographies of the Contemporary United States.* New York: Routledge, 2002.

Allerfeldt, Kristofer. *Race, Radicalism, Religion and Restriction: Immigration in the Pacific Northwest, 1890–1924.* Westport: Praeger, 2003.

Alper, Don. "The Idea of Cascadia: Emergent Transborder Regionalism in the Pacific Northwest–Western Canada." *Journal of Borderland Studies* 11: 2 (1996): 1–22.

Ammerman, Nancy. "Golden Rule Christianity: Lived Religion in the American Mainstream." In *Lived Religion in America: Toward a History of Practice,* ed. David Hall, 196–216. Princeton: Princeton University Press, 1997.

Anderson, Benedict. *Imagined Communities: Reflections on the Origin and Spread of Nationalism.* Rev. ed. London: Verso, 1991.

Anderson, Kay. *Vancouver's Chinatown: Racial Discourse in Canada, 1875–1980.* Montreal and Kingston: McGill-Queen's University Press, 1991.

Applegate, Celia. "A Europe of Regions: Reflections on the Historiography of Sub-National Places in Modern Times." *American Historical Review* 104: 4 (1999): 1157–82.

Arnup, Katherine. *Education for Motherhood: Advice for Mothers in Twentieth-Century Canada.* Toronto: University of Toronto Press, 1994.

Avella, Steven. "Catholicism in the Twentieth-Century American West: The Next Frontier." *Catholic Historical Review* 97: 2 (April 2011): 219–45.

Ayers, Edward. "What We Talk About When We Talk About the South." In Ayers et al., *All Over the Map,* 62–82.

Ayers, Edward, and Peter Onuf. "Introduction." In Ayers et al., *All Over the Map,* 1–10.

–. "Preface." In Ayers et al., *All Over the Map,* vii-viii.

Ayers, Edward, Peter Onuf, Patricia Nelson Limerick, and Stephen Nissenbaum, eds. *All Over the Map: Rethinking American Regions.* Baltimore: Johns Hopkins University Press, 1996.

Baer, Douglas, Edward Grabb, and William Johnston. "The Values of Canadians and Americans: A Critical Analysis and Reassessment." *Social Forces* 68: 3 (March 1990): 693–713.

Bainbridge, William S. "Atheism." *Interdisciplinary Journal of Research on Religion* 1: 1 (2005): 1–24.

Barman, Jean. *The West Beyond the West: A History of British Columbia.* Rev. ed. Toronto: University of Toronto Press, 1996.

Baskerville, Peter, and Eric Sager, eds. *Household Counts: Canadian Households and Families in 1901.* Toronto: University of Toronto Press, 2007.

Behiels, Michael, and Marcel Martel, eds. *Nations, Ideas, Identities: Essays in Honour of Ramsay Cook.* New York: Oxford University Press, 2000.

Belshaw, John. "The West We Have Lost: British Columbia's Demographic Past and an Agenda for Population History." *Western Historical Quarterly* 29 (Spring 1998): 25–47.

Bendroth, Margaret. *Growing Up Protestant: Parents, Children, and Mainline Churches.* New Brunswick, NJ: Rutgers University Press, 2002.

Bendroth, Margaret, and Virginia Brereton, eds. *Women and Twentieth-Century Protestantism.* Urbana: University of Illinois Press, 2002.

Bercuson, David. "Labour Radicalism and the Western Industrial Frontier, 1897–1919." *Canadian Historical Review* 58: 2 (1977): 154–75.

Bernard, H. Russell. *Research Methods in Anthropology: Qualitative and Quantitative Methods.* 3rd ed. Walnut Creek: AltaMira Press, 2002.

Berton, Pierre. *The Comfortable Pew: A Critical Look at Christianity and the Religious Establishment in the New Age.* Philadelphia: Lippincott, 1965.

Bibby, Reginald. *Fragmented Gods: The Poverty and Potential of Religion in Canada.* Toronto: Irwin, 1987.

–. *Restless Gods: The Renaissance of Religion in Canada.* Toronto: Novalis, 2004.

Blanshard, Paul. *Religion and the Schools: The Great Controversy.* Boston: Beacon Press, 1963.

Block, Tina. "Everyday Infidels: A Social History of Secularism in the Postwar Pacific Northwest." PhD diss., University of Victoria, 2006.

–. "'Families that pray together, stay together': Religion, Gender, and Family in Postwar Victoria, British Columbia." *BC Studies* 145 (Spring 2005): 31–54.

–. "'Going to church just never even occurred to me': Women and Secularism in the Postwar Pacific Northwest." *Pacific Northwest Quarterly* 96 (Spring 2005): 61–68.

–. "Religion, Irreligion, and the Difference Place Makes: The Case of the Pacific Northwest, 1950–1970." *Histoire sociale/Social History* 43: 85 (May 2010): 1–30.

–. "Ungodly Grandmother: Marian Sherman and the Social Dimensions of Atheism in Postwar Canada." *Journal of Women's History* 26: 4 (Winter 2014): 132–54.

Booth, Charles. *The Northwestern United States.* New York: Van Nostrand Reinhold, 1971.

Bowen, Kurt. *Christians in a Secular World: The Canadian Experience.* Montreal and Kingston: McGill- Queens University Press, 2005.

Braude, Ann. "A Religious Feminist – Who Can Find Her? Historiographical Challenges from the National Organization for Women." *The Journal of Religion* 84: 4 (October 2004): 555–72.

–. "Women's History *Is* American Religious History." In *Retelling U.S. Religious History,* edited by Thomas Tweed, 87–107. Berkeley: University of California Press, 1997.

Brown, Callum. *The Death of Christian Britain: Understanding Secularisation, 1800–2000.* London: Routledge, 2001.

–. *Religion and the Demographic Revolution: Women and Secularisation in Canada, Ireland, UK and USA since the 1960s.* Woodbridge: Boydell Press, 2012.

–. *Religion and Society in Twentieth-Century Britain.* Edinburgh Gate: Pearson, 2006.

–. "The Secularisation Decade: What the 1960s Have Done to the Study of Religious History." In *The Decline of Christendom in Western Europe, 1750–2000,* edited by Hugh McLeod and Werner Ustorf, 29–46. Cambridge: Cambridge University Press, 2003.

Brown, Richard Maxwell. "The Other Northwest: The Regional Identity of a Canadian Province." In *Many Wests: Place, Culture, and Regional Identity,* edited by David Wrobel and Michael Steiner, 279–314. Lawrence: University Press of Kansas, 1997.

Bruce, Steve. *God Is Dead: Secularization in the West.* Oxford: Blackwell, 2002.

Bukowczyk, John. "The Transforming Power of the Machine: Popular Religion, Ideology, and Secularization among Polish Immigrant Workers in the United States, 1880–1940." *International Labor and Working Class History* 34 (1989): 22–38.

Burkinshaw, Robert. *Pilgrims in Lotus Land: Conservative Protestantism in British Columbia, 1917–1981.* Montreal and Kingston: McGill-Queen's University Press, 1995.

Canipe, Lee. "Under God and Anti-Communist: How the Pledge of Allegiance Got Religion in Cold War America." *Journal of Church and State* 45: 2 (Spring 2003): 305–23.

Carroll, Jackson, Douglas Johnson, and Martin Marty. *Religion in America: 1950 to the Present.* New York: Harper and Row, 1979.

Chaves, Mark. *American Religion: Contemporary Trends.* Princeton: Princeton University Press, 2011.

Christiano, Kevin. "Church and State in Institutional Flux: Canada and the United States." In *Rethinking Church, State, and Modernity: Canada between Europe and America,* edited by David Lyon and Marguerite Van Die, 69–89. Toronto: University of Toronto Press, 2000.

Christie, Nancy, ed. *Households of Faith: Family, Gender, and Community in Canada, 1760–1969.* Montreal and Kingston: McGill-Queen's University Press, 2002.

–. "'On the Threshold of Manhood': Working-Class Religion and Domesticity in Victorian Britain and Canada." *Histoire Sociale* 36: 71 (2003): 145–74.

Christie, Nancy, and Michael Gauvreau. "'Even the hippies were only very slowly going secular': Dechristianization and the Culture of Individualism in North America and Western Europe." In Christie and Gauvreau, *The Sixties and Beyond,* 3–38.

–, eds. *The Sixties and Beyond: Dechristianization in North America and Western Europe: 1945–2000.* Toronto: University of Toronto Press, 2013.

Clark, Norman. *Washington: A Bicentennial History.* New York: W.W. Norton, 1976.

Comacchio, Cynthia. "'The History of Us': Social Science, History, and the Relations of Family in Canada." *Labour/Le Travail* 46 (2000): 167–220.

Cook, Ramsay. *The Regenerators: Social Criticism in Late Victorian English Canada.* Toronto: University of Toronto Press, 1985.

Cox, Jeffrey. *The English Churches in a Secular Society: Lambeth, 1870–1930.* Oxford: Oxford University Press, 1982.

Cronin, Kay. *Cross in the Wilderness.* Vancouver: Mitchell Press, 1960.

Cruikshank, Julie. "Oral Tradition and Oral History: Reviewing Some Issues." *Canadian Historical Review* 75: 3 (1994): 403–18.

Crysdale, Stewart, and Les Wheatcroft, eds. *Religion in Canadian Society.* Toronto: MacMillan of Canada, 1976.

Cuba, Lee, and David Hummon. "A Place to Call Home: Identification with Dwelling, Community, and Region." *Sociological Quarterly* 34: 1 (1993): 111–31.

Curtis, Bruce. *The Politics of Population: State Formation, Statistics, and the Census of Canada, 1840–1875.* Toronto: University of Toronto Press, 2001.

Davenport, Thomas. *Virtuous Pagans: Unreligious People in America.* New York: Garland, 1991.

Davie, Grace. *Religion in Britain since 1945: Believing Without Belonging.* Oxford: Blackwell, 1994.

Denzin, Norman, and Yvonna Lincoln, eds. *Handbook of Qualitative Research.* Thousand Oaks: Sage, 1994.

Dierenfield, Richard. *Religion in American Public Schools.* Washington: Public Affairs Press, 1962.

Drury, Clifford Merrill. *Presbyterian Panorama: 150 Years of National Missions History*. Philadelphia: Board of Christian Education, Presbyterian Church in the United States, 1952.

Dubinsky, Karen. *Improper Advances: Rape and Heterosexual Conflict in Ontario, 1880–1929*. Chicago: University of Chicago Press, 1993.

Edgell, Penny, Joseph Gerteis, and Douglas Hartmann. "Atheists as 'Other': Moral Boundaries and Cultural Membership in American Society." *American Sociological Review* 71: 2 (April 2006): 211–34.

Ficken, Robert, and Charles LeWarne. *Washington: A Centennial History*. Seattle: University of Washington Press, 1988.

Findlay, John. "A Fishy Proposition: Regional Identity in the Pacific Northwest." In *Many Wests: Place, Culture, and Regional Identity*, edited by David Wrobel and Michael Steiner, 37–70. Lawrence: University Press of Kansas, 1997.

Findlay, John, and Kenneth Coates, eds. *Parallel Destinies: Canadian-American Relations West of the Rockies*. Seattle: University of Washington Press, 2002.

Fitzgerald, Maureen. "Losing Their Religion: Women, the State, and the Ascension of Secular Discourse." In Bendroth and Brereton, *Women and Twentieth-Century Protestantism*, 280–303.

Frederick, Arthur, and Ross Sanderson. *The Columbia Basin Project Area and Its Churches*. Seattle: Washington State Council of Churches, 1950.

Friesen, Gerald. "The Evolving Meanings of Region in Canada." *Canadian Historical Review* 82: 3 (September 2001): 529–45.

–. "Homer's Odyssey and a Region of Rednecks: What Communication History Can Tell Us about Canada as a Country of Regions." *British Journal of Canadian Studies* 15: 1/2 (2002): 27–41.

Fuller, Robert. *Spiritual but Not Religious: Understanding Unchurched America*. New York: Oxford University Press, 2001.

Furniss, Elizabeth. *The Burden of History: Colonialism and the Frontier Myth in a Rural Canadian Community*. Vancouver: UBC Press, 1999.

Garreau, Joel. *The Nine Nations of North America*. Boston: Houghton Mifflin, 1981.

Gastil, Raymond, Norman Clark, Richard Etulain, and Otis Pease. "The Pacific Northwest as a Cultural Region: A Symposium." *Pacific Northwest Quarterly* 64 (1973): 147–62.

Gee, Ellen. "Gender Differences in Church Attendance in Canada: The Role of Labor Force Participation." *Review of Religious Research* 32: 3 (1991): 267–73.

Gidney, Catherine. *A Long Eclipse: The Liberal Protestant Establishment and the Canadian University, 1920–1970*. Montreal and Kingston: McGill-Queen's University Press, 2004.

Ginzberg, Lori. "'The Hearts of Your Readers Will Shudder': Fanny Wright, Infidelity, and American Freethought." *American Quarterly* 46: 2 (June 1994): 195–226.

Gleason, Mona. *Normalizing the Ideal: Psychology, Schooling, and the Family in Postwar Canada*. Toronto: University of Toronto Press, 1999.

Glenn, Norval. "The Trend in 'No Religion' Respondents to U.S. National Surveys, Late 1950s to Early 1980s," *Public Opinion Quarterly* 51: 3 (1987): 293–314.

Golz, Annalee. "Family Matters: The Canadian Family and the State in the Postwar Period." *Left History* 1: 2 (1993): 9–49.

Grabb, Edward, and James Curtis. *Regions Apart: The Four Societies of Canada and the United States*. Oxford: Oxford University Press, 2005.

Grant, John Webster. *The Church in the Canadian Era: The First Century of Confederation*. Toronto: McGraw-Hill Ryerson, 1972.

Griffith, R. Marie. *God's Daughters: Evangelical Women and the Power of Submission*. Berkeley: University of California Press, 1997.

Groth, Paul, and Chris Wilson. "The Polyphony of Cultural Landscape Study: An Introduction." In *Everyday America: Cultural Landscape Studies after J.B. Jackson*, edited by Chris Wilson and Paul Groth, 1–22. Berkeley: University of California Press, 2003.

Hackett, David, Laurie Maffly-Kipp, R. Laurence Moore, and Leslie Woodcock Tentler. "Forum: American Religion and Class." *Religion and American Culture* 15: 1 (2005): 1–29.

Haddaway, C. Kirk, Penny Long Marler, and Mark Chaves. "What the Polls Don't Show: A Closer Look at U.S. Church Attendance." *American Sociological Review* 58 (December 1993): 741–52.

Hall, Catherine. *White, Male, and Middle Class: Explorations in Feminism and History.* New York: Routledge, 1992.

Hall, David, ed. *Lived Religion in America: Toward a History of Practice.* Princeton: Princeton University Press, 1997.

–. *Worlds of Wonder, Days of Judgement: Popular Religious Belief in Early New England.* New York: Knopf, 1989.

Harris, Cole. *The Resettlement of British Columbia: Essays on Colonialism and Geographical Change.* Vancouver: UBC Press, 1997.

Hartman, Mary, and Lois Banner, eds. *Clio's Consciousness Raised: New Perspectives on the History of American Women.* New York: Harper Torchbooks, 1974.

Hartmann, Susan. "Expanding Feminism's Field and Focus: Activism in the National Council of Churches in the 1960s and 1970s." In Bendroth and Brereton, *Women and Twentieth-Century Protestantism*, 49–69.

Hill, Samuel. "Religion and Region in America." *Annals of the American Academy of Political and Social Science* 480 (1985): 132–41.

Hirt, Paul, ed. *Terra Pacifica: People and Place in the Northwest States and Western Canada.* Pullman: Washington State University Press, 1998.

Hoge, Dean, and David Roozen. "Research on Factors Influencing Church Commitment." In Hoge and Roozen, *Understanding Church Growth and Decline*, 42–68.

–, eds. *Understanding Church Growth and Decline, 1950–1978.* New York: Pilgrim Press, 1979.

Holbrook, Stewart. *Far Corner: A Personal View of the Pacific Northwest.* New York: MacMillan, 1952.

Holbrook, Stewart, Nard Jones, and Roderick Haig-Brown. *The Pacific Northwest*, ed. Anthony Netboy. Garden City: Doubleday, 1963.

Irwin, Lee. "Native Voices in the Study of Native American Religions." *European Review of Native American Studies* 12: 2 (1998): 25–40.

Ito, Kazuo. *Issei: A History of Japanese Immigrants in North America.* Translated by Shinichiro Nakamura and Jean Gerard. Seattle: Japanese Community Service, 1973.

Janovicek, Nancy, "'If you'd told me you wanted to talk about the '60s, I wouldn't have called you back': Reflections on Collective Memory and the Practice of Oral History." In *Oral History Off the Record: Toward an Ethnography of Practice*, edited by Anna Sheftel and Stacey Zembrzycki, 185–99. New York: Palgrave Macmillan, 2013.

Jessett, Thomas. *Pioneering in God's Country: The History of the Diocese of Olympia, 1853–1967.* 2nd ed. Seattle: Diocese of Olympia Press, 1967.

Johansen, Dorothy, and Charles Gates. *Empire of the Columbia: A History of the Pacific Northwest.* 2nd ed. New York: Harper and Row, 1967.

Kay, Jeanne. "Landscapes of Women and Men: Rethinking the Regional Historical Geography of the United States and Canada." *Journal of Historical Geography* 17: 4 (1991): 435–52.

Killen, Patricia O'Connell. "The Geography of a Religious Minority: Roman Catholicism in the Pacific Northwest." *US Catholic Historian* 18: 3 (Summer 2000): 51–72.

–. "Writing the Pacific Northwest into Canadian and U.S. Catholic History: Geography, Demographics, and Regional Religion." *Historical Studies: Canadian Catholic Historical Association* 66 (2000): 74–91.

Killen, Patricia O'Connell, and Mark Shibley. "Surveying the Religious Landscape: Historical Trends and Current Patterns in Oregon, Washington, and Alaska." In Killen and Silk, *Religion and Public Life in the Pacific Northwest,* 25–50.

Killen, Patricia O'Connell, and Mark Silk, eds. *Religion and Public Life in the Pacific Northwest: The None Zone.* Walnut Creek: AltaMira Press, 2004.

Kirkley, Evelyn. *Rational Mothers and Infidel Gentlemen: Gender and American Atheism, 1865–1915.* Syracuse: Syracuse University Press, 2000.

Knowles, Norman. "Christ in the Crowsnest: Religion and the Anglo-Protestant Working Class in the Crowsnest Pass, 1898–1918." In Behiels and Martel, *Nations, Ideas, Identities,* 57–72.

–. "New Perspectives on the History of Religion in British Columbia." *Journal of the Canadian Church Historical Society* 38: 1 (1996): 4–8.

–. "Religious Affiliation, Demographic Change and Family Formation among British Columbia's Chinese and Japanese Communities: A Case Study of Church of England Missions, 1861–1942." *Canadian Ethnic Studies* 27: 2 (1995): 59–80.

Kosmin, Barry, and Ariela Keysar, eds. *Secularism and Secularity: Contemporary International Perspectives.* Hartford: Institute for the Study of Secularism in Society and Culture, 2007.

Kosmin, Barry, and Ariela Keysar, with Ryan Cragun and Juhem Navarro-Rivera. *American Nones: The Profile of the No Religion Population – A Report Based on the American Religious Identification Survey 2008.* Hartford: Institute for the Study of Secularism in Society and Culture, 2009.

Kosmin, Barry, and Seymour Lachman. *One Nation Under God: Religion in Contemporary American Society.* New York: Crown Trade Paperbacks, 1993.

Laird, Lance. "Religions of the Pacific Rim in the Pacific Northwest." In Killen and Silk, *Religion and Public Life in the Pacific Northwest,* 107–38.

Lane, Belden. "Giving Voice to Place: Three Models for Understanding American Sacred Space." *Religion and American Culture* 11: 1 (Winter 2001): 53–81.

Langford, Tom, and Chris Frazer. "The Cold War and Working Class Politics in the Coal Mining Communities of the Crowsnest Pass, 1945–1958." *Labour/Le Travail* 49 (Spring 2002): 43–81.

Laverdure, Paul. *Sunday in Canada: The Rise and Fall of the Lord's Day.* Yorkton: Gravelbooks, 2004.

Leier, Mark. "W[h]ither Labour History: Regionalism, Class, and the Writing of BC History." *BC Studies* 111 (1996): 61–75.

Liddell, Ken. *This Is British Columbia.* Toronto: Ryerson Press, 1958.

Limerick, Patricia. "Region and Reason." In Edward Ayers et al., *All Over the Map,* 83–104.

Lipset, Seymour. *Continental Divide: The Values and Institutions of the United States and Canada.* New York: Routledge, 1990.

Livingstone, David. "Science and Religion: Foreword to the Historical Geography of an Encounter." *Journal of Historical Geography* 20: 4 (1994): 367–83.

Lomnitz-Adler, Claudio. *Exits from the Labyrinth: Culture and Ideology in the Mexican National Space*. Berkeley: University of California Press, 1992.

Lyon, David, and Marguerite Van Die, eds. *Rethinking Church, State, and Modernity: Canada between Europe and America*. Toronto: University of Toronto Press, 2000.

Maffly-Kipp, Laurie. "Historicizing Religion in the American West." In Peter Williams, *Perspectives on American Religion and Culture*, 11–21.

Manzer, Ronald. "Public Philosophy and Public Policy: The Case of Religion in Canadian State Education." *British Journal of Canadian Studies* 7: 2 (1992): 248–76.

Marks, Lynne. "Exploring Regional Diversity in Patterns of Religious Participation: Canada in 1901." *Historical Methods* 33: 4 (2000): 247–54.

–. "Heroes and Hallelujahs – Labour History and the Social History of Religion in Canada: A Response to Bryan Palmer." *Histoire Sociale* 34: 67 (2001): 169–86.

–. "'Leaving God Behind When They Crossed the Rocky Mountains': Exploring Unbelief in Turn-of-the-Century British Columbia." In Baskerville and Sager, *Household Counts*, 371–404.

–. *Revivals and Roller Rinks: Religion, Leisure, and Identity in Late-Nineteenth-Century Small-Town Ontario*. Toronto: University of Toronto Press, 1996.

Marshall, David. *Secularizing the Faith: Canadian Protestant Clergy and the Crisis of Belief, 1850–1940*. Toronto: University of Toronto Press, 1992.

Marty, Martin, Stuart Rosenberg, and Andrew Greeley. *What Do We Believe? The Stance of Religion in America*. New York: Meredith Press, 1968.

May, Elaine Tyler. *Homeward Bound: American Families in the Cold War Era*. New York: Basic Books, 1988.

McDowell, Linda. *Gender, Identity, and Place: Understanding Feminist Geographies*. Minneapolis: University of Minnesota Press, 1999.

McGowan, Mark. *The Waning of the Green: Catholics, the Irish, and Identity in Toronto, 1887–1922*. Montreal: McGill-Queen's University Press, 1999.

McKay, Ian. "A Note on 'Region' in Writing the History of Atlantic Canada." *Acadiensis* 29: 2 (2000): 89–101.

–. *The Quest of the Folk: Antimodernism and Cultural Selection in Twentieth-Century Nova Scotia*. Montreal: McGill-Queen's University Press, 1994.

McKenna, Marian, ed. *The Canadian and American Constitutions in Comparative Perspective*. Calgary: University of Calgary Press, 1993.

McLeod, Hugh. *Piety and Poverty: Working-Class Religion in Berlin, London and New York, 1870–1914*. New York: Holmes and Meier, 1996.

–. "Reflections and New Perspectives." In Christie and Gauvreau, *The Sixties and Beyond*, 453–68.

–. *The Religious Crisis of the 1960s*. Oxford: Oxford University Press, 2007.

McLeod, Hugh, and Werner Ustorf, eds. *The Decline of Christendom in Western Europe, 1750–2000*. Cambridge: Cambridge University Press, 2003.

McManus, Sheila, Dimitry Anastakis, Jeet Heer, Karen Marrero, and Joseph Tohil. "Challenging the Boundaries of Geography: A Roundtable on Comparative History." *Canadian Review of American Studies* 33: 2 (2003): 139–60.

McNally, Vincent. "Challenging the Status Quo: An Examination of the History of Catholic Education in British Columbia." *Historical Studies: Canadian Catholic Historical Association* 65 (1999): 71–91.

–. "Church-State Relations and American Influence in British Columbia before Confederation." *Journal of Church and State* 34: 1 (1992): 93–110.

Mercier, Laurie. "Reworking Race, Class, and Gender into Pacific Northwest History." *Frontiers* 22: 3 (2001): 61–74.

Meyerowitz, Joanne, ed. *Not June Cleaver: Women and Gender in Postwar America, 1945–1960.* Philadelphia: Temple University Press, 1994.

Miedema, Gary. *For Canada's Sake: Public Religion, Centennial Celebrations, and the Re-Making of Canada in the 1960s.* Montreal and Kingston: McGill-Queen's University Press, 2005.

Mol, Hans. *Faith and Fragility: Religion and Identity in Canada.* Burlington: Trinity Press, 1985.

–. "Major Correlates of Churchgoing in Canada." In Crysdale and Wheatcroft, *Religion in Canadian Society,* 241–54.

Morgan, Murray. *The Northwest Corner: The Pacific Northwest, Its Past and Present.* New York: Viking Press, 1962.

Morrissey, Katherine. *Mental Territories: Mapping the Inland Empire.* Ithaca: Cornell University Press, 1997.

Morton, Suzanne. "Gender, Place, and Region: Thoughts on the State of Women in Atlantic Canadian History." *Atlantis* 25: 1 (Fall/Winter 2000): 119–28.

Mueller, Samuel, and Angela Lane. "Tabulations from the 1957 Current Population Survey on Religion." *Journal for the Scientific Study of Religion* 11 (1972): 76–98.

New, William. *Borderlands: How We Talk About Canada.* Vancouver: UBC Press, 1998.

Newman, William, and Peter Halvorson. "The Church Membership Studies: An Assessment of Four Decades of Institutional Research." *Review of Religious Research* 35: 1 (1993): 55–61.

–. "Updating an Archive: 'Churches and Church Membership in the U.S.,' 1952–1980." *Review of Religious Research* 24 (September 1982): 54–60.

Newman, William, Peter Halvorson, and Jennifer Brown. "Problems and Potential Uses of the 1952 and 1971 National Council of Churches 'Churches and Church Membership in the United States' Studies." *Review of Religious Research* 18 (1977): 167–73.

Noll, Mark. "What Happened to Christian Canada?" *Church History* 75: 2 (2006): 245–73.

Oliver, Marjorie, and Ron Kenyon, eds. *Signals for the Sixties.* Toronto: United Church of Canada Board of Information and Stewardship, 1961.

Orsi, Robert. "Everyday Miracles: The Study of Lived Religion." In Hall, *Lived Religion in America,* 3–21.

–. *The Madonna of 115th Street: Faith and Community in Italian Harlem, 1880–1950.* New Haven: Yale University Press, 1985.

–. *Thank You, St. Jude: Women's Devotion to the Patron Saint of Hopeless Causes.* New Haven: Yale University Press, 1996.

Owram, Doug. *Born at the Right Time: A History of the Baby-Boom Generation.* Toronto: University of Toronto Press, 1996.

Palmer, Bryan. "Historiographic Hassles: Class and Gender, Evidence and Interpretation." *Histoire Sociale* 33: 65 (2000): 105–44.

Pangle, Thomas. "The Accommodation of Religion: A Tocquevillian Perspective." In McKenna, *The Canadian and American Constitutions,* 3–24.

Parr, Joy, ed. *A Diversity of Women: Ontario, 1945–1980.* Toronto: University of Toronto Press, 1995.

Parr, Joy, and Mark Rosenfeld, eds. *Gender and History in Canada.* Toronto: Copp Clark, 1996.

Pasquale, Frank. "The 'Nonreligious' in the American Northwest." In Kosmin and Keysar, *Secularism and Secularity,* 41–58.

Patai, Daphne. "Ethical Problems of Personal Narratives, or, Who Should Eat the Last Piece of Cake?" *International Journal of Oral History* 8: 1 (1987): 5–27.

Perry, Adele. *On the Edge of Empire: Gender, Race, and the Making of British Columbia, 1849–1871.* Toronto: University of Toronto Press, 2001.

Petigny, Alan. "The Spread of Permissive Religion." *Canadian Review of American Studies* 39: 4 (2009): 399–422.

Punch, Maurice. "Politics and Ethics in Qualitative Research." In Denzin and Lincoln, *Handbook of Qualitative Research,* 83–97.

Putnam, Robert, and David Campbell. *American Grace: How Religion Divides and Unites Us.* New York: Simon and Schuster, 2010.

Reimer, Samuel. *Evangelicals and the Continental Divide: The Conservative Protestant Subculture in Canada and the United States.* Montreal and Kingston: McGill-Queen's University Press, 2003.

–. "A Look at the Cultural Effects on Religiosity: A Comparison between the United States and Canada." *Journal for the Scientific Study of Religion* 34: 4 (1995): 445–57.

Robinson, John. *Honest to God.* Philadelphia: Westminster Press, 1963.

Roof, Wade Clark, and William McKinney. *American Mainline Religion: Its Changing Shape and Future.* New Brunswick: Rutgers University Press, 1987.

Roozen, David, and Jackson Caroll. "Recent Trends in Church Membership and Participation: An Introduction." In Hoge and Roozen, *Understanding Church Growth and Decline,* 21–41.

Roy, Patricia. *A White Man's Province: British Columbia Politicians and Chinese and Japanese Immigrants, 1858–1914.* Vancouver: UBC Press, 1989.

Rutherdale, Myra. *Women and the White Man's God: Gender and Race in the Canadian Mission Field.* Vancouver: UBC Press, 2002.

Rutherdale, Robert. "Fatherhood and the Social Construction of Memory: Breadwinning and Male Parenting on a Job Frontier, 1945–1966." In Parr and Rosenfeld, *Gender and History in Canada,* 357–76.

Sandwell, Ruth. "Peasants on the Coast? A Problematique of Rural British Columbia." *Canadian Papers in Rural History* 10 (1996): 275–303.

Sangster, Joan. "Doing Two Jobs: The Wage-Earning Mother, 1945–1970." In Parr, *A Diversity of Women,* 98–134.

Schmidt, Leigh Eric. *Consumer Rites: The Buying and Selling of American Holidays.* Princeton: Princeton University Press, 1995.

Schwantes, Carlos. "The Case of the Missing Century, or Where Did the American West Go After 1900?" *Pacific Historical Review* 70: 1 (2001): 1–20.

–. *The Pacific Northwest: An Interpretive History.* Rev. ed. Lincoln: University of Nebraska Press, 1996.

–. *Radical Heritage: Labor, Socialism, and Reform in Washington and British Columbia, 1885–1917.* Seattle: University of Washington Press, 1979.

Shibley, Mark. "Religion in Oregon: Recent Demographic Currents in the Mainstream." *Pacific Northwest Quarterly* 83: 3 (July 1992): 82–87.

–. "Secular but Spiritual in the Pacific Northwest." In Killen and Silk, *Religion and Public Life in the Pacific Northwest,* 139–68.

Shields, Rob. *Places on the Margin: Alternative Geographies of Modernity.* London: Routledge, 1991.

Shortridge, James. "Patterns of Religion in the United States." *Geographical Review* 66: 4 (1976): 420–34.

–. "A New Regionalization of American Religion." *Journal for the Scientific Study of Religion* 16: 2 (1977): 143–53.

Silk, Mark. "Religion and Region in American Public Life." *Journal for the Scientific Study of Religion* 44: 3 (2005): 265–70.

Silk, Mark, and Andrew Walsh. *One Nation, Divisible: How Regional Religious Differences Shape American Politics.* Lanham, MD: Rowman and Littlefield, 2008.

Smith, Patrick. "Cascading Concepts in Cascadia: A Territory or a Notion?" *International Journal of Canadian Studies* 25 (2002): 113–48.

Smith, Timothy. "Religion and Ethnicity in America." *American Historical Review* 83: 5 (1978): 1155–85.

Soden, Dale. "Contesting for the Soul of an Unlikely Land: Mainline Protestants, Catholics, and Jews in the Pacific Northwest." In Killen and Silk, *Religion and Public Life in the Pacific Northwest,* 51–78.

Sparke, Matthew. "Excavating the Future in Cascadia: Geoeconomics and the Imagined Geographies of a Cross-Border Region." *BC Studies* 127 (2000): 5–44.

Stark, Rodney, and William Bainbridge. *The Future of Religion: Secularization, Revival, and Cult Formation.* Berkeley: University of California Press, 1985.

Stewart, Bob. "That's the B.C. Spirit! Religion and Secularity in Lotus Land." *Canadian Society of Church History Papers* (1983): 22–35.

Stout, Harry, and D.G. Hart, eds. *New Directions in American Religious History.* New York: Oxford University Press, 1997.

Strickland, Ron, ed. *Whistlepunks and Geoducks: Oral Histories from the Pacific Northwest.* Corvallis: Oregon State University Press, 2001.

Strong-Boag, Veronica. "'Their Side of the Story': Women's Voices from the Ontario Suburbs, 1945–1960." In Parr, *A Diversity of Women,* 46–74.

Stump, Roger. "Regional Migration and Religious Commitment in the U.S." *Journal for the Scientific Study of Religion* 23: 3 (1984): 292–303.

Sutton, William. "Tied to the Whipping Post: New Labor History and Evangelical Artisans in the Early Republic." *Labor History* 36: 2 (1995): 251–81.

Szasz, Ferenc. "The Clergy and the Myth of the American West." *Church History* 59: 4 (1990): 497–506.

Taft, George. "Socialism in North America: The Case of BC and Washington State, 1900–1960." PhD diss. Simon Fraser University, 1983.

Taylor, Quintard. *In Search of the Racial Frontier: African-Americans in the American West, 1528–1990.* New York: Norton, 1998.

–. "'There Was No Better Place to Go': The Transformation Thesis Revisited, African American Migration to the Pacific Northwest, 1940–1950." In Hirt, *Terra Pacifica,* 205–19.

Thompson, Paul. *The Voice of the Past: Oral History.* 3rd ed. Oxford: Oxford University Press, 2000.

Tweed, Thomas, ed. *Retelling U.S. Religious History.* Berkeley: University of California Press, 1997.

Valverde, Mariana. "Building Anti-Delinquent Communities: Morality, Gender, and Generation in the City." In Parr, *A Diversity of Women,* 19–45.

Veevers, J.E., and D.F. Cousineau. "The Heathen Canadians: Demographic Correlates of Nonbelief." *Pacific Sociological Review* 23: 2 (1980): 199–216.

Warren, Sidney. *Farthest Frontier: The Pacific Northwest.* Port Washington: Kennikat Press, 1949.

Weaver, Jace, ed. *Native American Religious Identity: Unforgotten Gods.* Maryknoll: Orbis Books, 1998.

Weisenfeld, Judith. "On Jordan's Stormy Banks: Margins, Center, and Bridges in African American Religious History." In Stout and Hart, *New Directions in American Religious History,* 417–44.

Welch, Kevin William. "Church Membership in American Metropolitan Areas, 1952–1971." PhD diss. University of Washington, 1985.

Welter, Barbara. "The Feminization of American Religion: 1800–1860." In Hartman and Banner, *Clio's Consciousness Raised,* 137–57.

Westfall, William. "Voices from the Attic: Crossing the Canadian Border and the Writing of American Religious History." In Tweed, *Retelling U.S. Religious History,* 181–99.

Widdis, Randy. "Borders, Borderlands and Canadian Identity: A Canadian Perspective." *International Journal of Canadian Studies* 15 (1997): 49–66.

Wigen, Karen. "Culture, Power, and Place: The New Landscapes of East Asian Regionalism." *American Historical Review* 104: 4 (1999): 1183–1201.

Williams, Peter, ed. *Perspectives on American Religion and Culture.* Malden: Blackwell Publishers, 1995.

Williams, Rhys. "Religion, Community, and Place: Locating the Transcendent." *Religion and American Culture* 12: 2 (June 2002): 249–263.

Williams, Sarah. *Religious Belief and Popular Culture in Southwark, 1880–1939.* Oxford: Oxford University Press, 1999.

Worster, Donald. "Wild, Tame, and Free: Comparing Canadian and U.S. Views of Nature." In Findlay and Coates, *Parallel Destinies,* 246–73.

Wrobel, David, and Michael Steiner, eds. *Many Wests: Place, Culture, and Regional Identity.* Lawrence: University Press of Kansas, 1997.

Wunder, John. "Pacific Northwest Indians and the Bill of Rights." In Hirt, *Terra Pacifica,* 159–88.

Wuthnow, Robert. *The Restructuring of American Religion: Society and Faith since World War II.* Princeton: Princeton University Press, 1988.

Yow, Valerie Raleigh. *Recording Oral History: A Practical Guide for Social Scientists.* Thousand Oaks: Sage, 1994.

Zelinsky, Wilbur. "An Approach to the Religious Geography of the United States: Patterns of Church Membership in 1952." *Annals of the Association of American Geographers* 51 (1961): 139–93.

Index

Note: (t) after a page number indicates a table.